Mandy Sayer is the autho
which are the short story
memoir *Dreamtime Alice*, which won the National Biography
Award and the New England Booksellers' Discovery Award in
the US. She lives in Sydney.

Praise for *Dreamtime Alice*

'A remarkable memoir . . . Sayer keeps our sympathy, exuding pluck, native smarts, and good cheer. She is sure to win the hearts of readers.' *Publishers Weekly*

'With its opening line, "I had my first orgasm when I was nine years old, four days before Christmas 1972", *Dreamtime Alice* grabs you by the throat and hurtles you through a story that is as touching and sad as it is funny and unbelievable . . . a beautiful story that is full of wonderful surprises and haunting writing; you shouldn't miss it.' Mark Rubbo, *Herald Sun*

'You're going to love Alice – her sassy voice, her bad father, her wonderful adventures. And most lovely of all – her language. Mandy Sayer's storytelling is unforgettable music.' Maxine Hong Kingston, author of *Woman Warrior*

'A riveting memoir . . . a no-holes-barred portrait of a lifestyle and its denizens that few of us will ever know so intimately . . . *Dreamtime Alice* is one of the most engrossing non-fiction narratives since John Berendt's *Midnight in the Garden of Good and Evil*.' *Canberra Times*

'A painstakingly rendered memoir.' *Wall Street Journal*

'Mandy Sayer seems to have inherited her father's talent for storytelling; her language and her imagery are as captivating as the stories themselves.' *Nine to Five*

'The memoir, permeated with a sense of the precariousness of life, is full of lyrical passages and indelible images . . .' *The Australian*

'A vivid, bawdy, funny and frequently lyrical memoir . . . Shrewd and street-smart, she has a marvellous eye and ear for detail and beautifully evokes New York City and New Orleans. There are scenes of sharp poignancy.' *American Way*

'This engrossing recollection of the years the author spent tap-dancing to the drumming of her father . . . on the streets of New York and New Orleans brings us into an unfamiliar and beguiling milieu: a world of men and women who, though they play for pennies, think of themselves as artists. Ms Sayer miraculously conveys in this memoir the courage and pathos of her struggle to win her father's love.' *The New Yorker*

'The life that Sayer describes is fascinating, almost surreal in its colourful squalor.' *Washington Post Book World*

'Sayer's imagery is superb . . . beautifully written . . . offers a brutally honest look at the unique and complex relationship between a father and a daughter. An enchanting read.' *Sunday Telegraph*

'Compelling . . . remarkable . . . so engrossing a story you'll have to keep reminding yourself it's true.' *Detroit Free Press*

'A reminder of just how dynamic a memoir can be. Sayer has crafted a spellbinding story of family mythology and betrayal that delights in the melody of each and every word rather than in its exotic subject matter . . . The book is the literary cousin to all those old tap routines.' *Interview*

'There is magic in the way that Mandy, nearly drowning in desperate cicumstances, bobs back up again and again . . . You root for this street performer when she really starts to work on her craft, turning sidewalk hoofing into art.' *San Francisco Chronicle*

'Sayer has found her true metier . . . What succeeds best is her depiction of the cracked kaleidoscope of American urban life . . . With this memoir of her half-horrid, half-thrilling trip through the looking glass, Mandy Sayer at last claims her rightful place as the top-billed star of her own life story.' *USA Today*

'A powerful, boldly provocative memoir . . . A rich tapestry . . . brilliantly coloured . . . Sayer's enchanting mix of pluck and naiveté will win hearts; her haunting, lyrical way with words will garner plaudits. *Dreamtime Alice* is her triumph.' *Arizona Daily Star*

'Sayer never strikes a wrong note. You won't be bored for a moment.' *Mademoiselle*

'Alice works on so many levels, carries so much emotional baggage, features so many wild and memorable characters, and is so often wise in its observations on life that, at 368 pages, it seems barely enough.' Matthew Condon, *The Age*

'A joy to read . . . Sayer tells her story colourfully, humorously and without a skerrick of self-pity . . . The book is a rare and wonderful thing in its own right. Trees would have died happy for once, if they'd known they would end up as the pages of such a special work of art.' Diana Simmonds, *The Bulletin*

'Sayer has turned her time in the trenches into a universal women's war story.' *Sydney Morning Herald*

'Biographical writing is about the new self re-creating the old. Sayer uses the defensive shift to the third-person Alice figure, and her considerable experience as a fiction writer, to write candidly about the more intimate details of her past.' *The Australian's Review of Books*

'A book that delicately portrays the elusive nature of all human bonds, in particular the tangled one between offspring and parent.' *New York Daily News*

'Weird families make fabulous copy, and Sayer's bohemian background is more complex than most . . . The writing is lyrical and loopy, like saxophones scaling the blues.' *The Australian Way*

'Mixing her narrative . . . with her father's own wild tales and stories, of the characters they met, *Dreamtime Alice* draws you into Sayer's experience with an invigorating rush.' *Marie Claire*

Also by Mandy Sayer

Fiction:
Mood Indigo
Blind Luck
The Cross
15 Kinds of Desire

Non-fiction:
Dreamtime Alice

Other:
In the Gutter, Looking at the Stars: A Literary Adventure through Kings Cross (co-ed. with Louis Nowra)

Velocity
A Memoir

MANDY SAYER

V
VINTAGE

Author's Note

The people in this memoir are real and the events described took place. Of course, some names have been changed.

A Vintage Book
Published by
Random House Australia Pty Ltd
20 Alfred Street, Milsons Point, NSW 2061
http://www.randomhouse.com.au

Sydney   New York   Toronto
London   Auckland   Johannesburg

First published by Random House Australia 2005

Copyright © Mandy Sayer 2005

All rights reserved. No part of this publication may be reproduced, stored in a retrieval system, or transmitted in any form or by any means, electronic, mechanical, photocopying, recording or otherwise, without the prior written permission of the publisher.

National Library of Australia
Cataloguing-in-Publication Entry

Sayer, Mandy.
Velocity.

ISBN 1 74051 385 1.

1. Sayer, Mandy – Childhood and youth. 2. Sayer, Mandy –
Family. 3. Women novelists, Australian – Biography.
I. Title.

A823.3

Cover photograph courtesy of Australian Picture Library
Cover design by Gayna Murphy, Greendot Design
Author photograph by David Mariuz
Typeset in 11.5/17 pt Janson Text by Midland Typesetters, Maryborough, Victoria
Printed and bound by Griffin Press, Netley, South Australia

10 9 8 7 6 5 4 3 2 1

For Louis

*. . . he who has stood the surprise of birth
can stand anything.*

William Faulkner, *Mosquitoes*

Prologue

I knew all the beer gardens in Sydney by the time I was eight: the Tilbury in Woolloomooloo, the Bondi Hotel, the pub that overlooks the beach at Watsons Bay. Some were merely a stretch of courtyard with a few tables and chairs and plastic ferns that never wilted, no matter how many cigarettes were butted out against them. Others, like the landscaped terraces of the Newport Hotel, were alive with the scents of jasmine and jonquils and I could hide behind tree trunks and pluck the petals of stolen daisies. My parents weren't the types who took their children to the circus or – heaven forbid! – an art gallery, though they might have if there'd been a bar inside the big top, or a beer hall at the end of the sculpture garden. I didn't really mind; when they drank they relaxed and seemed to love each other more, my father's jokes were funnier and my mother's confidence and natural elegance suddenly blossomed.

In the 1960s, after playing drums in as many as three jazz bands a night, my father, Gerry, would arrive home late with a case of Dinner Ale and a conga line of musicians snaking along behind him through the back door of our Stanmore house. My mother would wake up in the front room, take the rollers out of her hair, put on lipstick and join them as someone began beating out a boogie-woogie on the piano. Soon my older brother, sister and I would be crawling out of bed to join in with the dancing and laughter, and as ashtrays filled and bottles emptied, I wanted this bliss to go on forever. These times were better than when they fought over money, or when the silences between them caused Gerry to sleep in the spare room. As the party raged on, I'd walk around the coffee table, dipping my dummy into the dregs of beer and scotch when I was sure no one was looking.

As we grew older our parents must have wanted to broaden our horizons: on Sunday afternoons we'd drive out to near Windsor, to a rambling country pub. There, we could watch bellbirds nest, finger the fine fur of a caterpillar, and swing on the branches of willow trees. Gerry and my mother would sit at one of the tables on the hotel's wide wooden veranda, chasing cold Resch's with nips of Green Ginger Wine. Whenever I ran back to show them a treasured find – a baby ladybird, a bright cockatoo feather – and saw them holding hands and kissing, I'd back away and leave them alone, glad that they were happy.

Of course, the most popular beer garden was the one in our back yard: fold-out aluminium chairs with nylon webbing, a yellow banana lounge, a pockmarked styrofoam esky – all submerged in the swaying grass that enraged the neighbours because my father rarely cut it. The open windows framed speakers from the record player, through which Frank Sinatra sang, 'I've Got the World on a String' and 'Pennies from Heaven'. Sometimes my parents would rise from the chairs and begin flattening the grass with their feet as they danced. If they let us turn on the garden hose we were happy playing with it for hours, and could calculate the precise time at which we could spray them with water without being rebuked: four schooners into the afternoon. At six schooners they'd laugh and turn the hose back on us. After that, anyone was fair game, even the ornery bloke who peered between the slats of the paling fence, purse-lipped and shaking his head. The good thing about the backyard beer garden was that it was only a short stagger to the house, and the car remained in the garage, embanked by three walls of empty bottles that grew higher as summer progressed.

The height of the season was the Musicians' Picnic. For one day a year it turned out to be the biggest beer garden in the world. Since musos work long hours over Christmas and New Year, in the lull of January the union compensated their families with this annual celebration in a tract of cleared bushland on the edge of Sydney. Chops and rissoles hissed on barbies while the men pumped kegs in time to scratchy recordings of Count Basie and Louis Armstrong that flooded through the PA system. For the children there were long trestle tables laden with fairy bread, meringues and GI cordial. The head of the union – a former trumpeter – usually flogged tickets for the chook raffle. A miniature train threaded between scribbly gums and hibiscus. Each time we chugged by and waved, our parents swayed and leaned a little more, as if the ride's revolutions made them dizzy. When the men grew flushed with sunburn and beer they'd set up their instruments in the shade of a peppercorn tree – fifteen, twenty, even a thirty-piece band jamming with such intensity that when my brother pushed me from the pony's back on our ride to the river and I found myself lost, the sound of 'Route 66' and my father's booming bass drum drew me back through the forest of stringybarks and geebungs, back to the clearing where mothers danced with toddlers in their arms and older children quarrelled over manning the keg gun.

There were no breathalysers in those days – I don't remember our Volkswagen even being fitted with seat belts. My mother didn't know how to drive and my father's personal test for whether he was sober enough to get behind a wheel was if he could say, with the added handicap of his harelip and cleft palate, 'The British Constitutional Truly Rules' – a phrase that was a challenge even when he hadn't had a drink. There must have been one year after the annual picnic when he'd slurred the words so much that he had the sense to install his bandleader, Jeff, in the driver's seat and to pile into the back with us kids. The car had only crawled a few feet, however, when Jeff suddenly realised he was too pissed to steer, but assured us he was able to manage the accelerator and brakes. And it was my twelve-year-old brother, sitting on the bandleader's lap, knuckles white against the black wheel, following the sequence of instructions – 'Turn left here . . . change lanes after the lights . . .' as Jeff worked the pedals – who finally got us home.

You'd think such rampant boozing would have ended up killing one of us but, as irony would have it, the only time my father had an accident was when he was off the grog: a boy ran in front of his car on Anzac Parade and Gerry swerved to miss him, crashing into a telegraph pole. Even the resulting eight months in hospital was an occasion to extend the family tradition; each day my mother would smuggle a bottle of scotch into Royal Prince Alfred, push his wheelchair out into the garden and they'd sit beneath the canopy of a plane tree, sipping from medicine cups, smoking and telling jokes, while I collected beetles and occasionally showered them with petals.

Those two great boozing nature-lovers separated years ago – after twenty-three years of marriage, not even the grog and an overgrown back yard could hold them together forever. But my mother, now in her 70s, has a courtyard in front of her terrace flowering with buttercups and gardenias, a well-stocked bottle shop just around the corner. And it wasn't the alcohol that got my father in the end – at eighty he still had a perfect liver – but the Camel plains he'd smoked during his drinking bouts. The penultimate beer garden that he and I enjoyed together was amidst the ferns on the veranda of the Sacred Heart Hospice in Darlinghurst, sipping Carlton Colds with Howard, a Koorie suffering from emphysema, who passed on to me the sage advice that I should 'never mix morphine with metho'.

The last beer garden, of course, was Gerry's private room – the height of summer, the open double doors framing a cloudless sky, curtains billowing, the sound of Duke Ellington pulsing through the speakers of the CD player. He was no longer able to speak and to sit up and hold a drink, but he managed to squeeze my hand, part his lips. I dipped a cotton bud into my glass of wine and placed it on his tongue, sensing there was something about the ritual that pacified him in the face of what he knew was ahead. He sucked on the bud for a few moments and then squeezed my hand again, gazing with glazed blue eyes at the bunch of opening irises I'd given him earlier, as if they were the most exquisite blooms he'd ever seen.

1

I am three years old, sitting in my wet cozzie on the steps of the Coogee Bay Hotel. It's morning and my dad has taken us to the beach. Mum hasn't come because she's sick in bed. The sun's warm on my face. There's sand in my pants. My brother and sister are playing chasey on the grass. Dad told us to wait here while he buys us a drink. I asked him if I could have a pink lemonade but he didn't answer back. Gene pulls Lisa's hair and she screams.

OK, kids! *My dad walks down the steps and sits beside me. He's holding a tray.*

Gene hurt me! *says Lisa.*

I never, *says Gene.*

Forget about that, *says Dad.* Get stuck into this!

He hands Lisa a glass, then Gene. They're quieter now and sit on the steps next to us. He gives me a glass, too, and keeps one for himself. I look at the colour. It's not pink lemonade. More like the colour of wee, but with bubbles. Gene and Lisa start drinking it and so I take a sip. It tastes funny. When I swallow it makes me feel dizzy, like when I spin in a circle for too long. I take another sip. My dad is pulling faces.

He's pretending to be Yogi Bear on TV. We all start laughing and now he's being the little bear called Boo-Boo who walks too slow and complains a lot. We laugh even more and Lisa coughs and the drink starts bubbling out of her nose. I'm so giddy I feel I could fly like the seagulls, high, high up into the sky, all the way to heaven.

When we finish I stand up but I can't walk properly. My brother lifts me and carries me on his back. He tosses me into the back seat of the car. Everyone else gets in, too. Dad gets his keys out and turns to us all.

Listen, kids. When we get home, whatever you do, don't tell your mother.

I was conceived in May 1962, roughly an hour after my father swallowed a block of hash at a party of jazz musicians. He was just about to roll a joint in the living room when a band of police began kicking down the front door in their attempt to raid the house. He automatically picked up the block – about the size of a postage stamp – and drank it down with his glass of beer. While others were being hauled off for possession, my father walked free, back to our Stanmore home and the bed he shared with my mother. That night he experienced, as he would always say, *the best fuck of my life*. And then he would add, *I could feel a part of me swimming out of myself and into your mother, like a big pair of wings*. And when he rolled off her, he announced, *Now that's a baby*.

Often, as I was growing up, he would declare to me, with great affection, *I'm so glad I swallowed that block of hash!* He attributed any talent or eccentricities I had to that wafer of Lebanese Gold. It obviously did me no harm, as my mother's pregnancy was easy, particularly after she backed out, at the last minute, of an abortion my father had arranged. Gerry had never wanted any children – partly because he was a musician and they always had financial problems, and partly because of the harelip and cleft palate he'd been born with, which had resulted in him spending the first seven years of his life in hospital, enduring scores of painful operations. He knew the condition was hereditary and, as he put it simply, *I wouldn't want anyone to go through what I went through.*

I think it's fair to say it was probably an even mix of altruism, practicality and selfishness that prompted him to sell his prized Zyldjian cymbals to pay for the termination. My mother got as far as the front gate of the Maroubra surgery and, realising she was a few minutes early, crossed the road and sat on the beach, where she remained for over an hour, growing more enraged at what she'd been talked into doing. After an hour or so, she tore up the money and threw it into the water. Not only was she going to keep me, she decided, she was going to make damn sure he lost his treasured cymbals forever.

When she arrived home, still pregnant and without the money, he was so angry he moved into the spare room and didn't speak to her for three weeks. The power struggle between them stretched back to the mid-1950s, when she fell pregnant for the first time. Disturbed by the news, Gerry visited a doctor in Ashfield and obtained some yellow liquid that, after being ingested, would cause her to abort. Instead, she threw it down the toilet and my brother was born seven months later, a colicky and difficult child who cried a lot and kept them up each night for weeks at a time. *He was a bugger of a kid*, they both agreed. As a toddler he liked to throw his glass milk bottles down the stairs and would laugh when he heard them smash. My mother spent several months knitting him a three-piece suit in her spare time. When she first dressed him in it, he'd only had the suit on for five minutes before she looked around to see it completely destroyed. He'd gone outside and rolled in a stretch of damp tar that had been used to pave the footpath.

When she fell pregnant again, two and a half years later, she must have felt worn down, and hence a little less resistant to the bottle of yellow liquid my father presented to her once more. They were having money problems and barely managing the handful that was my infant brother. The news must have been a shock to them both, as they didn't find out until she was almost five months gone. I can't imagine how hard it must have been for her to take the first sip, and then the next, and the next. It must have been like drinking poison. They waited for the first signs of miscarriage – the cramping, a gush of blood – minute by minute, hour by hour, but nothing happened.

A boy was born eight weeks premature and lived only for nine hours. During the birth, my mother struggled to survive herself, due to severe haemorrhaging, which was complicated by a transfusion of the wrong blood type, sending her entire system into shock. The guilt, for both of them, must have been excruciating.

After that experience, Gerry redevoted himself to the family religion of Catholicism, attending 6 am mass every day, begging for forgiveness. His efforts must have been rewarded because several months later my mother was up the duff again. Right throughout the pregnancy he continued his daily churchgoing, praying for a healthy baby, which was delivered between Christmas and New Year 1958 – a small, sweet, even-tempered girl who was the antithesis of her older brother. She never cried; she slept peacefully. She was so good, in fact, that my mother frequently forgot to feed her.

The healthy presence of this daughter must have assuaged Gerry's guilt, otherwise I'm sure he wouldn't have sold his cymbals to try and prevent yet another birth. Of course, my mother would never quite get over the hand they'd both had in the death of their second son. They were left not speaking to one another during the early weeks of her fourth pregnancy.

My mother's water broke one night when she was at home, watching an episode of 'Perry Mason'. Gerry was playing in a nightclub and was not available to assist her, and it was our next-door neighbour, Bill, who drove her to the Salvation Army Hospital in Marrickville, where both she and my sister had been born. When Bill dropped her off, the staff were overworked, mostly attending a hysterical Italian woman who was in the midst of a difficult and complicated first birth. When my mother announced she was carrying her fourth baby, they directed her to a room on her own, telling her to change into a gown and rest. *You're experienced*, they said. *You know what to do.*

Fifteen minutes later I was lying in her arms, the umbilical cord still connecting us. *You just popped out like a cork*, she always says, *no doctor, no gas, no nothing*. When a nurse rushed in to grab an oxygen tank for the Italian woman, she found my mother sitting up on the side of the bed, counting my fingers and toes and, shocked at the speed and ease with which I was born, ordered her to lie down until she cut the cord. I was born on St Valentine's Day, 1963, twelve pounds heavy and twenty-four inches long. The hash must have had some beneficial qualities.

I was welcomed home by a few relatives. As my mother lifted me from the Volkswagen, they stood in a line singing a song my maternal grandmother had written: *My little Mandy . . . from Toni-Pandy . . . how I love to hear you singing . . . Yakka-dakka-dakka-doo . . .* My brother, by then eight years old, must have sensed my arrival was imminent, because he fled his classroom and ran home in time to see me being carried into the living room. He's often remarked, when he saw me for the first time, he *fell in love*. This was the beginning of an unusually close bond between us that lasted many years. From that day he became my second mother, changing my nappies, cutting my fingernails, parading me around the house like a prize he'd won at school.

Before I was born, my father had gutted our large bathroom and renovated it into a soundproof music studio where he could practise, rehearse and teach his students, which proved handy for my mother after my birth. She subscribed to a popular idea of the time: that if a fed and changed baby still keeps crying when you put her down in her bassinet, you leave her alone to scream herself stupid. I apparently spent up to two hours a day in the soundproof room, while my mother prepared dinner and listened to the radio, impervious to my cries.

I must have grown used to that room because, when I began to crawl, I was often found in there, sitting beneath the drum kit, intrigued by the sounds the skins made. When I blew on the steel snare it whispered back, like wind rustling through fallen leaves.

Oddly enough, apart from my brother, the second person I developed a close bond with as a baby was neither the grandmother who'd written me a song, nor my mother, but the very man who'd dreaded my birth. Apparently, I grew stubborn and petulant around 2 pm every day, before my father arrived home for lunch. He must have had some kind of day job then, because he had only half an hour to consume his food. Anticipating his arrival, I refused to eat my own lunch and would not lie down for my afternoon nap until he appeared in the dining room, lifted me up and threw me into the air, after which he'd sit me on his knee and feed me bits of his own lunch while he ate. It was a ritual my mother tried to break: *She won't eat her own food . . . She won't sleep . . . You've only got thirty minutes . . .* But Gerry didn't seem to mind the imposition and my will turned out to be stronger than hers. After he left each day I happily went to my cot and slept the rest of the afternoon away.

When I was three I fell deeply in love with two different men: Lurch, the flat-headed grumbling butler from the TV show 'The Addams Family', and the severely handicapped man who sold newspapers from his wheelchair on a corner of Parramatta Road, whom I also nicknamed 'Lurch'. I'd crawl into his lap, chanting *Lurch! Lurch!*, kiss his dribbling lips over and over, and squeeze him so tightly his eyes began to bug. It was also at this time that I decided I wanted to have a baby – preferably a black one, and fathered by Lurch (either one of them). My mother gracefully skirted the genetic impossibility of such a proposal and instead pointed out that *You have to be married* to have a baby. I suddenly burst into tears and was inconsolable for five or so minutes. When she finally calmed me down and asked me what was wrong, I declared, still snuffling and shaking, *Yes, but who'd marry ME?*

Soon I was discovered by the postman out on the front veranda, pretending it was a stage. I was singing a song and dancing, wearing nothing more than my mother's high heels. Perhaps I was trying to attract a husband.

I've been told that most of the time I was an optimistic child. I'd never been scared of the dark, unlike my older sister. At three, I'd walk seven-year-old Lisa through our creaky Federation house each night so she could go to the toilet on the back veranda, which had become an alternative bathroom since the music room had been created. I had even more confidence when it came to the abilities of my brother. As he walked me down to the local shops one day, a group of much older boys began picking on him, trying to start a fight. *Come on, Gene!* I encouraged. *You could knock those guys stupid. Go on! Knock 'em down!* I obviously had more confidence in him than he did in himself, because he had to drag me away before I got him into more trouble.

I happily sat on the front of his handmade billy cart, between his parted legs, and hurtled with him down the steep hill at the side of our house, wind whipping my hair. The cart had no brakes and he had to quickly steer it into a hairpin turn at the bottom of the street before we hit the intersection. My parents suspected I had *a taste for danger*, which was confirmed when I was taken to Luna Park and turned my nose up at the more gentle rides. While my mother and sister enjoyed the smooth undulations of the merry-go-round and the river caves, I dragged my father onto the Big Dipper, over and over, and when I grew bored with that it was onto the Wild Mouse, which was in fact so wild that my father later complained it had left his arms purpled with bruises.

At two and a half I developed a serious kidney disease and was told that I would drop dead if I got out of bed and walked. I suppose at that age I had no idea what *drop dead* meant, and whenever my mother was out of eyeshot I'd leap out of bed and play with my green plastic ball. But of course I wasn't totally immune to fear. My mother refused to hospitalise me and, each day for six months, she'd take me by bus to Camperdown Children's Hospital, where I was jabbed with needles. The doctor wore earplugs because I screamed so much.

It was after I recovered from my illness that I became infatuated with elephants, probably due to the cute images on TV of Disney's floating pink Dumbo, who had wings and blew bubbles from his trunk. I then became obsessed with the idea of actually *riding* an elephant, like Tarzan, and prattled on about it so much that my mother finally gave in and agreed to take me and my sister to Taronga Park Zoo. The trip involved a walk to the bus stop, a forty-minute ride to Circular Quay, a half-hour ferry ride, and yet another bus ride to the front gates of the zoo, during which I would ask, almost every three minutes, that proverbial question: *When are we going to get there?* When we arrived, my mother, almost demented by my pestering, made a beeline to the stairs and platform from which children mounted the elephants. Unfortunately, the rides wouldn't begin until 2 pm and she and my sister had to endure my carping for yet another three hours as we circled the cages of what I considered boring animals: tigers, monkeys, birds.

By 1.30 pm she could no longer stand my pining and had me and my sister join the queue of children on the staircase that would lead to the hallowed spot on an elephant's back. I waited impatiently in the summer heat, gripping the handrail, sweat pearling down my face, craning my neck to catch my first glimpse of a *real* elephant. I had waited hours, days, weeks for this.

The old grey beast, led by a staff member, finally lumbered into view and up to the platform. I took one look at the bloated creature and screamed my lungs out, burst into tears, and went tumbling headfirst down the stairs in my efforts to get away from the animal I had, for so long, desired.

What's the matter? my mother asked, as she scooped me up into her arms. *Is the elephant too big?*

No, I replied, still sobbing. *It smells like a toilet!*

My father was not there to help her cope with our one childhood outing to the zoo. His nightly gigs kept him out late. It wasn't unusual for him to work until midnight; then he'd have to pack up his drums and load them into the car and drive back from wherever he was playing, which could be as far as fifty miles away. Sometimes he went to the Musicians' Club afterwards to unwind with a few of his muso friends. Often, he wouldn't get to bed until two or three in the morning, which meant he'd usually wake up around lunchtime – far too late to join a family outing.

When we kids played in the mornings, a perpetual mantra accompanied us through the house – *Be quiet! Your father's trying to sleep!* – we'd have to tiptoe and stifle our laughter for hours until he appeared at the dining room table. One particular morning I dropped a glass on the floor and the noise was so loud I was banished to the back yard. I was swinging on the back gate, feeling sorry for myself, when I saw our car turn the corner and pull up at the kerb. A man wearing a tuxedo and bow tie crawled out, grinning widely, his blond hair wild and curly.

Mum! I cried, feeling vindicated. *Dad's not asleep. He's been out all night!* And my father laughed and laughed, swept me up in his arms, and danced me back into the house.

She never got upset when he stayed out late. She realised he was like most other men, enjoying the company of his mates after work. And curiously, this was never a point of contention between them in all their years together. My mother knew the last thing on my father's mind would have been another woman – one was enough, along with three kids, to distract him from his greatest love, which was music.

He showed his affection in his own inimitable way – teaching me to recite my name and address in the event that I found myself lost. In spite of his harelip, he'd inherited the family gift of mimicry, and would entertain us with various voices when he told jokes at the dinner table. He was a tactile man who loved brushing our hair and having his locks combed in return. When he'd arrive home late after his gigs and everyone was asleep, he'd quietly open the doors to our rooms and simply watch us sleeping.

It was after one such night that my mother woke up to a crash so loud she thought part of the roof had fallen in. She leapt out of bed and went running down the hall to find the eight-foot mahogany door to my bedroom lying on the floor, with only a pair of shiny black shoes sticking out from beneath it. She pulled the door sideways and found Gerry, flat on his back, virtually unconscious. He'd come home drunk, and had proceeded to perform his usual routine of checking on us as we slept, when he'd lost his balance turning the knob and pulled the entire slab of wood off its hinges. She wrestled him up and into bed. The next morning, she was more than amused to hear him cry, from the other end of the house, *Betty! Look what these bloody kids have done now!*

My mother was usually the disciplinarian, or rather, she had to be. She insisted that we exhibit perfect manners, especially in public. On crowded buses we had to offer our seats to the elderly without being prompted. Every request we made had to be accompanied by a *Please* and, if fulfilled, a heart-felt *Thank you*. If we dared to speak back to her we were banished to our room for several hours. We girls were always in bed by seven-thirty sharp. None of us had the temerity to swear, even when she was out of earshot. I was often reprimanded for staring at strangers, particularly if they had a disability. Of course, every now and then we grew loud and exuberant at home. She would become exasperated, lose her temper, and demand that Gerry *do something about the bloody kids* who were driving her *insane*. At such times he'd quietly call us into the living room, sit us in a circle and say, with the equanimity of a monk, *Your mother's going mad again. Just cool it for a while.* This happened so infrequently – our father telling us what to do – that we sat before him in silence, obediently nodding in agreement.

While there were unspoken understandings between his generation and ours, no such composure existed between Gerry and our grandmother, who had never approved of her beautiful nineteen-year-old daughter marrying a rambunctious jazz drummer with a harelip who was eleven years her senior. My mother had had many wealthy and eligible suitors during her teenage years – one, John Vrondotis, heir to a national shoe chain, fell to his knees and wept when she told him she was about to wed Gerry, who'd already stood her up at the altar twice before he finally went through with the ceremony.

The animosity between him and his future mother-in-law was there from the start, from the day my sixteen-year-old mother-to-be first brought him home to meet the family. My grandmother's opening question was, *What kind of work do you do?* After hearing his reply, she asked, *Yes, but what do you do to earn money?* When he repeated his original answer, she remarked, *What? Is that all you do for a living – bang a drum?*

Yes, he replied. *But you have to bang it in the right places.*

He always knew that she loathed him, and the feeling – to put it simply – was mutual. It probably didn't help that she was English and he was from a staunch Irish family.

When she visited she kept up a pretence of liking him intensely, probably for the sake of my mother, who'd always been the favourite of her own four children. Gran would sweep through the back door, kiss and embrace him warmly, and declare, *Oh, my favourite son-in-law!* During one such greeting, when I was about four, I saw Gerry pull her aside, out of earshot of my mother, and say, in a low voice, *I know you can't stand me. And I can't stand you. So let's cut the bullshit, Floss.* I was astonished by his forthrightness and grew tense, anticipating a scene between them, but as my mother walked into the kitchen, Gran merely smiled and kept up the ruse. She laughed loudly and pecked him on the cheek. *Oh, Gerry*, she cried, *you're such a card!*

It was that kind of response that made him dislike her even more. He was usually a non-judgemental and forgiving man, but he could never abide anyone he considered to be *two-faced*. Because of this, he took pleasure in trying to rile her in other, more subtle ways. Every time she visited from then on he would deliberately emerge from the shower completely naked and stroll through the house on his way to his bedroom. *G'day, Floss*, he'd remark casually as he passed her in the kitchen. The hard, frozen look he received was infinitely preferable to him than the platitudes and false love she'd affected in the past.

By this time, both of his own parents were dead, and Floss would be the only grandparent I would ever know. My mother hadn't seen her own father since she was seven years old, since the day he fled to Tasmania with a female co-worker.

Fortunately, Floss wasn't around to witness some of Gerry's other forms of behaviour: the jam sessions in the living room, a handful of boozy musicians playing into the early hours of the morning, while we kids skipped and danced and tripped over, giddy with excitement. His friends and students were always dropping into the house, sharing their latest American jazz records and drinking scotch. Sometimes the smell of burning rope wafted from beneath the door of the music room, and one night I woke up to find my father sitting on the side of the bed, pulling on a big pipe, as the same acrid stench filled the room. People began dropping by more and more often, asking to see Gerry, until my mother finally realised what was being transacted. She found his stash hidden down a narrow passage that ran along the side of our house and, without saying a word, simply left the four ounces of marijuana on his bedside table. When this gesture made no difference to his habits she began combing the house until she discovered his latest hiding place and flushed the grass down the toilet. *What if we got busted?* she'd wail. *I've got three kids to look after*.

Each couldn't wear down the other's will. She started drinking more, though now it was by herself. The dope, Gerry often said, always relaxed him. *It opens my ears!* he'd say. The marijuana made him hear music more intensely and hence he thought it made him a better musician. When she argued back he usually played his last card: *At least when I'm stoned I can wash and dry the dishes. After half a bottle of scotch, you break them all.*

When my mother kicked Gerry out, she replaced him with a truck driver from a brewery who provided her with an endless supply of free beer. My older brother loathed him. Weeks earlier, he'd spied Mum kissing my father's best friend in a corner of the kitchen, and was anxious about being party to such an obvious betrayal of the father he adored. This new man – the truck driver – only further deepened his unease.

My strongest memory of this man is the time he drove us all to a sprawling old mansion on a dairy farm that was owned by a friend of his. I grew carsick during the journey and vomited all over my mother. By the time we pulled up at the farm, we both smelled like rancid milk. It was the first time I had ever visited the country. The house we were staying in seemed more like a castle. Inside, the floors were paved with flagstones and a wide, sweeping staircase curved up to the second floor. While our mother and the truck driver mixed their first drinks in the games room, we kids wasted no time racing up the stairs and sliding down the huge wooden banisters.

The following day, we roamed the farm unchecked; I helped a man milk a cow, squeezing its tits, shocked to witness the steaming liquid squirting out of the animal's enormous stomach. The farmhand lifted a ladle of the fresh, creamy concoction to my lips and I took a sip, but I was unable to shake the thought that what had just been inside the cow was now inside me, and it was so warm and sickeningly thick that I spat it out, disgusted. *I like the milk from the bottle best.*

In the absence of my father, I began to rely on my eleven-year-old brother more and more. He became my teacher, my protector, and he loved me with the same intensity with which he loathed my older sister, who'd been his rival from the day she'd been born. When she was three years old he'd tried to kill her by shoving her headfirst down a drain in the lane behind our house; it was only her terrified screams that saved her. My mother came running down the alley and finally pulled her out, scratched and bleeding.

Luckily enough, he cherished me, and that day on the farm was when I became conscious of this dynamic between us.

We'd found a barbed-wire fence and on the other side of it was a shallow stream hemmed by golden sand. We crawled beneath the wire and began wading in the clear water. Soon we were making boats from twigs and leaves and sailing them along the current. I remember hearing the sound of rustling foliage. I looked up to see a herd of enormous bulls charging towards us from the other side of the stream. My sister screamed; my brother automatically scooped me up and threw me over the fence like a football and then crawled between the strands of barbed wire, leaving Lisa to run off down the stream on her own, the bulls stampeding after her.

Fortunately, she had a lead on them and was able to dive under the fence before she was mauled. Back at the mansion, shaken and out of breath, we burst into the games room to find the truck driver kissing our mother against a snooker table. When we told her about the bulls she didn't believe us. I decided I didn't like the country, where the milk was disgusting and animals tried to kill you. I couldn't wait to return to the security of the city.

In all the years my parents were together, I never saw my father express a skerrick of jealousy towards the many men who desired my mother. He was always composure personified, as if he were above such clichéd emotions. I think, perhaps, it was a consequence of his handicap, the taunting he'd endured as he was growing up: at an early age he probably decided he would not let anyone or anything overwhelm him again. But while the truck driver was living with us, Gerry was sharing a Bondi flat with one of his young music students, Brian Fitzgibbons, and he forced Brian to spy on my mother regularly and return with any news. When Brian reported back that she was involved with a brewery truck driver, Gerry was disappointed. *Couldn't she take up with a bloke with a bit of class?*

He was probably undergoing something close to an early midlife crisis at the time, and what followed was highly unusual in Australia in the 1960s: he began seeing a psychiatrist and experimenting with LSD under the doctor's supervision. Years later, he often told me that, after several gruelling trips on clear clinic acid, he'd experienced two epiphanies: the first was that he really *was* born to be a jazz drummer, and the second was that he'd married the wrong woman. After those two great realisations, I don't know exactly what it was that made him attempt a reconciliation. I know there was pressure from his friends to *do the right thing*. But perhaps the biggest motivation, he once told me, was the sight of his eleven-year-old son, weeping uncontrollably in his arms and begging him to come home.

He couldn't return alone, however, and insisted that Brian move into the family home with him, as a friendly buttress against his decidedly shaky marriage. The joy I experienced when my father returned was heightened by the fact that this new member of the household adored me as much as my father and brother did. I think I gravitated towards the company of men because my sister monopolised the attention of my mother, and when Lisa wasn't doing that she was usually terrorising me, pretending to be a witch and threatening to kill me. I preferred the breezy playfulness of my father and Gene, and Brian was so kind and attentive towards me I decided that, even though he was in his early twenties, I would marry him before I started school.

A certain composure settled over the house. Brian's weekly board, coupled with his way with children, reduced the strain between my parents. He allowed me to help myself to his lime cordial in the fridge any time I wished, much to the chagrin of my mother. He bought me a pair of pink bunny slippers for my fourth birthday. One day when he was baby-sitting, he served a plateful of my mother's spaghetti bolognese for dinner – a dish that I detested – and when I asked him if I had to eat it, I was stunned when he shrugged and replied, *Not if you don't want to.*

Our fragile paradise ended only a few months later, the night my father's Volkswagen hit the telegraph pole on Anzac Parade and every bone on the left side of his body was shattered. At first, the doctors predicted that he would not survive; and when he lived they said he would never walk again, and when he walked they said he'd never again play drums. He proved them wrong on the last prognosis, too, but it would take years for him to achieve it because, along with all those bones, his confidence as a musician was also broken. He let his hair and whiskers grow in the hospital, and I remember nestling in the crook of his arm and brushing his long, multicoloured beard, thinking he must be related to Santa Claus.

The eight months Gerry spent in hospital sent my parents spiralling into debt. My mother began working nights as a waitress at the Hasty Tasty Cafe in Kings Cross. At dawn, the local police used to pick her up in the paddy-wagon and drive her home so she could get my brother and sister up in time for school.

It was such a strain on her – physically, emotionally, financially – that when my father was eventually released from hospital, she began pining for another kind of life, one that would not take him away from his family every night, one that was stable, normal, and paid a regular income. In short, she wanted him to give up music and become a businessman. And he, no doubt damaged in many ways by the trauma of his accident, finally acquiesced. But even then, I sensed it was like putting a ladybird in a matchbox and expecting it to live – I knew the result because I'd already tried it. The day he sold his pearl-grey drums and a man with a beard drove off with them, I pressed my face against the paling fence and wept.

2

I am five years old, sitting in the classroom on my first day of the second school I've started in three months. I am scared and need to wee. But I'm too nervous to ask anyone where the toilet is. I've had a bad morning. Now that I'm a big girl I'm supposed to know how to tie my shoelaces. I tried and tried but it never worked out right and I sort of wedged the laces into a bunch that made them look like they were tied when my mother inspected them. But as soon as I was out the front door of our new house they fell apart and tripped me up.

I've already forgotten the teacher's name. She is handing out small pink books and says she is going to test us on the quiz on page 9. I press my legs together, trying not to wee. I haven't seen the pink books before, let alone the questions inside them. This school is bigger than the last one. There are more rules, like wearing white socks and belts and where you're allowed to play outside. All the other kids have been here since the start of the year and know what to do and when to do it. They sit up straight with their hands on the desk and I do that, too, because I want to seem just like them.

There is a blunt pencil in front of me and I pick it up. I miss my old school and my teacher at Annandale Public. She had big teeth like Princess Anne and her name was Miss Homehorse. This new teacher puts a pink book in front of me but I don't touch it until all the other kids have one and she says, very loudly, You may begin.

    I act like the other kids and open it up to page 9. Once I see the questions and the shapes before me my heart beats faster and I feel even more scared. This is a test. It is Very Important. I can already hear the scratching of lead against the sheets of paper we're supposed to be working on. All the other children seem to know what to do. I am terrified of getting into trouble if I don't do this right. But I can't think properly because I need to wee so much.

    The girl beside me has already done half the test and I haven't even begun. A thought crosses my mind: I could copy from her paper. But something tells me this would probably be a sin. And then I have another idea: if I let out just a little bit of wee, just for a few seconds, I would feel better, and then maybe I could do the test. I glance about – no one is looking. I bow my head and let my muscles loosen. It begins as a spurt but in no time grows into a steady stream and now that it's started and is running down my chair, I can't stop it. I grip my pencil and watch with horror as it rolls out from under my desk and down the middle of the aisle towards the teacher standing at the front of the room. I comfort myself with another idea: she probably won't notice it – or maybe if she does, she won't be able to figure out who did it. I see the thin yellow stream trickling up towards the points of her high-heeled shoes. She looks down. I cower in my seat, still unable to stem the flow. She spots the little dam at her feet and I watch with growing fear as she begins to follow it, like a line of breadcrumbs, down the aisle and around the desks, until she is standing above me, frowning down at my untouched test, my wet and stinking uniform, my shoes and untied laces resting in a pool of wee on the floor.

Mandy, *she says kindly*. If you need to go to the toilet, all you have to do is raise your hand.

I was taken to a small room by the teacher and handed a clean uniform. There were no spare knickers on the shelves and the teacher merely placed my soiled ones and my wet socks in a plastic bag. I was picked up by my mother a few minutes later. I was astonished. Not only was I not in trouble for failing to do the test, I was not in trouble for peeing all over the classroom floor. In fact, the teacher and my mother were being nice to me, as if I'd accomplished something miraculous. And then I had a second school uniform and no undies on and my mother was buying me an ice cream as she led me back to our new house. And as I walked I marvelled at this discovery: *If you need to go to the toilet, all you have to do is raise your hand.*

From that day on, when I raised my hand in class, an expression of relief, almost happiness, came over the teacher's face and she excused me from the classroom, content that I had learned well the first and crucial lesson she'd taught me. After I'd been excused on three occasions an extraordinary idea occurred to me: *The teacher could have no way of knowing if I really need to go to the toilet or not.* So, when I was ambivalent about an activity or exercise, or just plain bored and wanted a break, my hand would rise into the air. I'd see her smile and nod gently, and within seconds I was gliding out the door and into the playground, where I'd roam beneath the jacarandas for a seemingly appropriate time before returning to the classroom that always smelled of glue and rotting bananas. This habit would hold me in good stead at school for another three years, until I realised that, by the age of eight, children are expected to be in control of their bladders.

Our new home was very different from the Victorian Federation in which we'd lived in working-class Stanmore. We'd *moved up in the world*, to the North Shore suburb of Lane Cove. My parents now owned a business: a combined barber, sports, toy and tobacco store on the main street, and we lived in the apartment above. Combining cigarettes and sports goods seems a little odd to me now, but again, this was the late 1960s, and to my parents it must have seemed extremely practical: a customer could buy a carton of Benson & Hedges, pick up a new cricket bat, purchase a fluffy bear for his daughter and then get a crew-cut – all in the one store! The night we moved in, our parents allowed us kids to run downstairs to the shop and pick out a toy each from the stock. My brother chose a football; my sister, a monkey in a red pinafore. I picked a tiny black doll, with a blue-and-white checked dress and bandy legs, whom I named Bindi. I finally had the black baby I had so desired. But I still didn't have the husband.

There were three barber chairs at the back of the store, where I'd find my father in a white coat, scissors snipping around the hairline of some pinch-faced boy or pensioner. My mother worked the cash register at the front, flirting happily with the male customers. According to her, our lives were going to be different and better in this well-heeled, moderate suburb. No more jazz musicians, no more late parties, no more gigs to take my father away at night.

But I was disappointed. This new world seemed so ordered. No one unconventional dropped in. Nothing exciting happened. Gerry no longer played music because he'd been forced to sell his drums. He was still recovering from his injuries and had to wear sculpted wooden clogs to help his bones set properly. Every week a doctor would arrive and my father would lie on his bed and I'd watch the specialist stick wires over his chest, all of which were linked to a machine. I was frightened for my father, because by then I had an idea of what death was – I'd already seen the ladybird expire in the matchbox, a dog hit by a car, the corpse of a neighbour's canary on the floor of its cage, lying stiffly against moist pellets of grey-black shit. And I was scared I would come home from school one day and find my father on his bed, as silent and rigid as that tiny yellow bird.

Meanwhile, my sister regularly tried to kill me. When she knew my mother wasn't around, she'd suddenly appear before me, her long white hair teased and wild, eyes preternaturally wide, and hiss, *I'm a witch!*

No you're not, I'd reply uncertainly. *You're Lisa*.

She'd raise her hands and begin backing me into a corner. *I'm not Lisa. I'm a witch and I've come to kill you.*

You're Lisa, I'd repeat, a tremble in my voice, trying to convince myself that this was true.

She'd cackle ominously and cry, *I've killed your whole family, including Lisa. That's why I look like her. AND NOW I'M GOING TO KILL YOU!* Suddenly, her hands would fly up and grip my throat, trying to strangle me, until I was screaming and sobbing hysterically.

It was only then that she'd release her grip, gushing apologies, telling me it was a game, scared our mother would hear the noise and investigate its cause. For the next few minutes my sister would be unusually nice to me, allowing me to sit on her part of the bunk bed, which was the top, letting me play with her monkey doll, perhaps braiding my hair, all in an attempt to keep me quiet about what had just transpired.

The pathetic aspect of this routine was that, for years, she was able to convince me she really *was* a witch every time she pulled the charade, and I assumed that, every time those smooth white hands gripped my neck, I really *was* about to die.

I wasn't particularly close to Lisa because she didn't like me very much. I wasn't very attached to my mother, either, because she was often busy with the home, the business, and the demands of my sister, who was predisposed to illness. Throughout her childhood, Lisa would often miss two days of school each week because she had a *terrible case of bronchitis*. She also suffered nosebleeds so heavy that she would soak entire bedsheets with her haemorrhaging. She was quite tiny for her age and I used to marvel at how so much blood could come out of someone so small and pale.

I began to realise that illness – real or fake – was a powerful way of avoiding things. It was kind of like pretending, when I was bored at school, that I needed to go to the toilet, but on a much grander scale. One day, after I'd begun the first grade at Lane Cove, I was nominated to collect all the workbooks from everyone's desk, which I did – only to find, to my horror, that mine had suddenly vanished. Heart racing, I looked everywhere: the cupboard, the shelves, underneath all the desks, anticipating the deep trouble I would be in when the teacher realised I had lost such a valuable item. Panicking, I shoved all the books in the appointed cupboard and fled the school at the end of the day. I was already anticipating the punishment I would receive from my new teacher, Miss Fallow, a grim young woman with dark curly hair and acne-scarred skin who used to smoke at her desk while we worked. She'd already screamed at me once or twice before and I was terrified of her. In fact, if anyone raised their voice to me, it would unnerve me so much I would always burst into tears.

My mother had screamed at me once, back at Stanmore, for accidentally spilling some chips on a newly vacuumed floor, and banished me to the room I shared with my sister for the whole afternoon. I was so shaken by the experience that I cried hysterically for hours. I then wrenched off the ring she'd recently given me for my fifth birthday and threw it across the room. The gold bangle on my left wrist remained a treasured gift, given to me by my father, who never yelled at or even got mildly angry with me. It was only after I'd rid myself of the unwanted symbol of my mother that I realised it would get me into further trouble. I searched the room frantically – under the beds, behind the toy box, beneath the wardrobe, but only came up with balls of dust and two lost marbles. At the end of the day, when she entered my room, gentle and conciliatory, it wasn't long before she noticed my hand and asked, *Where's your ring?* I looked at my hand, feigned surprise and announced, *It must have fallen off my finger*.

She took the news calmly, and I experienced terrible pangs of guilt as I watched her patiently pull back each piece of furniture and scour every inch of the bedroom twice. Finally, she shrugged and gave up. *Oh well*, she said kindly. *I'm sure it'll turn up*.

It never did. Which is why I was now convinced that the workbook had also vanished forever, and when my pockmarked, chain-smoking new teacher discovered it was lost, there would be hell to pay. The next morning, when I woke up, I wondered how I could make myself ill. I was sure I could pretend I didn't feel well, but I would have to manufacture some genuine, obvious symptoms to convince my mother my condition was so serious that she would have to keep me home from school. I remembered the first thing she always did whenever I wasn't feeling well: her hand would automatically shoot up to feel my forehead, trying to detect a temperature. Suddenly I had an idea. I reached into my toy box and pulled out my plastic slide projector and turned it on. I huddled beneath the blankets for five or so minutes, the hot bulb of the projector pressed hard against my forehead.

Oh my God! exclaimed my mother, after I'd announced I felt sick and she'd rested her hand above my eyebrows. *You're staying in bed. You're burning up!*

Relief soon bled into an overwhelming sense of guilt, especially when she made a bed for me in the living room so I could watch television, and when both she and Gerry made regular trips up from the shop with sandwiches and toys. This anxiety caused me to tone down my so-called 'symptoms' but I couldn't repress them too much because that meant I would have to return the next day to the wrath of Miss Fallow.

The next morning, my fever suddenly returned, courtesy of the toy slide projector, and my mother, growing concerned, gave me yet another day's reprieve from the dreaded infants' school. Again, I enjoyed the bed in the living room, the gifts of sweets and toys. I wondered how long I could keep this going without her calling a doctor or taking me to hospital. On the third morning, I ditched the projector, knowing full well it was a sin to be so deceitful. But maybe it wasn't so bad to press your stomach against the edge of the kitchen table until it caused you a deep, sharp pain, and then you could truly tell your mother you had pains in your tummy without feeling as if you were lying.

Of course, I tried it, pushing my belly hard against the imitation wood until I could stand it no more. But when I complained of the genuine pains I was experiencing, my mother shook her head and told me I'd had enough time off school. She obviously assumed that no child could be ill if he or she didn't have a hot forehead and wasn't *burning up*.

I returned with dread to Miss Fallow's classroom, to the smell of her cigarettes and cheap perfume, only to find, when I opened the cupboard, my very own workbook sitting on top of all the others, my name printed on the cover. It was nothing less than a miracle, and I put it down to the fact that I did not deceive my mother for as long as I could have: God was rewarding me for acknowledging how bad I'd been.

I experienced a final reprieve from Miss Fallow's temper due, curiously enough, to my taste in music. One afternoon we six-year-olds were assigned the task of bringing one record from home to play in class the following day. That night I looked through my father's large collection and selected my favourite album. But the next morning, as one kid after another had their records played, I was convinced I had made a terrible mistake. I'd never heard recordings like these before: 'Oh Where, Oh Where Has My Little Dog Gone?'; 'Five Little Ducks Went Out One Day'; a woman with a wobbly voice singing a medley of nursery rhymes. I was trembling slightly when my turn came and I passed my record over to Miss Fallow. But when she lowered the needle onto the revolving turntable and Frank Sinatra, accompanied by the Count Basie Big Band, came blaring out of the speakers, I was amazed to see, through the spiral of blue cigarette smoke, an expression of absolute delight on my teacher's face. It was the first time I had ever seen her smile.

I was further stunned when the bell rang for play-lunch and she pulled me aside and asked, in a low voice, *May I borrow your record and take it home?* I bit my bottom lip, not knowing what to say. It was my father's record and I only had permission to borrow it for the day. But then I realised I was now finally in Miss Fallow's good books and if I loaned her the record she might not yell at me anymore and would not keep me in at lunchtime, practising writing capital Ds. I fingered my belt buckle. *All right*, I finally replied, and fled the room.

Much to Gerry's annoyance, she did not keep it for a night or two. Despite gentle reminders, days stretched into weeks, and weeks into months, until she finally relinquished it towards the end of the year. But, to her credit, Miss Fallow maintained our silent understanding and, after she'd been loaned the album, she was nothing but kind towards me.

My second-grade teacher was a young, vivacious woman just out of college. She was short as a twelve-year-old girl and had as much enthusiasm as any child in the classroom, and it was through her joy and encouragement that I began to write and read voraciously.

One morning Miss Frost passed out small, hardback orange dictionaries and encouraged us to compose *an entire sentence*. She was trying to teach us the difference between verbs and nouns. We were instructed to look up every word in the dictionary to make sure we were spelling it correctly. I quickly decided upon the statement I wished to set down: *I like looking at the painted starfish at the bottom of the sea*, and went thumbing through the dictionary, carefully copying each word into my notebook. As Miss Frost wandered between the desks, checking on everyone's progress, she casually leaned over my shoulder to peruse what I had written. Suddenly, she swept up my notebook and marched to the front of the classroom. I did not know if I had done something wrong or something right. *Boys and girls*, she announced. *Listen to this*. The other children obediently put down their pencils and looked up. *This is a very good example of an adjective*, she announced. *Remember, an adjective is a describing word*. I began to relax. Obviously she liked my adjective, *painted*. Miss Frost cleared her throat: *I like looking at the pointed starfish at the bottom of the sea*, she announced. *Pointed*, she remarked, *that is a very good describing word for a starfish*.

I sat there feeling guilty again. Should I tell her I'd made a mistake and had looked up the wrong word, or happily accept the praise? I swallowed, finally deciding on the latter. It was the first sentence I had ever written.

My best friend at school was Kerryn Harrison, a cute, slightly chubby girl with short curly ash-blonde hair. Kerryn's former best friend was Barbara, an earnest young thing with freckles and long red hair which she always wore in two perfectly braided plaits. Barbara played the violin and was so intelligent she was in the 'A' class of the grade. It wasn't hard to steal Kerryn away from Barbara, especially when I showed her how to make bird calls with the mouthpiece of a recorder, and when I shared with her my secret of how to get out of class when you were bored. We always walked around the playground arm-in-arm, kissed each other sometimes, and announced to the other kids we were going to get married.

Youse can't get married! taunted the boys. *Youse two are girls!* We thought about this, and wondered if it were true.

The good thing about my father giving up music was that he was usually either in the shop or upstairs at home and I began to know him better. During my sixth birthday party, he appeared in the kitchen, wearing one of his white hairdressing coats back-to-front, his hair teased up to look like some mad professor, and announced to me and my eleven friends that he was Dr Mustafoo. Brandishing a teaspoon, he performed a comic routine during which the teaspoon became variously a stethoscope, a dentist's drill, and a microscope as he moved from child to child, examining them and pulling invisible lice from their hair and pretending he could look into my ear and see right through my head. All the kids were in stitches and my popularity suddenly soared, especially when my parents, half drunk by this time, let us run wild through the closed shop downstairs and play with all the toys. Later, my five-year-old friend William entertained us in the lounge room by playing the cornet. Gerry genuinely thought he was *a natural*, and should take the instrument up professionally.

I played with William after school and on the weekends. He was the younger brother of my brother's best friend and lived only a block away. William had a blunt bowl-cut of straight blond hair, and slanted blue eyes that made him seem like a very fair Asian child. The reason I liked him so much was that he would never cower from any adventure I dreamed up, no matter how outlandish or illegal it might have been. Sometimes we'd steal flowers from a particular garden, knock on the front door of the same property, and sell them back to the unwitting woman who'd grown them. For a while there I liked sneaking into other people's houses, even if they were at home. I'd creep up the back stairs and slip through the screen door and have a look around, perhaps play with a toy left on the floor or finger a row of figurines. I also liked to inspect bathrooms, and was amazed by how many variations could exist of an area that was basically for weeing and bathing: painted or wallpapered; tiled or partly carpeted; some had enormous claw-footed baths, others just a tiny shower recess. And then there were the extras: crocheted toilet seat covers, plastic prescription jars, soaps carved into the shapes of shells and flowers.

Obviously, I was curious about how other people lived and William, well . . . William just liked to follow me around. I realised we were too young to be a threat to anyone and, if we were discovered, would not be considered thieves, or even trespassers. Once, however, an old man heard us playing in his garage and yelled at us to come out: he was going to *call the police*, he was going to have us *arrested*. William and I cowered further behind a wall of stacked beer kegs, trembling, as the man screamed and ranted. Finally, I signalled to William to make a run for it. But as we burst out of the garage, I accidentally tipped over one of the empty beer kegs and, as we dashed towards the fence, it went rolling down the steep driveway and crashed into the old man before he had a chance to catch us.

At night, I sat on my father's lap as my parents sipped scotch. The whole family would watch popular television shows like 'Bewitched', and 'I Dream of Jeannie'. On hot summer nights we'd move the sofa, chairs and television out onto the patio and later sleep out there on fold-out mattresses. It was around this time that my mother decided Gerry wasn't doing enough male-bonding with my brother, and forced him to take Gene on weekend camping trips, which bothered me because I wasn't allowed to go along and was left at home with my sister. The trips annoyed Gerry, too, because he didn't know the first thing about camping and would often return bruised and cut, his fingernails stripped to the quick.

My mother then suggested that my father join the local Better Businessmen's Bureau. After enduring much harping and cajoling, he finally attended his first social gathering of the local group. After one beer, however, he reeled out of the building aghast, vowing never to return. When he arrived home, he wailed, *All they want to talk about is what kind of mark-up I have on razor blades! I said to them, guys, I came down here to have a beer and forget about all that crap. You can stick your razor blades up your arse.*

I suppose he was trying to atone for the financial and emotional strain he'd caused our mother following his near-fatal car accident, but even at seven years old, I could tell the effort it took him was destroying whatever it was that had kept them bound together.

How would you like your hair cut? I heard him ask an elderly man one day.

Short, the man replied.

OK. No worries. He whipped a white towel around the man's neck and picked up a pair of scissors.

. . . But I don't want it SHORT, the man added.

I saw my father pause. He put down the scissors and pulled the towel from the man's neck. *All right, mate. Let's start again. How do you want your hair cut?*

Oh, you know. I want it short.

Gerry nodded, slipping the towel back into place.

But, you know, not . . . SHORT.

Gerry sighed. I could see he wanted to jab the man with the scissors in his hands. He rolled his eyes and ran a hand through his own hair.

OK, mate. One last time. I'm going to ask you how you'd like your hair cut and you're going to answer me with just ONE WORD: trimmed, medium or short, all right?

The man nodded.

So how do you want your hair cut?

Short.

Fine, short it is. Gerry picked up the scissors and made his first snip at the man's hairline.

. . . But not short, the man murmured again.

That's fucking IT! My father threw down the scissors. *Just because you've escaped from a mental asylum, don't try and send me there!* He wrenched off his white coat. *I'm going down the pub!* he cried to my mother. He strode past me as if I weren't there, and pushed his way through all the bewildered customers, past the razors and combs, the tennis racquets, golf balls, the Mickey Mouse dolls and stuffed rabbits, the display case filled with pipes and cartons of Marlboro and on, striding towards that shimmering oasis of the hotel at the end of the street.

3

I am running towards a brick wall. I spin sideways and throw myself against it. The pain forks up my arm and shoulder, but I don't hear a bone breaking. I back away to get a better running start, draw in a deep breath, and charge towards the wall again, ramming my elbow against it. The impact makes me reel back and fall to the ground. I see my skin is cut and grazed now; blood forms a tiny red bracelet around my wrist. An ache crawls up towards my neck, but I know it's not pain enough. I pick myself up and back away once more, preparing for another attempt. Suddenly, my mother's at my side, demanding to know what's wrong, why I am bleeding so badly. But I can't get the words out to answer her. She bathes my wounds with disinfectant. She asks me again as she wraps my arm with gauze.

Finally, I tell her I fell over in the paddock behind the hotel.

What did you fall on? asks my mother. *A broken mirror?*

I don't answer her, of course. And most of all I can't tell her that I've done this to myself on purpose.

*

Just weeks after my eighth birthday, my aunt dropped my mother, sister and me off in front of the residential wing of a sprawling brick pub called the Mulga Hotel. It stood on the dusty main street of a remote western suburb. As we pulled our bags from the boot of the car, the front door swung open and a glamorous woman with long red hair appeared before us. She was wearing a pink negligee, and clutched the filmy material against her throat.

Sir Charles, no! she cried. Suddenly, an enormous, muscular Great Dane came bounding out from behind her, barking as it ran down the stairs. The silver-haired dog was as big as a Shetland pony, almost as tall as I was, and I pressed back against the bonnet of my aunt's car, terrified.

The woman pulled the dog back by his collar and calmed him down. She introduced herself as Natalie. I noticed she had skin as pale as a peeled apple and she looked as haughty and mysterious as a silent film star. She exuded the scent of something sweet – it reminded me of honey. We picked up our bags and followed the pink cloud of her translucent nylon into a hallway and up a flight of stairs. The first room on the right was to be the room for my sister and me. It contained two single beds, a dresser, a wardrobe and a corner sink. It was the first hotel room I'd ever seen, and I found it sparse and depressing. The window overlooked the pub's curved driveway and the main street. Our mother's room was directly opposite ours, but smaller. Natalie then led us down the long hallway, lined on either side with wooden doors, and showed us the bathroom we were to share with the other hotel boarders: I was surprised to see three toilet cubicles, two shower recesses, two baths and, pressing through the thin material of the negligee, Natalie's two dark nipples.

We were shown the rest of the property. Downstairs was a dark, formal dining room filled with antiques: a large, round wooden table and matching chairs, an ancient organ with stops and pedals, overstuffed chairs, and the smell of mothballs and austerity. This was where the boarders – three men – always dined. Natalie pushed open a swinging door that led into a huge, sunny kitchen. Walking from one room to the other was like emerging from a crypt into the blinding light of day. I had never seen a kitchen so big. The windows overlooked a side yard, where I noticed two other Great Danes. Natalie pointed to the bigger one with a silver-grey coat and said, *That's Duchess*. Then she gestured to the smaller black one, who was digging a hole in the garden: *And that one's Mona*.

A round modern table sat to one side with lime-green swivel chairs. Natalie told us this was where my mother, sister and I were to take our meals, so as not to disturb the lodgers.

We followed her out of the kitchen and down the hallway to an open door, where the rather ordinary faded red carpet was replaced by a swirling purple pattern and the colour of the walls changed from beige to white. Once we stepped over this invisible border we were now in the apartment of Natalie, her husband, and her three boys. There were closed bedroom doors on either side of the corridor, which led into a large living room. Everything my gaze fell upon exuded an aura of grandiose excess: the sparkling chandelier, the mirror above the fireplace with its heavy, gold-leaf frame, the two marble statues of naked nymphs, the glass coffee table so bright and buffed I could see my reflection in it. For someone who liked sneaking into strangers' houses and observing how different people lived, I was near swooning. In all my wanderings I had never encountered a home as palatial as this one.

But there was more: the French doors opened out to a patio, which overlooked a rectangular pool. Natalie told us we were free to swim in it any time, but we'd have to walk through their private apartment in order to access the yard. We followed her down a path that ran the length of the garden and she opened a gate to her right, and then yet another entirely different world unfolded before my eyes.

Horses. There was a tan one only a few feet away, drinking from a trough of water. *That's Roving Eye*, said Natalie. And that's *Marine Boy*, she added, nodding to a dark brown one in the next corral. The corral after that contained a white one, who was called *Great Expectations*. I was astonished. What more could these people own? A Rolls Royce? A jet? A private cinema? All in all, they owned seven racehorses. Natalie informed us they were her husband's greatest passion, and we were never to feed them without permission from Pat, the trainer. The horses were on a strict diet and exercise regime and their calorie intake had to remain consistent.

I wondered what kind of children were so blessed as to have been born into such wealth and opulence. On top of her other many duties, my mother had been hired to look after them, which meant I would now have to share her with three other kids. It didn't seem fair to me, as they already had two parents to themselves and my sister and I now had only one between us.

We followed Natalie back through the apartment and into the kitchen. Suddenly, I heard the front door slam and the big dog, Sir Charles, barking loudly. A rather tall, lanky boy, not quite in his teens, walked into the room. He had dark red hair and the bluest eyes I'd ever seen; he was followed by a smaller boy, about my age, who had straight red hair with a blunt fringe and an unusually wide mouth that seemed to contain more teeth than was normal. He was followed by a chubby, fair-haired boy who was probably a little younger than me. He had his mother's round, gentle face.

Boys, said Natalie, *this is your new housekeeper.* My mother smiled nervously and said hello. I could tell she was straining to make a good first impression. She was already wearing an apron and had rolled up her sleeves, ready to begin work. *And these are her girls, Lisa and Mandy.* We all sized each other up. *This is Ian.* Natalie gestured at the older one, who was frowning and had his jaw firmly set. *This is Peter*, she said, pointing at the middle one, who bugged his eyes and pulled a face. *And this is Nigel*, she added, patting the head of her smallest son. *Now be nice, boys. I'm sure you're all going to get along fine.* And then she floated out of the room, the folds of her pink negligee billowing behind her.

The boys stood there, looking my mother up and down as she poured them glasses of milk. There was something grim and hard in their faces, as if she smelled bad or was wearing her dress back-to-front.

How long you reckon you're gunna last? said the older one, Ian, his fists clenched inside his trouser pockets.

My mother turned around, surprised, yet trying to maintain her smile. She opened her mouth to speak, but before she had a chance to reply, the middle one, Peter, sneered, *I'll give her three weeks.*

Yeah, agreed Ian. *None of 'em ever last longer than that.*

*

My parents didn't have a fight before they split up; in fact, they didn't even argue. The separation was as gradual as the movements of two icebergs drifting in opposite directions. The day Gerry had stormed out of the shop, heading for the pub, was the beginning of the end, but it was more than a year before they sold the car, the furniture, the paintings, our bicycles, and said goodbye to one another.

They'd been losing money running the store. They sold the business after two years and we moved into a rented house in a cheaper part of Lane Cove. It was the worst-looking house in the street, covered in dark grey stucco and surrounded by overgrown grass and paspalum. My mother began working full-time in a lolly factory and Gerry bought another hairdressing business on the ground floor of a large building in Kent Street, in the city. It was a small shop with only two chairs and no sports goods or tobacco to complicate transactions. Fortunately, I didn't have to change schools with this move and for a while life seemed settled and close to happy. Gerry drank less and began to smoke more pot; my mother brought home free lollies from the factory and, because there was a constant supply, I became rather popular with the neighbouring children.

My brother was planning to quit school that year, at the age of fifteen, because he wanted to work at a small vineyard owned by the father of his best friend. At the same time, my sister began menstruating. I didn't quite know what that meant at the time, but was aware of the mysterious package in our wardrobe that had been placed there by our mother. *Feminine Hygiene* was printed on the box. Around the same time, Lisa wanted to attend a school dance, and the subject of her chosen ensemble was being discussed at the dinner table. She made the announcement that she intended to wear lace-up boots and a mini-skirt. Gerry shook his head and told her she was too young to wear something as provocative as that, and an argument escalated between them. Lisa, close to tears, began begging him to allow her to wear the outfit. *No,* he insisted, *I already said you're too young.* I decided to leap to my sister's defence. *No, she's not, Dad. She's already got her pyramids.*

He burst into laughter, and my mother and brother echoed him, as if I'd just told the funniest joke they'd heard in years. My unwitting blunder buoyed his spirits so much that he finally relented and allowed Lisa to wear the skirt and boots – *only because you've got pyramids,* he kept repeating, still laughing. Even so, Lisa was furious with me for blurting out her secret in front of everyone and, before we went to bed that night, she punched me hard on the arm.

I woke up one Saturday morning and found Gerry wasn't home. *Is he at work?* I asked. My mother shook her head. *I don't know where he is. But don't worry, he'll be back.* She seemed fairly confident and I wondered if she knew more than she was telling me. I waited two days, three. The car was still in the driveway. Most of his clothes were in his wardrobe. He'd left behind his favourite boots. I waited a week, still no word. The second week passed. Every afternoon when I came home from school, I'd run from room to room, expecting to discover him. But it was like chasing a ghost and I wondered if he had in fact died and my mother was trying to protect me from the news.

By the second weekend, I was beside myself with worry, convinced that he'd passed away without even saying goodbye.

But right when I was resigning myself to this notion, I heard a knock on the front door early one morning and suddenly he was before me, sunburnt and grinning. *How's it going, Sunshine?* he said, sweeping past me as if he'd only been away a few minutes to buy a packet of cigarettes.

Where've you been? I called after him.

He paused in front of the closed door of the main bedroom. *You know what I did?*

I shook my head and brushed the sleep out of my eyes.

I went out to the airport, walked up to the counter and said to the chick, the next plane that's leaving – where's it flying to? And she said, Darwin. I said, fine, give us a one-way ticket. And off I went, just like that! Just on the spur of the moment.

He seemed infinitely proud of this display of spontaneity, as if it were some distinguished accomplishment or heroic deed. As he turned the doorknob and disappeared into the bedroom, I realised that it was his birthday and he had just turned fifty.

There was no reprimand or anger awaiting him when he dived into bed beside my mother. In fact, she was thrilled to see him again and I was surprised to glimpse them lying against the pillows, kissing and cuddling like newlyweds. But from that day on, their routine began to alter. Gerry gave up drinking and went on a health kick, living on salads and nuts. At night, when he arrived home from work, he and my mother would sit in the kitchen with the door closed. He'd eat his special meal, my mother would drink beer, and they would have one of their *discussions*. I had no idea what they were discussing in there every night; I only knew we kids were forbidden to trespass into these talks.

One evening, about two months after Gerry's return from Darwin, the kitchen door swung open and they both walked solemnly into the living room. *Kids*, announced Gerry, *we've got something to tell you.* His voice sounded unusually serious. My mother switched the television off. *Your mother and I are separating.* We glanced between them, disbelieving. *She's going to get a live-in housekeeping job. I'm moving into the back of the barber shop.*

The back of the barber shop? I wondered. There was no back of the barber shop. It was all shop. *Gene's leaving school and is going to work in the vineyard.*

I shifted uncomfortably. *Where will we live?* I asked, meaning Lisa and myself.

Oh, he said, as if the question hadn't occurred to him before. *You girls'll go with your mother.*

The reason, they both assured us, was that they just couldn't afford to keep a family under the one roof anymore. A housekeeping job would provide my mother with a small income and relieve them both of the burden of paying rent and bills.

This separation was supposed to have been amicable and possibly temporary, and they went to great lengths to explain that they still loved each other, but as time went on I began to suspect it was a lot less friendly and practical than they wanted us to believe. Firstly, once we moved to the Mulga Hotel, Gerry never visited us and, for some inexplicable reason, our mother would not allow us to visit him. My father's goodbye had been disturbingly brief: a quick kiss on the cheek before he crawled into a borrowed car crammed with his few possessions and drove through the front gates and out of my life. The first thing I remember doing in the hotel bedroom was writing him a letter, describing the pub and the horses and the swimming pool, and telling him how much I missed him. He had vowed he would write back to me.

When I asked my mother for his address, and for some money to a buy a stamp, she offered to post the letter for me. In fact, she became insistent and I finally handed over the sealed envelope, making her promise she would mail it that very afternoon. I waited a week, two weeks, but there was never any reply. I wrote a second letter, a third. My mother cheerfully offered to post the letters again, and I passed them to her, certain I could trust her.

It was during this interlude that I first began to experience frenzied fits of crying, a deep, visceral hysteria that sometimes continued for hours. I found these episodes frightening because they were so sudden and because, no matter how hard I tried, I had no way of controlling them. Also, they were embarrassing, and I certainly didn't want my sister or those three awful boys seeing me in such a state. When I felt an episode coming on I'd walk down the second-floor hallway and lock myself in the broom closet, thrashing around on the floor until it passed, leaving me exhausted.

I was beginning to feel that this separation idea was a cheap trick, a sham, that my father had abandoned me forever and I would never see him again. My mother was working up to fifteen hours a day: cleaning, feeding the horses and dogs, cooking entirely separate meals three times a day for Mr and Mrs Ronson, we children, and the boarders upstairs. She was beginning to drink heavily, usually scotch. It was easy to see why no housekeeper had lasted longer than three weeks: the work was demanding and the two older boys – Ian and Peter – were uncontrollable, lighting fires in the garden, putting laxatives in the boarders' drinks, exposing their genitals while we kids were having breakfast. Their parents never seemed to emerge from the main bedroom – they were always inside there, day and night – and the few times I did see Natalie she was invariably swathed in one of her negligees. My mother left meal trays at their door and, like a hotel maid, returned later to collect the dirty dishes. I wondered how and when Natalie and Mr Ronson went to the toilet. Maybe they had one of their own in there, along with the television set I glimpsed one day when the door was left slightly ajar.

My mother enrolled me in the third grade of the local public school, which caused some consternation to the principal because I was seven months younger than all the other kids and she presumed I wouldn't be able to cope with the work. The principal suggested I repeat the second grade, especially since this was my third school in as many years, but my mother stood her ground and into the third grade I went.

The class work was easy but the other children proved to be tough. Girls mocked my unfashionable pointy-toed school shoes. My uniform wasn't short enough. I lived in *a pub!* My mother was *a housekeeper!* And I was the tallest child in the class, taller than any of the boys. I remember sitting alone, in the shade of a withered plane tree, watching the other kids play tag, eating my vegemite sandwiches and wondering if I would ever have friends again.

The most popular girl in my class was Robina Wagner. She was not particularly pretty or intelligent, but she had one characteristic that elevated her above the average eight-year-old: a broken arm. She wore it in a sling made of translucent red material and, at any time during recess or lunch, she could always be found surrounded by a group of adoring girls who liked to autograph their names on her cast. One glance at the white plaster around her arm could arouse envy in any girl even mildly lonely: the monickers, the drawings of flowers, the messages of good luck and best wishes were a testimony to the camaraderie in which she basked each day. When the girls ran out of space on the cast, they moved onto the red sling, their proclamations looping upwards towards the knot at the back of her neck. By this time she didn't look so much like a girl with an injury as a walking monument to the many and varied friendships she enjoyed.

After my unsuccessful attempt at breaking my own arm, in order to become popular like Robina, I did what many isolated and vulnerable people do: I found God. I experienced a certain amount of solace and distraction in preparing for my First Holy Communion. There were weekly scripture classes at school, augmented by classes on Saturday mornings at the church, and of course Sunday mornings were devoted to mass, which was still being recited in Latin. I enjoyed the ritual of putting on my best dress and walking a mile along the dusty main street, then sitting in the church, inhaling the scent of furniture polish and watching the way the light pressed through the stained-glass windows. If I just stayed with God, I decided, I would be all right – or so I thought at the time.

My mother was steadily drinking more and more and I noticed she now kept a small bottle of mouth freshener in her apron pocket. One morning, after she had given me some pocket money, I walked across the street to the newsagency and bought a 1972 Almanac for the Star Sign of Gemini. I thought it might cheer her up, perhaps give her hope for the year ahead. When I presented her with the gift, however, she flew into a rage, slapping my legs and screaming at me for having spent all of my weekly allowance so quickly and on a book that was utterly useless.

I fled upstairs and spent another afternoon locked inside the broom closet.

It was around this time that my mother's older brother and sister-in-law heard about our circumstances. They arrived at the hotel one Saturday morning unannounced, pretending they were just passing through our remote western suburb. My mother, surprised, greeted them and made them tea in the kitchen of the hotel. She wasn't close to her brother and his wife – in fact I couldn't remember them having visited us before – and I wondered why Phil and June were suddenly in our lives. We only ever saw them once or twice a year, when we visited Floss and Auntie Joan – they all lived within a mile of each other. Phil and June had three boys; their only daughter, Cherie, was a year younger than me and would throw spectacular tantrums when she didn't get her way. Whenever she came near me I would always run and hide.

Every time I'd met June she'd been wearing a slim black cocktail dress; her dark hair swept up into a high, lacquered beehive. This day was no different, even though it was ten o'clock in the morning. Uncle Phil had lost more hair and his paunch was a little bigger. He'd made his money collecting bottles, which he'd done for over twenty-five years. He was what you called a Bottle-o. I didn't think you could make very much money picking up empty beer and soft-drink containers, but they owned a three-bedroom house, a caravan, a boat; their kids had a pet goat in the back yard. I sat before them in the kitchen, wondering how many bottles it must have taken to pay for all those things. Millions, I guessed. Hundreds of millions.

After finishing tea, June wanted to see the rest of the hotel, and Mum and I led them through the Ronson's apartment, onto the patio, showing them the pool, the dogs, the horses. June inspected the property closely, scrutinising every detail, as if she were considering buying it. When they walked back inside, I remained behind and played in the yard. About ten minutes later, my mother called me in to say goodbye to them. At the front door, June pecked my cheek and Uncle Phil patted me on the head. They climbed back into their station wagon and drove away.

What was that all about? I asked. *They've never visited us before.*

They thought they could give you a better life, said my mother. *They wanted to adopt you.*

My stomach tightened. I couldn't think of anything worse than being separated from my mother.

What about Lisa? I asked.

My mother shook her head. *They just wanted you. They thought you'd make a good sister for Cherie.*

I could feel the blood draining from my face. My head began to hurt.

My mother took my hand. *Don't worry, love*, she said. *I wouldn't give you up for the world.*

In the meantime, my sister was heading into adolescence. While kids at my school merely ignored me, the ones at her high school were highly antagonistic because she looked so ethereal and petite: long fair hair, blue eyes, milky-white skin. After her first day there a girl picked a fight with her and I was horrified to see them punching and brawling in the dusty paddock behind the hotel. Soon she *fell in with a bad crowd*, and she and her friends took to frequenting public telephone booths and ripping the directory books to shreds. She changed her clothes up to six times a day, and the hems of her skirts rose with every passing week.

One day at school, when we were being taught the steps of a progressive waltz, I was swung on to the next partner in the circle and, as soon as I was in his arms, he boasted, *I've seen your sister in the nude!* I flushed with embarrassment – after all, she was only thirteen. *You have not*, I replied, though I knew instantly my voice lacked a certain conviction. *I have!* the boy insisted, as he guided me into the reverse steps. *Through the screen door at Prue Crampton's house. She was in there with my brother!*

The only person I was remotely friendly with was Nigel, the youngest and gentlest of the Ronson boys. On Sundays, after I arrived home from church, he and I would sneak into the closed public bar of the hotel. We'd crawl around on the floor, searching for small change dropped by the previous night's customers who'd been too drunk to care or know. The carpet smelled of stale booze and cigarette smoke as our hands patted along its damp texture, seeking out copper and silver coins that would later buy us Icy Poles or a frozen chocolate Heart.

Even though they were only nine and twelve, the two older boys, Ian and Peter, were so obsessed with sex they would take any opportunity to demonstrate their insatiability. Whenever Peter experienced an erection he'd promptly pull down his pants and wave his hard, tiny willy in front of me, as if it were a trophy. They'd tease Nigel for having befriended me, and kept taunting him with the question, *When are you gunna root her, Baby-boy?* They also liked to taunt me: *You're a nobody. Your mother's just a housekeeper, just a slave, really. And you're just a slave's daughter. You'll end up just like her. Working for rich people like us.*

When I met their father for the first time I realised that they were merely milder and younger versions of this overbearing man. Balding, bug-eyed and extremely overweight, he had the apoplectic face of a heavy drinker and teeth the colour of wet cement. He rarely emerged from the bedroom he shared with Natalie, but when he did he was always dressed in a pair of carpet slippers and loose boxer shorts, affording an uninterrupted view of his enormous, bloated belly. Every sentence he uttered contained an expletive. *I told you fucking kids not to feed the fucking horses! Roving Eye's put on fucking weight. Now, which one of you little bastards did it? I wanna fucking know!* It was awful to imagine the beautiful, honey-scented Natalie in bed with him all day.

He was equally offensive towards his staff. Once, I overheard him saying to my mother, *You're damn lucky to have this job. Who else'd take on a woman at your age with two bloody kids?* She worked up to fifteen hours a day, six days a week. He paid her fifty-eight dollars a fortnight, plus our keep. Ronson treated his own father-in-law, whom he employed as a handyman, with the same amount of contempt. Everyone called Natalie's father Poppa, even my mother. He was a kind, gentle man, with snowy white hair and a limp. And he was always wearing overalls. I used to like hanging around his tool shed on the weekends, watching him repair barstools and helping polish up the horses' saddles. When his wife visited and brought gifts for the boys, she invariably gave presents to my sister and me as well.

Through Mr Ronson's horseracing connections my mother came into contact with various men who were *filthy rich*. One afternoon she was serving drinks to Mr Ronson and his friends on the patio as they argued about which one of them owned the best car. Mr Ronson had a Mercedes with a sunroof; Natalie drove a silver convertible Alfa Romeo; a jockey who sometimes rode for Ronson boasted a late model white Porsche; another man, in his 60s, with thin, greying hair and a pencil moustache, drove a vintage black Jaguar. As they continued bantering, Mr Ronson turned towards my mother and asked, *Well, what do you think, Betty? Which one would you pick?*

None of them, she replied, setting the last glass on the table.

Whaddya mean? asked a disbelieving Ronson.

Well, to me a car isn't a status symbol. It's a means to get you from A to B. If I had my choice I'd choose something functional and easy to run. Like a Datsun. Yes, I'd probably choose a Datsun.

Ronson waved her away. *Oh, what the fuck would you know?*

The older man who drove the vintage black Jaguar was so obviously impressed by her that he later walked into the kitchen and asked her out. My mother was still very attractive, with semi-tanned skin and blonde hair that she wore swept up into what she called *a French roll*. Percy was the first of several men she began dating. He grew so besotted with her that one day he turned up unannounced at the hotel and summoned her to the bar. When she arrived, he pointed through the double glass doors. She turned and took a few steps forward: there in the driveway was a brand new Datsun Bluebird. *Here's the keys*, said Percy, dropping them into her hand. She stood stock-still and began to flush with embarrassment. *No thanks*, she replied, and palmed the keys back.

That night, when she told Mr Ronson about the purchase, Ronson snorted and shook his head. *You're fucking mad. To Percy, that's just like buying a box of matches.*

Yes, agreed my mother, *but I'm not a box of matches.*

There were some advantages to living amongst the wealthy. Occasionally, the class and social lines blurred and I was privileged to have experiences from which I would otherwise have been excluded. Riding in Mr Ronson's Mercedes Benz, the sunroof down, a tape of The Monkees blaring as Natalie drove and sang the lyrics, her red hair wild in the wind. Going to the races once when Ronson's horses were running, and being allowed to lay fifty-cent bets with a bookmaker. One day Natalie was cleaning out a storeroom and gave me three old books from her childhood: they were big, musty annuals from the 1930s, with stories about English girls in boarding schools who have *pillow fights* and *high tea*, with framed coloured plates illustrating their various adventures. I had no books of my own and devoured these annuals, reading the tales again and again, as if they could release me permanently from the world of the Mulga Hotel. Of course, I'd done enough scripture study to know that the path to true redemption was through the Catholic church. As my mother hand-sewed my white lace Holy Communion dress, I dutifully attended all my classes in religious instruction – at school and on the weekends.

There was only one flaw in this holy regime. The elderly nun who taught me made it very clear that, before I was to make my communion, I had to attend confession twice a week and admit all my most recent sins. The problem was, I already had a fairly good idea of right and wrong and could never think of any trespasses I had committed. But I knew I couldn't creep into the box and sit there dumbly, saying nothing and wasting the priest's time, so twice a week I found myself cloaked in darkness, inventing sins that I could never, in my craziest dreams, have actually carried out. It started off with simple naughtiness: *I lied to my mother; I thought a bad thought; I didn't share my lollies with my sister.* But after a week or so I had run out of minor infringements and moved on to grander crimes. *I stole the fur coat of my mother's boss; I cut the brakes of a boy's bike; I set fire to my best friend's guinea pig.* Each session my misdeeds became more elaborate and fanciful, yet even then, the irony didn't escape me: I was actually committing the sin of lying in order not to commit another sin, which was the sin of not attending confession. Yet in my private, spiritual order I felt excused from damnation because I was still doing the increasingly hefty penances for the bad things I'd never done.

My communion dress was exquisite: long-sleeved, with a flowing skirt made of embroidered lace, and pearl buttons. My mother was brimming with pride when I tried it on, even though she never attended mass herself. The day of the ceremony was auspicious in another way, as my brother attended, and it was the first time I'd seen him since my parents had separated months earlier. After the service, we all returned to the pub and sat in the closed public bar. I peppered Gene with questions, eager to hear any news of our father. True to his word, Gerry was now sleeping in the back of the barber shop. And my brother was living with him, having tossed in his job at the vineyard.

But there's no back of the shop, I said, *it's just one tiny room in a big building.*

Dad rigged up a sheet, he explained, *there's just enough room behind it for a double mattress.*

But what about cooking?

Gene smiled. *Cafes.*

I thought about this for a moment. It didn't seem plausible. *But what about taking a bath?*

He smiled again. *Wynyard Station. There're old showers there for people who travel.*

I imagined my father and brother trawling the city streets each day, from cheap restaurants to public railway stations to corner pubs and then back to the minuscule barber shop to sleep together on a mattress on the floor. He'd given us up to be able to live in this way? He'd left behind any sense of luxury or even comfort, yet he was still cutting hair instead of playing music, and the sacrifice didn't seem to be justifying the reward. It left me feeling heavy and confused.

We'd been living at the Mulga Hotel for well over a year when Mr Ronson summoned a meeting of all the hotel's inhabitants and workers. Crowded into the kitchen were his two in-laws, Poppa and Nanna; Pat, the horse trainer; all the boarders; my mother, sister and me; the three boys and, of course, Natalie. Sir Charles, Ronson's regal and muscular Great Dane, sat beside him, panting.

Right, now I want youse to all bloody listen to this. He began pulling at his curly grey chest hair. *The dogs are in heat. They're mating, understand?*

I looked around the room and saw everybody nodding. Mr Ronson gazed at me directly. I nodded too.

Now, Sir Charles and Duchess – they're top breeders. What you call pedigrees. The best.

I nodded automatically this time, thinking of Duchess's sleek silver-grey fur, how big and lean she was.

But Mona, she's just a little runty bitch. A no-nothing.

I thought of the heavier, smaller, black Great Dane, and wondered why he was calling her a bitch.

So we got two girls in heat, understand? More nods. *But we only *want one of 'em to breed, right? The pedigree one – Duchess.* Ronson glanced at his wife, swathed in a cream lace negligee, and Sir Charles began panting harder, as if he understood what Ronson was talking about. A string of drool hung at the side of the dog's mouth, wavering.

Now Mona's gunna wanna get some action, too. And Sir Charles's gunna wanna – you know – oblige her. But we don't want Mona pregnant, that's the last thing we want. So this is what we're gunna do. Sir Charles hung his head a little and the icicle of drool suddenly dropped onto the carpet. *Duchess stays in that yard.* Mr Ronson pointed through the kitchen to the fenced side garden. *That's where they're gunna be breeding. And Mona –* Ronson cocked his thumb over his right shoulder, indicating the much bigger garden with the pool – *she's gunna be in that yard.*

Ronson paused and played with his chest hair again. *Now, Sir Charles and Duchess are allowed in the house whenever they want, but Mona's in quarantine out there.* Another cock of the thumb. *And whatever youse do, don't let Sir Charles out into Mona's yard! Understand?* A few murmured yeses wavered throughout the room. I leaned against the kitchen table, taking all the information in. I had never seen dogs mate before and was curious as to how they did it. Then Mr Ronson clicked his fingers. Sir Charles automatically stood up. As Mr Ronson and Natalie swept out of the room together, the dog followed them, the peaks of his ears twitching like two antennas.

After making my Holy Communion I continued confessing invented sins and repeating the prayers that were my penance, which varied between ten and twenty each time, depending on how bad I imagined I'd been, and how I'd described it to the priest. I wondered whether it would be a sin to watch the dogs mating, but it didn't overly concern me, because every time I went into the side yard, Sir Charles and Duchess were either eating or sleeping, and did not seem remotely interested in one another.

On the Saturday following Mr Ronson's lecture, I was playing in the paddock behind the hotel. Just near the sandpit, I came across Peter's bicycle left lying on the ground, a shiny blue ten-gear Speedwell. As I did not have a bike of my own, I was tempted to pick it up and ride it down to the fence and back, but I knew it was wrong to take or even borrow something without asking the owner first. I looked about: the boys were nowhere in sight, and therefore there was no one to ask. *No*, I thought, *it's still wrong to take it*. But as I stood there, eyeing the plastic streamers attached to the handlebars, another thought popped into my head: *It's all right to take the bike, because you can just confess the sin next week and be absolved*. Since I was already doing penance for far worse things than borrowing a bike without permission, this line of reasoning began to make more and more sense. I picked the bike up, swung my leg over the frame, and began pedalling across cracked earth and tufts of grass, steering my way clear of potholes and fallen branches. Diamonds of sunlight flickered through a flowering bloodwood. The wind raked my hair. But as I came closer and closer to the fence a feeling of dread overcame me, as if I were pedalling towards some sudden and untimely end. I knew, intuitively, that I was doing something I normally would have shied away from in my pre-religious years. I thought, *could I really steal Natalie's fur coat? Could I really set fire to a pet guinea pig?* The potential hideous acts

I might perform abruptly widened into an extended life of crime – robbing a bank, stealing a car . . . *Could I really murder Mr Ronson and be forgiven?*

My mouth was dry and suddenly I felt dirty and sullied by how the church was indirectly encouraging me to be sinful through its simplistic promise of absolution. I felt my fingers tighten around the brakes and some force inside me was steering the handlebars to the left and turning the bike around. I pedalled back towards the blond circle of the sandpit. I crawled off the seat and placed the bike back on the ground, in exactly the same position as I had found it. From that day on, I stopped going to church. It was beginning to confuse me too much.

The next day, a Sunday, I slept in and, when I woke up, I stayed in bed and reread one of my girls' annual volumes. Downstairs, I drank tea and ate toast. After breakfast, I decided to go for a swim and changed into my bathers. I remember my new blue thongs slapping against my heels as I passed the closed bedroom door of Mr and Mrs Ronson. I heard Natalie's high, girlish voice: *Don't, darling. Don't,* and the sound of a shower running. As I passed through the living room, I did not sense anyone or anything behind me but, when I opened the door that led to the patio, suddenly a great force rushed against me, knocking me sideways, and I saw Sir Charles running across the patio and into the yard. Within seconds, he was on his hind legs and mounting Mona, thrusting into her like a powerful piece of machinery. All I could do was stand there in horror and disbelief, my hand still gripping the doorknob.

You fucking stupid prick of a kid! How many times did I tell you? Mr Ronson was running through the living room, pulling up his pyjama pants. *You stupid, stupid fuck!* Outside, he grabbed the garden hose, turned it on full bore, and began blasting the dogs with water. *Pat! Where are you? Fucking come here, will ya? Pat!* The Irish horse trainer bolted through the gate. *Get her outta here, willya? Get her out!* Ronson aimed the torrent of water in Sir Charles's face and the dog reeled away from his mount. His enormous penis was still red and hard as Ronson forced him back against the fence. Pat grabbed Mona by the collar, dragged her through the garden, and into the stable yard.

When the gate was firmly locked, Ronson abandoned the hose and turned on me, screaming, *You fucking idiot bloody kid! I fucking told you not to let Sir Charles out! What are you – some kind of moron? Some idiot fucking moron?*

Suddenly, my mother was at my side. *How dare you speak to my daughter like that!*

I'll speak to her any way I like, 'cause you're an idiot, too, and I'll tell you another thing – you're sacked!

You can't sack me, she yelled back, *I'm quitting! Come on*, she said, grabbing me by the hand, pulling me away from Ronson and out of the room.

Well that's the best fucking news I've heard all day! he screamed after us down the hall. *And you better make your last pay go a long way – 'cause no one's gunna employ an idiot bitch like you with two fucking morons for kids!*

As we climbed the steps to our rooms, I was shaking. I tried to explain it was an accident, that I hadn't let the dog out on purpose, that I was sorry. I began bawling then and my mother sat me on the side of my bed and took me into her arms. She kissed me on the head, rocked me back and forth. *Don't worry, love. You did me a favour. I always hated this job.*

4

I am sitting in Mr Brown's living room, pretending I cannot hear my mother's moans. She's inside our bedroom, and sounds as if she's being tortured. What's she doing in there? *asks Stacey, Mr Brown's nine-year-old daughter.*

My face is hot with embarrassment. The television flickers as we watch cartoons. The bedsprings creak, her wail rising higher and higher.

They went in there to look at photos, *says Mimi, Stacey's younger sister. Mr Brown will be home from work soon and I know what she's doing in there is against the rules.*

They're not looking at photos, *scoffs Stacey.* They're making too much noise.

Maybe they're really good photos, *offers Mimi, raising her thumb to her mouth.*

I can hear him in there now, a soft staccato of pleasure, as if he's cooing to a baby. Stacey glares at the bedroom door. The coffee table is littered with empty bottles of DA beer and an ashtray brimming with butts. It occurs to me that I should clean all this up before Mr Brown arrives home. I jump from the couch, pick up two bottles and an empty packet of

Benson & Hedges, but I'm only halfway across the living room when I see the silhouette of my mother's boss framed by the kitchen doorway. In the dying light I can see Mr Brown's eyes narrow as he takes in the empty bottles, the glass coffee table speckled with grey ash and beer.

Kids, *he says*, what's going on?

My mother's shrieking now, as if she's giving birth to the biggest baby in the world. I try to think of something to say, a convincing lie – anything.

Guess what, Dad? *says Stacey, pointing to the bedroom door.* Betty's in there with her brother!

When Mr Ronson sacked my mother, she had no money in reserve. I thought she might contact her mother, or sister, or even Uncle Phil and Auntie June, but she didn't. Perhaps she was embarrassed, or too proud. Maybe she was scared they'd want to adopt me again, that she'd lose me to more stable guardians.

It was Natalie's parents – Poppa and Nanna – who eventually came to our rescue. They helped us load our few belongings into their car and drove us to an old holiday house they owned north of Sydney. It wasn't accessible by road and, after parking the car at the end of a dirt track, we had to carry our bags and shopping down a narrow path that ran along the Hawkesbury River. After about fifteen minutes, Poppa stopped in front of a drooping picket fence wreathed with ivy and flowering jasmine. *This is it*, he said, smiling. *Welcome to the Bush Palace.*

It was a cool, shadowy home, probably built in the 1920s, with high ceilings and a screened-in veranda that overlooked the river. At night, I could lie in bed and listen to its currents gurgling past my window. During the day, I took solitary swims and picked wildflowers, glad to have escaped the claustrophobic world of the Mulga Hotel. The Bush Palace and its surroundings were idyllic and serene and I imagined it was some sort of reward for having survived the Ronson clan.

While I swam and walked along the river, I became conscious of two things: the first was that there was no one person or friend that I was unhappy about leaving behind; the second was that I enjoyed being alone. My mother, however, was not so happy. My sister had refused to move again. Lisa railed and ranted about being uprooted once more until my mother finally relented and allowed her to move in with the family of her best friend, Prue Crampton. Now, my mother remained in the shadows of the holiday house, sitting in the same canvas chair, chain-smoking and grimly working her way through a bottle of scotch. There was no telephone in the house and she complained of *feeling isolated*, and sometimes, when her head began to sway and the long ash on her cigarette fell into the folds of her skirt, it seemed as if she were both mesmerised and shocked by her own loneliness, as if she couldn't quite believe or accept what her life had now become. I filled the house with flowers, tiptoed around her hangovers, but it didn't do much good. After three days she and I walked the path back to the car park and caught a bus into the nearest town. She called Poppa from a telephone booth. *Come and pick us up, Pop. I'm going mad out here.*

Poppa collected us that same evening and told us we could stay at another house he owned, up in the Blue Mountains. It had a phone and was close to a railway station, which would make it easier for my mother to look for another job. I wondered how many houses Poppa and Nanna owned, and how an elderly handyman could afford so many properties. But when we arrived, it became obvious that Poppa wasn't wealthy – just extremely generous. This second house – made of fibro, with two modest bedrooms, and surrounded by a tiny garden – was where he and his wife had lived for over thirty years, and where Natalie, their only child, had grown up. We were to stay at the house until my mother *sorted herself out*, he said. In the meantime, he and Nanna would live at the Mulga Hotel. Even then, the irony amused me: Ronson had sacked my mother and had kicked us out; his father-in-law had rescued us and had moved us into his family home, and now Poppa and Nanna would probably be sleeping in one of the very rooms from which we'd been evicted only a few days before.

I thought my mother would be heartened by this second opportunity, but she began to unravel even more. I stayed in the living room most of the time, feigning interest in the Munich Olympics, while she sat in the kitchen, drinking and, I imagined, trying to figure out what to do with the rest of her life. I felt sorry for her. In a matter of eighteen months her husband, son and older daughter had left her one by one; she'd been sacked from her job because of something I'd done – albeit accidentally – and now she didn't even have a home or a boyfriend or anything – only me. Each day she bought me a packet of marshmallows and allowed me to toast them on the one-bar electric heater. And I wondered whether this daily gesture sprang from a sense of gratitude toward the one person who hadn't deserted her, or perhaps even a covert sense of guilt, or both.

One night during our first week in the Blue Mountains the doorbell rang, which was surprising, since so few people knew we were staying at the house. When I opened the door I was astonished to see my father standing before me, grinning, his strawberry-blond hair long and wavy, almost a glowing halo under the porch light. *G'day, Sunshine!* he announced, casually pecking me on the cheek, as if we hadn't seen each other all day, rather than for over a year. Then my mother was in his arms, kissing him. *Where's Gene?* she gushed. *Is Gene with you?*

Gene's always with me, he assured her, *he's just parking the car*. It was only then, as I heard him reply to her, that I noticed for the first time that my father had a speech impediment. His voice was nasally, and certain words came out slightly mangled, as if English were his second language, and I was surprised to realise that, after nearly two years apart, I had difficulty understanding him. *We came up as soon as we got your telegram*, he said, holding out a yellow piece of paper.

Gene appeared behind him then – tousled blond hair, grubby jeans – shouldering a case of beer. He looked scruffier and years older, his forehead already lined. Within minutes a family reunion erupted in the living room, fuelled by beer and cigarettes.

To see my parents cuddling and kissing on the couch, tipsy with nostalgia, it was hard to figure out why they'd ever split up. I wondered how two people could completely ignore each other for so long and then slip back so seamlessly into such an intense kind of intimacy. *Not one day has passed that I haven't thought about you*, said my mother, squeezing his hand. *I thought about you every day too*, my father replied. *Every single day*. It was as if my brother and I weren't there, as if they were off on a second honeymoon, unencumbered by the presence of children. And then another notion perplexed me: if they loved and revered each other as much as they were saying, why did my mother wait so long to send him the telegram? And why hadn't he visited us at the Mulga Hotel? Then another, more pressing question popped into my head.

Why didn't you write back to me? I asked.

What? said Gerry, as if he hadn't heard me properly.

I wrote you letters. But you never wrote back.

I was expecting him to explain that he'd been busy, or that he'd lost his address book, or something plausible like that, but he merely looked surprised and said, *I didn't get any letters from you, love.*

I wrote to you three times, I insisted. *Mum addressed them and put the stamps on and posted them for me.*

He and I both looked directly at my mother, puzzled.

Oh, I said I would, she said airily, ashing her cigarette, *but I never posted them.* She rested a hand on Gerry's thigh and leaned towards him. *I thought they'd upset you. I didn't want to upset you.*

I remember standing rigidly before her, my heart racing. This was a side of my mother that I had never encountered before. She'd promised me she'd post them, over and over again, in that voice I had grown to trust. If she could lie so calmly – and about something that was so important to me – what else was she capable of doing? Was she lying when she said she didn't want to upset my father, or did she keep the letters as a way to hurt him, to punish him for leaving us?

After they'd exhausted all the beer, my parents disappeared into Nanna and Poppa's room and fell into the double bed. My brother and I went to sleep in a room that had once been Natalie's, and which was still decorated with a fluffy pink eiderdown, porcelain dolls, and a mobile of painted butterflies. As I lay in bed that night, I tried to let the confusion I felt towards my mother fade and to replace it with the happiness of being reunited with my father and brother. But the fairytale unwinding in my imagination only lasted another thirty-six hours. I don't know what my parents discussed between that first night and the morning, two days later, when Gerry and my brother crawled back into their Holden station wagon and drove away. She never told me, but I knew we were in trouble when she telephoned her sister Joan that very afternoon and asked her to come and pick us up.

We returned to my aunt's house, a three-bedroom fibro bungalow in a place called Ashcroft, which was a flat, barren public housing estate in Sydney's southwest. Joan's husband, a trumpeter, had died years before and she was now raising three children and a foster son on her own. My grandmother, Floss, lived in the adjoining suburb, Green Valley, in a Housing Commission bed sitter overlooking a paddock. She had high blood pressure and a bad heart, and before we visited her I was instructed by my mother not to mention our latest troubles.

Joan was four years younger than my mother and it was hard to believe that they were sisters. Joan didn't drink and wrote poetry in her spare time. She usually dressed in simple slacks and tops and wore cat's-eye glasses attached to a chain around her neck. She was what my mother would call *plain*. My father was a little gentler and called her *eccentric*. But Joan was always there for us when we had nowhere to go and I couldn't help but compare the two sisters. And it appeared to me that if being as beautiful and alluring as my mother attracted so much unhappiness, I decided I too would rather grow up to be *plain*.

At night I slept, top-to-toe, in a single bed with one of my cousins, Tracy. My mother slept with Joan. The day after arriving in Ashcroft, I was enrolled in the fourth grade of the local school. If I thought my classmates at my last primary had been rough, their behaviour quickly paled in the face of the foul language and crude, arbitrary bullying of these kids, who mostly came from struggling welfare families. What made it worse was that I had to wear my old school uniform, which was the subject of much teasing. I was so scared of these kids I hid myself away behind empty classrooms at lunchtime in order to avoid any further conflict. The playground was barren except for a few wilting trees and in the middle of the day the sun beat down in withering waves against hard clay and tufts of dry grass.

After my first day there, I arrived back at my aunt's place to find my mother gone. *Where is she?* I asked.

Joan shrugged, averting her eyes.

Did she say when she'd be back?

She shook her head.

Has she rung?

My aunt sighed. *She took a bus into Liverpool, but that was hours ago.*

I wanted to ask if my mother had been drinking, but decided not to, because I was only nine years old and in all likelihood the answer would be *No*, even if my mother had staggered blindly out of the house after downing a bottle of brandy.

I played with my aunt's ginger tabby; I walked circles around the back yard; when it grew dark I was called inside and I sat with my cousins and Joan at the kitchen table and we began eating chicken noodle soup.

Where's Betty? asked Tracy.

Joan shifted in her seat and glanced at me. *She's out looking for a job.*

At this time? asked Brett, her son, wiping his chin with the back of his hand.

I think she's looking for bar work. That's usually at night.

This seemed like a plausible explanation to the four other kids and thankfully the subject was dropped.

When I woke up the next morning my mother still hadn't returned and as I dressed in my old uniform my hands were trembling. Had she left me for good? Had she dropped me off with someone she knew would look after me? Had she fled into an entirely new life, unencumbered by a daughter? As I tied my shoelaces my thoughts grew even more fearful. She was unconscious in a gutter somewhere; she was in hospital; perhaps she'd committed suicide or had even been murdered. I started bawling then and my aunt, passing the bedroom doorway, came in and hugged me, stroked my hair, told me everything would be all right. But she never told me *how* it would be all right and I didn't dare to ask more questions.

My mother finally arrived home two days later. She was thinner, her face gaunt, her clothes smelled of stale cigarettes and her French roll sat crookedly on her head. She did not say where she had been, nor why she hadn't bothered to ring. But even then I could tell what had happened, though I had no name to describe it. I wondered who she'd slept with and if he'd been handsome, or if it had just been some guy who'd paid her some attention and who'd had a case of cold beer at home.

Fortunately, whatever demons were possessing her seemed to fade over the next few days. She drank only moderately, helped Joan in the kitchen, visited her own mother again and read the newspaper classifieds. By the following weekend she'd secured herself another live-in housekeeping job, and I was relieved for two main reasons: the first being that she seemed to have pulled herself together, and the second being that I wouldn't have to return to the dreaded Ashcroft School.

Mr Brown was a kind, gentle man, who wore loose suits and scuffed shoes. In his late forties, he was tall, thin and balding, and the first time I saw him standing on his front porch, framed by the doorway, I thought he was the saddest man I'd ever seen. The house was a huge, contemporary, two-storey home that Mr Brown, an architect, had designed and built himself. It was wedged into the side of a deep slope of bushland in a wealthy northern suburb called Frenchs Forest. One side of the living room was made entirely of glass, affording sweeping views of a valley and, beyond, the hazy outline of the city. After introducing himself with a slight bow, Mr Brown showed us to our quarters: a tiny room with two single beds, a small vanity and a wardrobe.

I decided immediately that this place was better than Ashcroft and the Mulga Hotel, and that Mr Brown would probably be a good boss for my mother, much better than the awful Mr Ronson. This was confirmed when I later met the two teenage sons, who were tall and tanned and exceedingly polite. They lived in their own apartment downstairs, and could not have been more different than Ronson's sons; in fact, by comparison, they almost seemed angelic.

But my optimism was shaken within an hour, when a pale-faced, white-haired girl raced into the kitchen, followed by an older girl about my age, screaming, *You bitch!* The taller one yanked the smaller one's hair – a scream erupted – and then they began kicking at one another's shins until Mr Brown burst out of his bedroom and pulled them both apart.

She started it!

Did not!

My mother ran a hand through her hair, and I noticed that it was trembling. The younger one was bawling by now and snot was running over her lips. *She tripped me over!*

I didn't!

Girls – said Mr Brown.

You did so!

You fell over, you stupid drip!

You're a liar!

She hit me on the head with a ruler.

Girls, just stop it right now! Mr Brown suddenly looked two inches taller. They both glared at the floor sullenly, as if they'd been denied presents on their birthday, or had been told that they'd never see their dog again.

This is our new housekeeper, Betty. Say hello.

The younger one was still snivelling. She seemed harmless enough but the girl my age had an unsettling air about her as she appraised my mother, and I knew she was the kind of child I would have avoided in a school playground.

Hello, they both droned.

And this is Mandy, her daughter.

I clung to the back of a dining room chair as they looked me up and down.

The little one wiped her snot with the back of her hand as Mr Brown rustled her hair. *This is Mimi*, he said. She looked about five or six and seemed as fragile as a porcelain doll.

And this is Stacey, he said, resting his hand on the head of the older one, whose face was covered in a mass of freckles. Her light brown hair was pulled back in a ponytail. As she studied me I saw her nose begin to wrinkle.

Now you can all play together. Won't that be fun?

It felt odd sharing a small room with my mother in a house of people we'd only just met. At least the Mulga Hotel had been spacious, with so many hallways and yards and extra rooms that it was easy to hide and enjoy some privacy. As I unpacked my clothes and hung them in the wardrobe I was already starting to feel a little cramped.

I was enrolled in the fourth grade of Frenchs Forest Public, the same school *the girls* attended. It had an enormous playground with plenty of shade, a sports oval, and modern classrooms. Even the grass seemed much greener there. The school was definitely superior to any other I had experienced but I soon found out that wealth and privilege did not necessarily guarantee nicer or better-behaved pupils. The taunting of *the new girl* was just as relentless as in previous schools. Again, my shoes were too pointy; I didn't carry the right school case; and a lot of kids thought I was weird because my father played the drums and did not live with me.

I did not know how long this new job of my mother's would last and was wary of making friends I might soon have to give up. Instead of lingering in the playground during recess and lunch, trying to ingratiate myself into a game of hopscotch or jacks, I retreated to the library and began reading books, mostly biographies of classical composers: Beethoven, Mozart, Chopin, Liszt. I harboured a hope that I could become a composer too, and in my spare time worked out simple melodies on my recorder and notated them on scraps of paper. As I pored over the biographies, however, I felt painfully inadequate. Most of the greats were playing the piano by the time they were three, were writing their first sonatas at five; entire symphonies were created by precocious eight-year-olds. And here I was, a full nine years old, and all I had produced were a few pathetic melodic lines on used envelopes and old gas bills. It was obviously too late for me to be a prodigy and I lamented my wasted childhood. Still, the biographies transported me away from the stifling atmosphere of the school and for a little while I could sweep through sumptuous, eighteenth-century courts and listen to imaginary harpsichords and violins.

I began borrowing the books and reading them at home in my room in order to avoid *the girls.* The six-year-old, Mimi, wasn't too hard to get along with, but she was always bursting into tears at the slightest mishap and I found her fragility annoying. And her nose was always running, which she never seemed to notice. But Stacey was worse: if Mimi loaned me her bike Stacey would inevitably push me off it; if I were playing my recorder, she would tell me to shut up; she treated my mother like a servant, refusing any discipline with a loud, *You're not my mother!*

This was shouted so often it started me wondering what, in fact, had happened to their mother. I noticed there were many feminine items about the house to suggest that she must have been around once: old makeup in the bathroom cabinet, a pair of mauve slippers in the laundry. Once I crept into Mr Brown's bedroom and saw a satin stole draped over the back of a chair. I wondered if she had died or was perhaps in hospital, and thinking about this cast the girls in a new light and for once I felt sorry for them both.

One night, in our room, I asked my own mother what had happened to Mr Brown's wife.

She ran off with his best friend, she replied. *They're on a cruise ship for six months, sailing around the world.*

I sat on my bed, wondering how a woman could so casually abandon her family and disappear with another man. *Is she coming back?*

My mother shrugged. *I doubt it.*

Meanwhile, my mother was obviously looking for another man too. One day she went on a shopping spree and returned with a long, halter-neck dress, gold high-heeled sandals, two new blouses, and a pair of orange underpants that had a STOP sign stitched onto the front.

Once her housekeeping was done for the day, she'd change into her bikini, smother herself with olive oil and vinegar, and lie on a blanket spread out over the front porch. She painted her toenails and fingernails bright red and put a new perm in her hair. Sometimes, a balding sports journalist would pull up in his car on a Saturday night and take her out to a club in the city. I was glad this job was so much easier for her than the one at the Mulga Hotel: she had some spare time, was earning more money, and there was never any tension between her and Mr Brown. In fact, they got along exceptionally well. Sometimes she was able to cheer him out of his melancholia with his favourite meal: Chicken Cacciatore.

He was such a decent, generous man that I could not understand why his wife had decided to ditch him, and a part of me was hoping that Mr Brown would fall in love with my mother so that she could find some peace and security in her life. As far as I could see, she was already doing all the things a normal wife would do: shopping, cooking, cleaning, looking after the kids, and since they seemed so at ease with each other, I didn't see any reason why they shouldn't be together. Of course, it would mean putting up with *the girls*, but Mr Brown was infinitely preferable to Mal, a balding journalist my mother had been dating. There was something about him that I disliked and mistrusted: he was always overly nice to me – but in a way that I felt was insincere and manufactured for the benefit of winning my mother over and possibly getting her into bed.

Whenever the girls received a postcard from their own mother they would swoon, reading it over and over, studying the photograph on the front as if it were a rare and mesmerising object of art. There were pictures of sequinned beaches at sunset, ancient bridges cloaked in fog, foreign cities streaked with neon. The two teenage brothers downstairs seemed indifferent to their mother's absence and would merely glance over the brief messages on the back of the postcards – no longer than a few sentences – before picking up their surfboards and heading out towards the beach. Stacey saved every card and began sticking them to the wall above her bed, and they gradually accumulated into a colourful collage of her mother's trans-global infidelity.

It made me wonder what had happened to my father, and why he and my mother had not stayed together after their happy reunion. I didn't bother to ask about it. Even though I loved my mother, I no longer trusted her answers, not after finding out she'd lied about posting my letters. It was around this time that I withdrew into myself even further and began to study people with a keener sense of curiosity than I ever had before. I realised that what a person said, or the image they wished to present to the world, was not necessarily even close to the truth of who they were, and I became fascinated by the behaviour of everyone around me, scrutinising gestures, tones of voice, noting small inconsistencies and swings of mood. I had always enjoyed this pastime, but now it seemed vital and necessary, like breathing. I even took to eavesdropping on the telephone conversations of my mother, Mr Brown, and his teenage sons so I could enter the secret worlds of other people and begin to understand them.

I also realised that there was a side of myself that I was trying to keep secret. At night, I kept my mother awake grinding my teeth in my sleep. The old anxiety attacks returned, but instead of being able to retreat to a broom closet, as I had done at the Mulga Hotel, there was nowhere to go to keep them hidden. The first attack at Frenchs Forest was so unexpected and abrupt that I found it deeply embarrassing. One morning I was walking with the girls along our street to the bus stop when my heart began racing and my breathing faltered. Suddenly, I dropped my school case, shaking and weeping hysterically, unable to walk any further. It had happened within a matter of seconds, like an internal tidal wave, and Stacey and Mimi, shocked by my sudden turn, ran back to fetch my mother.

Not long after this attack, I heard the doorbell ring and when I opened the door I saw my father standing before me, grinning and holding a carton of beer. My heart felt as if it were suddenly cartwheeling in my chest. He put the beer down. *How's my girl?* he asked, and kissed my forehead, my cheek, my nose. His blond hair was even longer than the last time I'd seen him and he was wearing thick spectacles that looked like lenses extracted from two magnifying glasses.

Did you have trouble finding it? asked my mother, rushing down the hall. My father embraced her tightly. I could tell already that she had phoned him, and had summoned him to Mr Brown's house. And as they kissed I realised that she'd always been in a position to contact him – that she could have done so at any time she'd wished – and I wondered if she'd been seeing my father on the side occasionally, without ever mentioning it to me.

Once they'd settled into the living room, they began drinking beer and smoking, and I soon realised it was an unsettling repeat of that first night in the Blue Mountains, as if, despite the separation, they were delirious in each other's company and very much in love. Gerry put his feet up on the glass coffee table; he brushed my hair; sang a chorus of the blues. As my mother walked into the kitchen, he told her she had a gorgeous bum. Then he gave me a gift – unwrapped, no card – but it didn't matter, I adored it: a gold choker with a pendant encrusted with red stones and a matching piece that was a combined bracelet and ring – the ring part fitted around my middle finger and the linked stones lay against the back of my hand, joining around my wrist. They were things a grown-up woman would wear and as I gazed at myself in the mirror I felt blessed and infinitely sophisticated.

When I returned to the living room I cringed to see Stacey and Mimi bursting through the door. They suddenly stopped short and took in the sight of my parents drinking. I sat on the arm of a chair, nervous. I was fairly certain that my mother was not permitted to entertain men in the house.

Girls, she announced, her cigarette drawing a hazy circle in the air. *This is my brother, Gerry.*

I was surprised how quickly she created and delivered this lie.

It came so easily to her, like ordering a beer. *Mandy's Uncle Gerry.* She shot me a look: I was to play along, which made me even more nervous, scared that I would somehow mess it up. The girls regarded him with a little suspicion. *He doesn't look like you*, said Stacey, shoving her hands in her pants pockets.

He's had lots of operations on his face, explained my mother. *And he's broken his nose three times.*

This seemed like a plausible explanation to the girls and I distracted them by touching my choker and holding up my ring-bracelet, boasting, *Look what he gave me.* They were wide-eyed and impressed and I let them each try the jewellery on and parade around in front of my parents.

But it wasn't long before I became distracted and made a big mistake. I sat on Gerry's lap and asked, *Dad, where are you living now?*

Stacey leapt on me immediately. *Dad?* she said. *You just called him Dad!*

I began to flush, realising I'd blown my mother's cover. *No I didn't.*

You did! You did so. Stacey turned to my mother. *She called him Dad.*

My mother smiled, unfazed. *Oh, that's just a game the two of them always play. He calls her Mum and she calls him Dad.*

I nodded, startled again by my mother's capacity for invention. *Yeah*, I added, *sometimes he calls me Mum.*

OK, Mum, chimed Gerry, confirming the so-called game. *Hop out to the fridge and grab us another bottle of beer.*

I slid off his knee and repaired to the kitchen, glad to have escaped Stacey's scrutiny.

By dusk my parents had exhausted all the alcohol and had

played over and over the only two records in Mr Brown's collection my father could stand: Cat Stevens and The Beatles. They were drunk and starting to get a little sloppy – a hand on a knee, interlocking arms – and I was more than relieved when my mother turned to Gerry and asked him if he'd like to see some photos she had in her bedroom. They pulled themselves up and disappeared together, closing the door behind them.

The din they made while they were making love was excruciating, as if they were both in great pain and required immediate medical assistance. I switched on the television and turned the sound up in order to camouflage the noise, but the ever-suspicious Stacey hovered outside the bedroom door, bowing her head and frowning. She wondered aloud what they were doing, why they were taking so long, why viewing photographs would make them act in such a way, and when Mr Brown appeared in the living room, taking in the empty bottles of beer, the brimming ashtrays, the sound of my mother's banshee cries, and when Stacey announced that my mother and her brother were in the bedroom together, making all that racket, I nearly collapsed with embarrassment.

To Mr Brown's credit, he didn't sack my mother over the incident. When she and Gerry emerged from the bedroom, dressed and a little more sober than before, she introduced him as her brother, and Mr Brown kindly kept up the ruse, shook my father's hand, and said he was pleased to meet him.

Gerry promptly left after that, drove away in his car, though I had no idea where he was going, where he lived, or if I'd ever see him again. But I was growing accustomed to this pattern by now, and at least this time he had left me with a memento: the two pieces of glittering jewellery.

Even so, only about a month passed before Mr Brown gave my mother notice. It had nothing to do with her work or behaviour, nothing to do with me or his children. When she broke the news to me – that she was being *let go* again – I felt exasperated. We'd only been in Frenchs Forest three months, the school year was just winding up, and in two and a half weeks it would be Christmas Day. We'd planned to spend Christmas with the Browns, but now, my mother explained, that was just not possible. I wondered where we would go, where we'd spend the holidays, how she'd find another job at this time of year.

But why? I demanded. *Why's he kicking us out?*

My mother sighed and sat me down on my bed. *His wife wants to come back to him. The cruise is over. She wants to move back in time to spend Christmas with the kids.*

5

Come on, *I hear my mother say*, let's do it now.

But what if she wakes up? *says her boyfriend.*

The light of our tiny hotel room is on. I am lying in one of the two single beds, my eyes squeezed shut, trying not to move. They've been drinking downstairs and they are drinking still and I can smell cigarette smoke.

She won't wake up, *assures my mother, her words a nasal slur.*

But what if she does? *he says.* If that girl saw us I couldn't live with myself.

There's a pause. I hear them kissing. My face is hot and I want to turn over. The pressure to remain still is overwhelming. If I move or open my eyes it will be embarrassing for us all.

Fuck me, *she says.* Mate with me now.

There's the sound of a zipper being opened, shoes being kicked off.

But the girl – perhaps we should –

She's a heavy sleeper, Mal, *she says.* I should know. Now come and lie down with me.

*

My mother knew I was disappointed about having to move again, especially since it was just before Christmas. So, instead of returning to Auntie Joan's house in Ashcroft, she took us both on a week's holiday to a huge, rambling hotel in the Blue Mountains called the Hydro Majestic. In the early part of the twentieth century the hotel had been a popular spa for celebrities and socialites, providing various hydro-therapies. By the time we fetched up there, however, at the end of 1972, the hotel was merely a crumbling relic of the sumptous grandeur for which it had once been known.

Your father and I used to come here all the time, my mother announced as the taxi pulled up at the front doors. Inside, the atmosphere and musty scent reminded me of a museum. The reception area was bigger than a tennis court, with worn, faded carpet and soaring ceilings held up by cream-coloured columns. A fire raged in a large brick hearth, and a row of windows overlooked a deep, shadowy valley. Apart from me and my mother, the only person in this enormous space was an elderly woman with curly mauve hair who sat behind a counter.

Our room was on the top floor of a faraway wing, and we had to negotiate a series of labyrinthine halls and stairs in order to finally find the right door. It was definitely one of the *cheap rooms*: there was just enough space for two single beds and a sink. Paint was cracking and peeling off the walls, and from the ceiling hung a bare light globe that could only be turned on and off by pulling a string. Still, I'd never been on *a holiday* before and I found this mausoleum-like hotel intriguing.

That night we were seated in the grand dining room – white tablecloths, dark wooden chairs, chandeliers. My mother chatted brightly with the other guests at our round table, most of whom were European, and my mother allowed me to drink a small glass of red wine with my meal, *like the French*. Afterwards we walked arm-in-arm down the long, sloping corridor until we found ourselves inside a ballroom.

I'd never seen anything like it before, except possibly in an old film: the floorboards gleamed; there were alcoves on either side of the room, framed by ornate latticework; the glass roof rose up into a meringue-shaped dome. On the stage, a thin, ancient woman played a grand piano, while an equally elderly man, dressed in a tuxedo, sawed away at a violin.

We were the only other people in the ballroom and I felt sorry for the musicians. But they happily bobbed and swayed as they performed, as if they were entertaining a crowd of hundreds. As we walked towards one of the alcoves, the violinist caught sight of my mother and he abruptly stopped playing and cried out her name.

Within moments the two musicians were hurrying down the stage stairs and greeting my mother. The woman had heavy rings on each finger and was wearing a long gold lamé dress. Up close, she looked even older, with a corrugated face dusted with thick white powder. *You just missed him*, she said to us both. *He was here the other day.*

I didn't know what she was talking about. *Who?* I asked, but she didn't seem to hear me. *He called in with a couple of musos. They were on their way to a gig. In Bathurst, I think. Wasn't it Bathurst, George?*

The man called George nodded. *He had a few beers. Then he jumped up on the table and did a tap dance!* George guffawed and shook his head. *Bloody card.*

I could feel my stomach tightening, now knowing exactly who they were talking about. *When? When did this happen?*

What's today? asked the woman.

Friday, I offered.

The woman rolled her eyes. *Then it must've been Wednesday.*

I couldn't believe I'd missed running into my father by a mere forty-eight hours. *Is he coming back?*

George guffawed again. *You never know with Gerry. You know he just vanished after the tap dance and didn't even say goodbye?*

The couple returned to the stage and began to perform again. There were no drinks available in the ballroom and, after my mother seated me at a table, she disappeared into the bar across the hallway, which did not permit children. This was the beginning of what turned out to be a nightly routine: dinner with a glass of wine in the dining room, our walk together to the ballroom and then I'd sit alone, often the only person in the audience, listening to the rickety music, while she retired to the bar. Every now and then she'd come out and check on me and bring me a lemonade. And sometimes there'd be a man on her arm, who'd twirl her across the dance floor for one or two tunes before they both disappeared back into the bar. I knew what she was up to: she was looking for a man, not just a man for the night, but someone who might fall in love with and take care of her forever.

I thought she had a pretty good chance of achieving this, given that it was a fairly expensive hotel and it attracted people who seemed, well, *comfortable*. At forty-one, she was beautiful, slim and statuesque, her blonde hair swept up into a perfect roll, pearl-drop earrings, her long evening dress and gold, high-heeled shoes. She could still walk into a crowded room and command everyone's attention, something that I'd seen her do often. But no one man seemed to be sticking to her that week – not for longer than two or three dances – and she began spending more and more time in the bar, even in the afternoons.

This mainly left me to my own devices. I often walked around the hotel property, observing the abandoned tennis courts overrun by paspalum and grass, the empty swimming pool with a crumbling concrete dolphin at one end, the paths meandering between geraniums and pansies. Other times I investigated different parts of the hotel, the dusty games room, the back of the ballroom stage, the winding staircases that led to various floors, the reading rooms filled with antiques and overstuffed chairs. Many times I got lost, especially when trying to find my way back to the room I shared with my mother. One day I even went horseriding, but the heat of the afternoon and the constant motion made me feel nauseous, and on my way back to the hotel I collapsed in the garden and vomited onto the grass.

I liked staying in such an old, elegant place, but I was growing uneasy about my mother's behaviour and about how much money she was spending. All our meals in the dining room, all the drinks she consumed, were merely *put on the tab*, and I worried that, at the end of the week, Mr Brown's generous payout would not be enough to cover our escalating bill. Also, we'd been at the hotel for five days straight and she still hadn't found a man. I thought about all the well-off men she'd turned down at the Mulga Hotel and wondered if she regretted having been so choosy.

Eventually, she phoned up her old sports journalist paramour, Mal, and invited him up to visit. I was disappointed that she'd resorted to him. Apart from the fact that I neither liked nor trusted him, I found his company irritating. He knew I was keen on becoming a writer and he was always trying to get me interested in journalism, even offering several times to take me along to the offices of the paper where he worked.

I don't want to work for newspapers, I'd say, shaking my head. *I want to write books.*

You can't make a living writing books, he'd counter.

That's right, you know, my mother would add. *If you want to be a writer, you'll have to be a reporter. You don't want to starve all your life.*

Mal arrived at the Hydro Majestic only three hours after he'd been summoned. And it was for this reason that I found myself pretending to be asleep that night in the glaring light of our room, frozen into a half-foetal position, listening to their sighs and gasps and moans, the creaking rhythm of the bed.

I could barely stand to look at Mal and my mother the next morning, entwined on the single bed, asleep. I wondered how she could have run her hands over his thin, reptilian body, and taken his tongue into her mouth. I dressed quickly and slipped out of the room before they woke up, wanting to avoid them.

But Mal eventually came in handy. He spent a second, quieter night in our room, and the morning that followed – the morning that we were to check out of the hotel – my mother arranged for him to help carry our bags to his car. I didn't know for sure if he'd contributed toward our hotel bill – though intuition was telling me that he had – and if that were the case I worried about what he would expect in return. I was perplexed as to where we were moving now, and hoped it wouldn't be in with Mal. In eight days it would be Christmas. I sat in the back of his Holden as it purred along the highway, glimpsing cottages wreathed with decorations and wishing one of those homes were mine.

We were driven down through the bush of the Blue Mountains, the roads hemmed by eucalypts and flowering vines. Mal pulled over once to show me some bellbirds in a tree, to listen to their melodic trilling, and this was probably the only time I liked him, because for the first time he wasn't trying to impress my mother, who sat in the car, smoking.

We drove on, into the valleys, across the plains of Sydney's outer west, through the dry and dusty suburbs, the outskirts of Penrith. When I asked her where we were headed, she was evasive. *We'll see when we get there*, was as much as she'd admit. By now, I was sure we were moving in with Mal and was anticipating a dreary Christmas.

Once we'd entered the city, however, Mal steered the car up William Street, towards Kings Cross, and my mother began giving him directions. *Get in the left lane; turn left here; no, further down, past that truck.* I realised then that we couldn't be heading towards Mal's, because he'd certainly know where his own house was. We drove down a street lined with enormous plane trees and leafy sunlight, and pulled up outside a deteriorating, three-storey Victorian mansion with a frangipani tree out the front. A steep driveway flanked the right side of the house. My mother turned to me. *I think this is where your father lives.* She pointed down the driveway. *Why don't you go down and see if he's home?*

I could hardly believe what she was saying, and half feared she might be fibbing or twisting the truth again. I leapt out of the car and strode down the driveway. On my left were barred windows and, further down, an overgrown yard. I walked onto the L-shaped veranda overlooking the garden and heard a familiar sound: the raucous laughter of two men. I followed the laughter to an open window and there, on the other side of a torn lace curtain, were my brother and father sitting at a small table, drinking beer.

Gene glimpsed me first, and suddenly parted the curtain and embraced me through the window, kissing my face and ruffling my hair. And then my father was at my side, twirling me around. When he lifted me up, I pressed my face into his neck, inhaling his familiar, earthy scent.

Mal helped us carry our bags into the tiny basement room. I could tell that my mother wanted to reconcile with Gerry, but the excuse she used was that she was *in between jobs* and she merely asked him if we could stay with him until she found another position. Gerry seemed to have no problem with this proposal and welcomed us in, pouring beers for her and Mal and offering them cigarettes.

I was intrigued by the room. The walls were covered, from baseboards to ceiling, with large black-and-white posters of film stars. I recognised a few of them: WC Fields, wearing a top hat, peering down at me from behind a deck of cards; a pouting Marilyn Monroe in a low-cut dress; Fred Astaire in top hat and tails, leaping into the air. There was a fireplace, a small wardrobe, a three-quarter bed. The sound of a piano bubbled out of the speakers of a cassette player. Cockroaches roamed in aimless circles across the cracked linoleum. A huge old fridge stood near the doorway, but the handle had broken off and every time my father got up to get another bottle of beer, he had to lever the door open with a fire poker. There was only one chair and my mother and Mal were obliged to sit on our suitcases; my brother had a milk crate; I sat on the end of the bed.

Mal finally slunk off, obviously disappointed by this new arrangement. That night my parents made love on the bed while my brother and I slept on top of a single sleeping bag on the floor. The next morning Gerry woke me with hot buttered toast and a cup of black coffee and we ate breakfast together while my mother continued to sleep. My brother had already left for work. He now had a job as an apprentice car mechanic in the city.

Even though we were crammed into a single room, as I sipped the sugary coffee and chewed my crusts I was deliriously happy. The holidays were going to be good after all, back here with my father and brother. But there were still some aspects of my mother's behaviour that I found confusing. She was obviously trying to reunite with Gerry on a more permanent basis, but she still continued to go out on dates with Mal at night. I used to watch her dressing in front of me and my father, doing her hair, applying her lipstick at the table, and wondered what on earth she was up to. Was she hedging her bets between the two men? Did the fact that my father could only secure casual work playing music – and was therefore often broke – make it hard for her to give up Mal? Or was she merely trying to make my father jealous?

When she left us at night, I enjoyed sitting on the bed and watching my father practise drum rudiments on a rubber pad. One time when Gene wasn't at home, Gerry stopped playing at a little after 10 pm and asked me to walk up to the Village Centre, about five minutes away, to buy him a hamburger with egg.

But I'm in my pyjamas, I said, gesturing to my dressing gown and slippers.

That's all right, he assured me, *no one cares around here.*

I thought for a moment. My mother would never have allowed me out so late on my own, especially in the back streets of Kings Cross. Gerry handed me a five-dollar note. *You can also get yourself an ice cream.*

As I strode the lanes between our house and Springfield Avenue I was terrified, convinced someone would leap from a dark doorway and strangle me, but after I'd given the order and returned unscathed with the food, I felt a curious sense of achievement. This was the beginning of a significant change in my life. What had once been forbidden or intolerable in the confines of suburbia with my mother was now not only permitted, but celebrated. And everyone and everything around me seemed to confirm this idea. Soon I was to discover that the elderly woman who lived in two rooms at the end of our veranda had papered her kitchen walls entirely with nude centrefolds from *Penthouse*. Next door to her was an 83-year-old scientist who still worked part-time at the CSIRO. Jack Allen, the obese jazz pianist who lived upstairs, would walk around his flat in the nude, wearing only a straw hat, reciting monologues from *Hamlet* and *King Lear*. Across the landing from him lived a bass player named Jerry Gardner, who smoked dope as he watched three portable televisions at once. At night, he'd hook his bass up to an extension cord and wander around naked in the back yard, practising Santana riffs.

Also upstairs lived Mick Fowler, a merchant seaman and dixieland musician, who'd sit in the garden, entertaining me by playing his banjo and kazoo and singing old songs like 'I Can't Give You Anything But Love', and 'Flat-foot Floogie with a Floy-Floy'. Sometimes the elderly landlady with wild grey hair

93

would stick her head out of an upstairs window and yell at him to shut up, and when he didn't she'd grow even more irate and begin to throw things at him: a hairbrush, a book; and when that didn't stop him there'd soon be dinner plates smashing against the concrete path, but these just seemed to egg Mick on and his voice would grow louder, his banjo solos more expansive. *Don't worry about the old bag*, he'd assure me, *she's just my mum.*

Interesting people were always dropping into our room: a saxophonist who wore a kilt and a pith helmet; Jack Allen's American girlfriend, who never wore underwear; members of the Children of God sect, who lived in a big house down the road. And when I began exploring the streets of the Cross on my own, I discovered rippling waves of neon, women in platform heels and satin hot pants, American sailors on R&R drunk and dancing around the El Alamein Fountain, a bouncer outside the Pink Pussycat dressed in top hat and tails, who'd shaved off half of his blond moustache and beard, and who attracted a crowd by tapping his cane and soft-shoeing against a wooden platform.

Finally, I understood why my father had needed to escape the suburban life my mother had always preferred. I felt as if I were treading through some bright, spangled wonderland. Sometimes I felt as if I were witnessing an extended theatrical performance, with an enormous set and a cast of hundreds, that was being staged for my eyes only. I was so inspired by this new environment that one hot afternoon, after my parents had made love and fallen asleep, I rose from the blanket on the floor where I was supposed to be napping, took some change from my father's pocket, and walked across the road to the milk bar to buy an exercise book. While my parents slept, I sat at the table and wrote my first short story – at least the first one outside of a school classroom. It was about a girl in a magical land where the mushrooms were as tall as people and where umbrellas were made from cabbage leaves.

When they woke up I showed them the story and they were so proud of me they invited the elderly woman with a taste for pornography, Jack Allen, his girlfriend, Jerry Gardner and Mick Fowler down to our room so it could be read aloud to an audience. I was too shy to do it myself, so my mother took the book and narrated the story, invoking the various voices of the characters, her voice modulating like a well-played piano, in a way that made the writing sound much better than it really was. Nevertheless, everyone applauded at the end, spouting praise and admiration, and my father swept me up on his knee and let me finish the rest of his beer.

Christmas passed with this kind of simple happiness. My mother did all the cooking out in the hallway on an ancient communal stove that emitted three tiny blue flutes of gas. When we didn't have enough money to buy food for a regular meal, we'd all make a game out of scrounging around the room and through our pockets for stray one and two-cent pieces that would eventually accumulate into about fifteen cents – enough to buy a bag of tomatoes or a few potatoes. And then my father would turn this basic fare into yet another game: we'd sit on the floor and pretend we were consuming caviar, duck and champagne.

One night I was allowed to attend one of Gerry's gigs and, before we left, my brother dressed me up in his *hippie gear*: a beaded headband, a gold peace-sign medallion hanging from a chain around my neck, and a fringed suede jacket that went down to my knees. The nightclub, called Bee-Bee's, was on

William Street, and I was fascinated to find that the ceiling and interior walls were sculpted into the texture and shape of a cave. I was allowed to sit at the bar with my mother and brother, sipping pink lemonade while listening to the band, and later, during the break, my father let me crawl behind his kit and perform a solo on the drums.

One afternoon, however, between Christmas and New Year, our sense of security was disturbed when my mother received an urgent telegram. As she read it, her face went white and she told me to leave the room. When I protested, she turned to me and pleaded, *Mandy, please leave!* I knew then it must have been something really bad. I walked into the hallway and hovered outside the cracked door, listening intently.

It turned out that my sister, who was about to turn fourteen, had been *raped*. I did not know what this meant, but intuited, by the shocked tones of my father, that it was something that was close to tragic – something I later noted that day in my journal: *a tragic thing has happened to my sister*.

I could hear my father ranting, *Who was the bastard? I'll kill him.* And when my mother tried to calm him down, he cried, *Oh Christ! She could be pregnant.* They carried on like this for quite some time, scarcely aware of me peering at them through a crack in the doorway. Later, they crawled into the Holden and said they'd be back in a few hours. I watched the smoke belch out of the exhaust pipe as the car tore up the driveway and wondered what could have been so bad to have galvanised them both in such a way.

They returned that night, a little calmer and quieter, but they didn't talk much in front of me and my brother. I half expected them to have brought back my sister from the family she was living with, but they didn't even mention her. The next day, however, my father rose early and went out for a while and when he returned he announced to us all that we were going to rent the basement room next door to the one we now lived in, holding up the keys as evidence. We followed him into the hallway, past the communal gas stoves to the door at the end of the hall. He pushed the key into the lock and the door swung open to reveal a small room with two barred windows that overlooked the driveway. The windows absorbed the northern light so the room was sunnier than the other one, and it had carpet – albeit ratty – and a built-in gas heater in one corner. It also contained a single bed and a wardrobe. This, I soon found out, was where my father and brother had stayed before the room we now lived in had become vacant.

That afternoon, as I helped my mother clean out the room, we discovered a few glass milk bottles behind the heater, filled with pale amber liquid. As my mother lifted one of them, she wrinkled her nose and shook her head. *Ugh!* she said. *God, they're disgusting!* At first I didn't know what she was talking about. Were the bottles disgusting, or what was inside them? It wasn't until much later in the day, as I turned the phrase over in my mind, that I figured out what she'd meant. Instead of walking out of the room, down the hallway and out along the veranda to the communal bathroom, when my father and brother woke up in the middle of the night they would wee into empty milk bottles. When my mother said *they're disgusting*, she was referring to Gerry and my brother. I didn't think it was such a bad thing, since I knew that in the olden days people who didn't have toilets used to keep potties under their beds. But I did decide my father and brother should have emptied the bottles before they'd moved out six months earlier.

I was told this new room was being prepared for my sister, who would soon be coming to live with us again. I was to share the single bed with her; Gene and my parents would stay in the front room. My feelings about this were mixed. Since something *tragic* had happened to her, I thought the best place for her was probably with her own family rather than her best friend's, but I dreaded her spearing the happy bubble in which I now floated, and didn't look forward to sharing a bed with her.

She wasn't moving in for a while, however, and in the interim I busied myself by buying five-cent dresses from the Wayside Chapel Opportunity Shop, further exploring Kings Cross, and filling my notebook with stories and poems. I joined the Kings Cross library and spent the afternoons lying on the floor, reading. When my father wasn't drinking he'd smoke marijuana and take me on long walks through the Botanic Gardens and we'd eat ice cream and dangle our feet in a pond. I rang in the new year of 1973 with a silver bell, standing in the doorway of a clothing store on Darlinghurst Road, watching fireworks lance the midnight sky.

But my mother was still dating Mal a couple of nights a week and I feared that all this joy could so easily evaporate, like the rain that steamed our footpath at the end of each humid summer day. My father never exhibited an iota of jealousy about these outings, and acted as if she were merely stepping out with her sister or mother in order to do a spot of shopping. And I wondered if this was a good thing or not, if this either increased or reduced their chances of staying together.

My confusion lessened one morning over breakfast, when Gerry was pouring his first cup of tea. The night before, I'd been left at home with my brother because Gerry had been playing a gig, and my mother had gone out with Mal. It had been decided that I would sleep in the front room – the original one – for the night, along with Gene and my mother, because the gig finished at one o'clock in the morning and my father didn't wish to disturb anyone when he arrived home.

That morning, Gerry sipped his tea and told the three of us what had happened when he'd driven down the driveway at a little after 2 am. Mal, having delivered my mother home some time before, was sitting on the veranda steps, sipping from a bottle of scotch, obviously waiting for my father's arrival. He followed Gerry down the hallway and into the new room that we'd recently begun renting. He called Gerry a *swine* and a *no-hoper*. How dare he make his beautiful wife live in a slum? She deserved better than a dump like this, he said, and demanded to know what Gerry was going to do about it. Gerry, unfazed, took off his dinner jacket and tie and began unbuttoning his shirt. *I'm not making her stay here, Mal. She can do what she wants.* This seemed to infuriate the drunken Mal even more and he demanded that Gerry follow him outside where they could both *have it out*.

I'm not interested in fighting, Mal. I've been working all night. I just wanna go to bed. Mal grew even angrier then and, as Gerry continued to undress he kept taking ill-timed swings, which my father easily ducked. Stripped down to his underpants, Gerry merely crawled into bed and left Mal standing there, swaying in the middle of the room. *Look, mate*, he said, *it's up to her what she does. Now, on your way out, can you turn out the light?*

We couldn't help but laugh as he related the story and I inwardly marvelled at the way in which he'd remained so calm and detached. I wondered if he really felt that way or if he were just a sublime actor, adept at masking what he truly felt. Either way, his aloofness paid off, because after Gerry finished telling us about it, my mother promptly marched out of the room. When she returned a few minutes later, she announced to us all that she'd just rung Mal and told him that she loved living in a filthy slum with her husband, and that these past few weeks had been her happiest in years. *Then I told him to piss off*, she concluded, *and to never contact me again.*

Relief settled over the four of us like a delicious scent. We celebrated with a second pot of tea.

A few days later, when my mother and I were on our way to visit my grandmother, she gave me a strict order: *When we get there don't tell Gran your Dad and I are back together. You know she's got a bad heart.*

I didn't like the idea of attending a school called *Plunkett Street Public*. It sounded so silly. Who ever heard of a school named after a street, especially one as weird as Plunkett Street?

To get there I had to walk down a long flight of stone steps from the back of Victoria Street to the port district of Woolloomooloo. The streets and back lanes were lined with crumbling terraces from the early part of the century, the verandas of which leaned steeply over the footpaths, as if they could drop at any moment. Most of the iron lace borders that lined the verandas had long since shed their last coat of paint and were rusting in the hot, salty air. Some houses had cracked or shattered windows – others were merely boarded up. Elderly men and women, still wearing their pyjamas, sat on front steps, fanning themselves with newspapers and TV guides.

Once on the main road, I'd stroll by the moored ships and the docks of Woolloomooloo Bay. And then there were three pubs, one of which was an early opener. At eight thirty in the morning, I'd pass wharf labourers and sailors leaning out of the open doorways of the Macquarie, clutching schooners of beer and smoking. My father had already joked that I was forbidden to nick into the Macquarie for a quick drink on my way to school each morning. As usual, he'd been half joking and half serious: he'd done a couple of gigs in that hotel, when he was filling in for Mick Fowler, who also played drums, when Mick had been away at sea. He had warned me that it was *a really rough pub*. When I asked, *How rough?* he shook his head and replied, *The roughest pub I've ever worked in*. I tried to imagine how this pub differed from, say, the Mulga Hotel, and asked my father for an example. *OK*, he said, and then explained about a raffle that had been conducted one night at the Macquarie amongst all the sailors and wharfies. *The first prize*, he said, *was a girl for the night. The second prize was a case of beer.* I nodded, taking this in. *But this is the kicker*, continued my father, trying to contain his laughter. *The bloke who won it, when he clapped eyes on the girl, he grabbed the guy who'd come second and wanted to swap him for the booze!*

From the Macquarie it was just a short walk around the corner and down the block to Plunkett Street Public, which was the smallest school I'd ever seen. In fact, from the outside it looked more like a tiny, two-storey office block, the walls of which were paved with flesh-coloured stucco and supported by columns of grey cement. Unlike other schools, there were no separate areas outside for younger and older students – everyone, from kindergarteners to sixth graders, ran around in the same bitumen playground and used the same toilets and bubblers. And there was no tuckshop: kids buying their lunch had to order it from the old corner milk bar across the road.

The next astonishing aspect of this school was that there were so few children living in the Kings Cross/Woolloomooloo area that no grade contained more than fifteen students. There were only four classrooms and four teachers, including the principal. First and second graders were united into a single room, as were third and fourth graders, and those of the fifth and sixth. The kids in kindergarten had a room and a teacher to themselves. That term I was beginning Year 5, and on my first day I found myself at a desk on the left side of the room along with the handful of others in my grade; the kids in Year 6 always sat to the right. Mr Swords, my teacher, a man in his late sixties with greying hair and a pointed nose, was also the school principal. He was always dressed impeccably – white shirt and tie – and he was adept at seamlessly alternating between the two grades as he taught dual lessons. Once he'd settled the room down and we were all hard at work, he'd nick into his adjoining office. And as I hunched over my multiplication sums or wrote a short story I could always smell the smoke of his Viscount cigarettes curling out from beneath his closed door. I recognised the odour immediately because it was the same brand my mother smoked.

Mr Swords was a good teacher in many respects, and during my time at Plunkett Street I grew to admire him more and more. At my enrolment, he explained to me and my mother that I wasn't obliged to wear a uniform, which was something, in all the schools I'd attended, that I'd never encountered before. Mr Swords explained that most of the students came from *disadvantaged backgrounds*, and he didn't feel comfortable demanding that parents spend a lot of money on uniforms and particular shoes when they were struggling to put food on the table. This seemed entirely sensible to me and I was glad I would finally be going to a school with kids from families as poor as mine. Not only did this even things out – there'd be no more taunts about my pointy shoes and unfashionably long hem – but every day I could wear a different dress and feel like an individual.

On my first day there it was excruciatingly hot and, after lunch, as we kids sat at our desks trying to understand Mr Swords' lesson about long division, we all began to wilt over our open exercise books. Chalk in hand, Mr Swords paused and eyed us. Then he put down the chalk, hitched up his trousers and declared we should *all go outside and cool off for a while.* I assumed this meant we could take a drink from the bubblers and perhaps stand in the shade, fanning ourselves, but suddenly there was a stampede out the door, down the stairs, and into the playground. By the time I got outside, the younger students from all the other grades were running into the playground, too. I looked around to see every available tap and bubbler spouting and frothing as all the kids filled empty cans, lunch boxes and plastic cups. Within moments, the hundred or so students were in the throes of a huge water fight, pelting and spraying each other with raucous abandon. After a bottleful was poured directly over my head, I wiped my eyes and looked across to Mr Swords and the other teachers, who were standing in the shade of the building, and I marvelled at the way in which they were simply watching us and smiling. After we were all soaking wet, we happily filed back into our respective classrooms, where puddles formed beneath our desks and the ink in our exercise books began to run.

I decided that I liked everyone at this new school – even the teachers. No one pretended to be better than anyone else and I suffered no animosity or exclusion for being *the new girl*. I drifted easily into a circle of friends – all of whom were in my year. There was Diane, a dark-haired chubby Maltese girl from a single-parent family; Lucy, a frail, blue-eyed blonde whose father had also long since left her and her mother; Lebanese Fatima and Italian Rita; and Maria, a round-faced Greek girl even taller than I was, who lived in one of the dilapidated terraces up the street with her parents and eight brothers and sisters. Maria was the only kid at Plunkett Street who wore a uniform – an old pleated winter one, obviously from another school. Her mother made her wear it because she didn't want the burden of having to wash and iron a different dress for her daughter every day. I was always impressed by Maria's openness and lack of guile. She admitted one day that the favourite game she and her sisters played at home was seeing how many cockroaches they could kill with their hands.

Mr Davidson, a young man with orange hair and a moustache, taught the third and fourth graders. He was probably the most normal teacher there – he wore belted shorts with long socks – and I imagined he could easily have fitted in at the other schools I'd attended. But Miss Cloyton, who taught the first and seconders, was more unusual. Probably in her early thirties, she wore high heels with short skirts and looked impossibly sexy. She smoked at her desk in the classroom, and to me seemed more suited for a career in film than in early childhood education. Once, when I was running an errand for Mr Swords, I passed the open doorway of her room and saw her sitting on a chair, instructing the kids, while a six-year-old boy stood behind her, dutifully brushing her long dark hair. Even at ten, I knew this was a bit of a lurk, but there was something about her gumption that I admired.

The only teacher I grew to have reservations about was the kindergarten teacher, Mrs Gorton, who was in her sixties. I'd been around enough drinkers in my life to know that she was a heavy one. There were the telltale signs: the baggy eyes, the red and swollen face, her cheeks spiderwebbed with broken capillaries. Sometimes when she was on playground duty I could smell the unmistakable stench of brandy on her breath. A few times at school I even saw her completely drunk, swaying against a fence during a sports carnival. This in itself wasn't so bad, but the consequences of her boozing weren't good. Many times at recess I discovered a tiny five-year-old bawling his or her eyes out in the playground. I didn't know if it was the result of being drunk at the time, or if it was just the irritating effect of a particularly bad hangover, but every weeping kindergartener confessed to me that Mrs Gorton had beaten them with a stick.

Mr Swords himself wasn't beyond giving his students a good whack, but he was always sober and most of the time we deserved it. At Plunkett Street, my classroom infringements continued to be remarkably consistent: talking and laughing at inappropriate moments. Unlike my former teachers, Mr Swords had the sense not to banish me outside for the duration of the lesson – a punishment I had always welcomed because it allowed me to go on long walks undetected and return to my spot outside the classroom before the bell rang. No, he'd merely make me hold out my left hand and spank me six times with a foot-long wooden paddle coated with a strip of sandpaper. That would always shut me up for a while – well, at least until the end of the lesson.

I also quietened down when my sister arrived at our rooms in Victoria Street. I was curious about any differences in her, how a person might be affected by an event that was deemed to be *tragic*. I watched her unpacking her clothes and brushing her hair, plucking her eyebrows, cleaning the lint out of her bellybutton, painting her toenails pink. All of these things I had seen her do before but now I was constantly alerting myself to any possible alterations in her behaviour. She seemed no more withdrawn, no paler, no more sad or happy than she had been before. And when she snatched my journal out of my hands and read what I had written about her – about the tragic thing – she snorted and tossed the book on the bed. *You don't even know what it is!*

I tried sleeping in the same bed as her, as our mother had arranged, but it was too small for both of us and the stubble that grew back on Lisa's shaved calves chafed my legs. Eventually, Jack Allen from upstairs gave us a second chair to sit on: a bright green vinyl beanbag, and it was this that became my new bed. At night I'd carry it from the front room to the back one and settle into its shifting contours, my overhanging calves and feet resting against the carpet. But sometimes even that didn't guarantee a night's sleep: directly above our room was Mick Fowler's, and he stayed up playing his banjo for hours and thumping his foot to the beat of the music. It was at these times that my irate sister would spring out of bed, grab a broom, and bash the top of it against the ceiling until Mick finally got the message and took off his heavy boots.

My sister began attending Dover Heights Girls' High, which was up on a hill overlooking Bondi Beach, and which required the catching of two buses each morning to get there. She had to wear a uniform and acquire a set of special textbooks and as she set off grudgingly each morning I felt blessed to be at the nearby freewheeling Plunkett Street Public.

The month during which my sister arrived – February – was also the month that my father was offered his first permanent, well-paying music gig since his car accident seven years before. A large new nightclub called the Barclay was being opened and he was asked to head the house band six nights a week. Elated and enthusiastic, he promptly summoned Jack Allen down to our front room. Jack arrived, along with his girlfriend, Jonah, and sat in our only chair. Gerry told him the news and said he wanted to form a jazz trio, with him – Jack – playing piano. There was only one hitch in this great opportunity and Jack suspected it immediately.

Where's the club? he asked, toking on his rollie.

Look, it's not that far, assured Gerry. *We can share the driving.*

Jack raised one eyebrow, gazing directly at my father.

I've worked it all out, Gerry continued, *it'll only be fifty minutes each way – an hour at the most.*

Jack picked up one of our saucers from the windowsill, rested it on the top of his enormous belly, and flicked his ash into it. *So what are we talking about here? Newport? Palm Beach?*

Gerry grinned and shook his head. *Wollongong!* he announced, as if Wollongong was some musical and artistic Eden. In fact, in 1973, it was a small industrial city about one hundred miles south of Sydney, and its most prominent feature was its enormous, belching steelworks.

Jack puffed on his rollie again. *Wollongong* – he repeated drily – *that's a very untheatrical town.*

Jonah paced the room and suddenly spun around. *I don't care* how bloody untheatrical the town is, *Jack. You haven't worked in weeks. You're taking the goddamn job!*

I knew even then that, when it came to music, my father was an extraordinary optimist. We needed the money, sure, but I could also tell that it was the opportunity to be able to play jazz six nights a week at the same venue that had caused his spirits to soar; the minor inconveniences, like having to drive two hundred miles a night, didn't really come into the equation.

After travelling back and forth to Wollongong for several days, however, it became obvious to both Jack and Gerry that they would have to make other arrangements. Jack began renting a cheap motel room not far from the club, while Gerry slept on a mattress in the back of his station wagon. He showered and ate at the club before he began performing each evening. And on Saturday nights, after he finished his gig at 11 pm, Gerry would speed back to Sydney and spend Sunday and Monday with us.

I missed him during the week but this new way of living had its advantages. Since Gerry wasn't there most of the time, my mother suggested to him that perhaps she shouldn't search for another housekeeping job and move out: she could stay and look after my brother, Gene, who would otherwise be by himself. She could cook him proper meals and make sure his clothes were washed. I had assumed my parents had already discussed this subject privately – whether they would stay together as a couple or not – and was surprised that after all this time they still hadn't made their intentions clear to one another. At that moment I realised that my mother was being deliberately subtle in the way in which she'd broached the subject. She wasn't saying things like, *We should never have split up*, or, *I love you and want you in my life*, but making a suggestion that seemed practical, even though I knew it was a flimsy excuse for us all remaining together. My brother was almost eighteen and had been caring for himself for the best part of three years. The other strange thing was that she'd raised the subject while I was sitting there, watching and listening, and even if my father had inwardly not wanted a permanent reconciliation with her I doubt he would have had the heart to say so in front of me.

I was relieved to see him nod. *OK*, he said. *That'd be fine*. And with those four simple words the matter was settled. But it was only later that night, as I lay in the dark on my beanbag, that I realised what had really happened. During their brief conversation they had both silently agreed that as long as my mother didn't demand that Gerry give up the drums again, she could stay as long as she wished.

Even if things hadn't worked out between them, my mother wouldn't have had to find another housekeeping job, anyway. A few months before, she'd discovered, through her sister, Joan, that she was entitled to the benefits of a new welfare program called the Deserted Wife's Pension. The pension would provide a third more money than she'd earned working sixty hours a week at the Mulga Hotel. All she'd had to do was front up at a government office, declare herself and her two dependants as *deserted*, make the application and have an interview. In the three months we lived at Frenchs Forest, the application had been processed, and by the time my father was working in Wollongong, she was receiving regular fortnightly payments.

But sometimes, even then, the extra money didn't seem to stretch far enough. I don't know what they spent it on, but I do remember those few lean days just before the cheque arrived, when we had little food and she had no money for cigarettes. It was then that she'd walk to the pawn shop up the road and hock, for five dollars, the jewelled watch Gerry had given her for their twentieth wedding anniversary. Once the cheque arrived, every second Wednesday, she would pay the accrued interest and always get the watch back, until one particularly expensive month saw her delaying its retrieval. By the time she fronted up at the shop with the money, the pawnbroker had already sold it. I found the loss heartbreaking, and I was amazed by how easily she seemed to shrug it off. Perhaps she was merely pretending, or didn't want to seem too sentimental.

Little did I know then that there was another, more threatening loss looming. We first heard the rumour from Mick Fowler's mother, who'd heard it from the woman next door, and the news spread through the house, from us to Mrs Cavanaugh to the 83-year-old scientist, to dope-smoking Jerry Gardner, and on to the neighbours – the unemployed tree-loppers, the abstract artists, the elderly pensioners, the Children of God – leapfrogging backyard fences like a virulent strain of influenza. It seemed impossible and somehow illegal but Mick's mother assured everyone that it was true: all the Victorian houses along the west side of Victoria Street had been purchased outright by a developer, who had plans to demolish them and build a series of high-rise apartment blocks with harbour and city views.

I tried to convince myself daily that our little strip of paradise would remain untouched, until one day I arrived home from school to find the official eviction notice sitting on the table. We had two weeks to vacate the premises.

I was surprised that my mother seemed unfazed by the notice; in fact, she seemed quite pleased. *Look at the inducements*, she said, tapping the print of the second paragraph. I bowed over the notice again and read that, as compensation, the redevelopment company was offering to relocate each tenant and pay the bond and first two weeks' rent of the tenant's new premises. I tensed and stopped breathing for a few moments. Did my mother already have plans to move us out to the suburbs again? Was all this happiness going to unravel so quickly? Had she merely been pretending that she loved living so modestly, amongst musicians and actors and hippies?

When my father arrived home that weekend, they discussed the issue and a compromise was reached. Now that we were all back together, it was obvious that we required a bigger place anyway. Gene needed his own room and it would be nice to have a bath all to ourselves. We would accept the offer from the company but would stay in Kings Cross, not too far from Victoria Street, if possible.

While the offer, in some ways, came for us at the right time, the same couldn't be said for Mrs Cavanaugh and the elderly scientist, who were eventually relocated into suburban nursing homes. I tried to imagine Mrs C taping pornographic pictures above her bed in the home, and wondered if the staff would permit her. Some neighbours moved down to rooms in Woolloomooloo because they couldn't afford anything more expensive. Jack Allen and Jonah packed up and shifted to a farm near Wollongong so Jack could move out of the cheap motel he was staying in and avoid the weekend driving. The day before they left, he came down to our room and removed all the black-and-white posters that had papered our walls, as they had always belonged to him. *Now that we're moving out the cockroaches can have their Olympic Games!* he announced, laughing. But to me the unpeeling of the posters was the final gesture, a kind of goodbye wave, to the happiest six months of my life.

We moved into a ground-floor flat at 7 Springfield Avenue, only a couple of lanes away from Victoria Street. Sure, it was in the same area, but it lacked the casual atmosphere and sense of community of our former basement home. The bedroom my sister and I shared overlooked a back lane dotted with garbage cans and stray cats. My brother slept in the small adjoining sunroom. The kitchen, bathroom and my parents' bedroom faced onto a small, gloomy lightwell. The lounge room was quite large, but contained no windows. The floors were covered with carpet the colour of mustard; the walls were a monochromatic beige. There were no neighbours practising music or Shakespearean monologues or strolling about in the nude. And even though a gay couple lived in the flat next door and a beautiful callgirl named Margaret lived upstairs, everyone in the building usually kept to themselves.

Another problem became evident once we moved to Springfield Avenue: we had no furniture. Even though the redevelopers had allowed us to take any items we wanted from the rooms we'd occupied, the only things that had been worth keeping were the two beds and a chest of drawers. But now that my mother was on a deserted wife's pension she was entitled to the services of a national charity called the Smith Family. I accompanied her to a local branch of the organisation, which was in a building in East Sydney. After a preliminary interview with a middle-aged woman, we were ushered into a huge warehouse filled with furniture and household goods and I was astonished to hear the woman announce that we could choose any items we wished and they would all be delivered the following day. I couldn't believe the charity was simply *giving* us anything we liked or needed.

I skipped between the long embankments of second-hand wardrobes, couches and desks, and traced entire avenues of seats and stools, imagining each piece in my room, or at least in my half of it. My mother picked out a big refrigerator, a laminex kitchen table with chairs, a bedroom suite for herself, three wardrobes, a bed for my brother, two mirrors, a coffee table, and a vanity. While she was doing that I discovered an old 1930s overstuffed tapestry lounge suite and eventually begged her to choose it over the modern vinyl one she'd been eyeing, which, to my great joy, she did.

But that was not all. She also selected pots and pans, a set of crockery and cutlery, towels, sheet sets, curtains, vases, all of which were delivered promptly and free of charge the next day, as the woman had promised, along with three large cardboard cartons of tinned foods ranging from mushrooms in butter sauce to creamed corn to condensed milk and Christmas pudding. I had not seen such a variety of food since we'd lived in Frenchs Forest with Mr Brown. There was only one problem: we didn't own a can opener and, after we moved to Springfield Avenue, it was the one thing we were forced to buy.

With our bond and first two weeks' rent paid in advance, along with the Smith Family's charity, my mother's pension, and my father's regular income, I expected our lives would settle down once more and money would be the least of our problems.

*

On the night of my parents' twenty-third wedding anniversary, my mother and brother travelled down to Wollongong and, in order to surprise Gerry and celebrate, turned up unannounced at the club where he played. We then bought a cat, a ginger-coloured Persian with a tail as thick as a feather duster. I was happy and doing well at school; and my sister had slightly softened towards me and sometimes allowed me to tag along with her and her two French girlfriends when they strolled around the Cross or went swimming at the Boy Charlton Pool. My mother got a part-time job as a barmaid in the Sliprail Bar of the Rex Hotel, a short walk away. On Saturday nights, she allowed me to sit up in bed with her and we'd both read for hours until my father arrived home from Wollongong sometime after midnight. And when he did we'd all roll around on the bed, laughing and joking, and catching up on each other's news. On Sunday mornings I lay in my own bed for hours and continued to read until my parents woke up.

It was around this time that Mr Swords sent a letter to my mother, asking her to make an appointment with him. This came as a great shock to her because, as she kept saying, *Mandy, you never muck up at school*. We both wondered what kind of trouble I was in and she was as nervous as I was when we arrived at the office together. Within seconds, however, all our fears were dispelled: dragging on a Viscount, Mr Swords explained that the best secondary high school in the area, Sydney Girls' High, offered a full scholarship for one student graduating from Plunkett Street each year. He was pleased to inform us that I'd been selected for the honour, which I would take up in eighteen months. My mother was so thrilled she bought me an ice cream on our way home. She wasn't so thrilled, however, when my sister left Dover Girls' High after her second term there. Lisa began going to technical college to study hairdressing and became an apprentice in a French salon called Nicole's, inside the Rex Hotel complex.

Our lives were now unfolding in a fairly happy and stable way. But some weekends my father didn't return from Wollongong and I worried that something was wrong. My mother would explain that he wanted to rest rather than drive, or had a weekend gig elsewhere, but since we didn't have a telephone, I wondered how he could have conveyed these messages to her. She began drinking more and suffering from strange physical ailments – insomnia, headaches, stomach ulcers, weight loss – that sometimes kept her in bed all day with the lights off. She summoned her old family doctor, Greg McGovern, who prescribed tranquillisers, sleeping aids, and the contraceptive pill to regulate her menstrual cycles. Gerry returned home maybe one or two weekends a month now, and there never seemed to be any tension or unhappiness between them, at least not as far as I could tell. One month, however, toward the end of winter, he failed to appear at all, and when I asked my mother if and when he was coming back, she looked away and said she didn't know.

It felt like the time when he disappeared and flew to Darwin, and I sensed that she knew far more than she was letting on, but she was now enclosing it in that dark bedroom of hers, along with her prescription drugs and bottles of brandy. For the first time in her life, she didn't get up in the morning to make me breakfast and pack my lunch and it was these times that I would secretly thank the Smith Family and set off with a tin of peaches or creamed rice and the can opener in my school case.

I now caught the bus to school. The fare was five cents but, in order to save money, I would sit upstairs on the second deck and pretend I had fallen asleep. Whenever the conductor came along the aisle, he never had the heart to shake me. I used the unspent fare at recess on something from the milk bar across the road from school.

Early one Friday night my mother was so drunk from a cocktail of brandy and Valium that when she stood up to go to the toilet, her knees suddenly buckled and she collapsed on the living room floor. She was ranting and gurgling unintelligibly, unable to get up, and as my brother struggled to help her to bed, he scolded her angrily, like an irate father dealing with a wayward daughter. *You can't take all those pills and drink! What's got into you?* She was like a huge, heavy puppet in his arms, and talking gibberish. *Don't let Mandy see you like this*, he pleaded. *Don't, Mum. Stop it*. But she was beyond any reasoning and, with the help of my sister, they dragged her down the hall and put her to bed.

It was not long after this that Gene found a studio for himself in Darlinghurst and shifted out on his own. I was deeply disappointed, but I couldn't really blame him. He was eighteen years old, had his own job, and it was depressing living in the flat with our mother.

One afternoon I came home from school and I couldn't find our Persian cat. When I asked my mother where he was, she shook her head and said Mickey had escaped out the front door and she hadn't been able to find him. I devoted hours, then days, looking for him, knocking on neighbours' doors, scouring our apartment building, tracing the back lane, then all the streets of Kings Cross. One day when she was tipsy she must have realised that I would not stop looking until I found him, and she finally admitted to me that Mickey had died. *Why didn't you tell me?* I asked, thinking of all the hours I'd wasted in my search. *Oh*, she replied, lighting a cigarette, *I didn't want you to get upset.*

What did you do with the body? I asked.

My mother shook her head. *You don't need to know that.*

Of course, I began to grow even more suspicious then, and wondered what other things she was keeping to herself. My father had vanished just as mysteriously, and without explanation, and my old fear of his death returned threefold. At night I imagined his face bloody and mangled in a car accident; in the mornings he was floating in a river; sometimes I could see him lying in a ditch by a country road, as rigid as a fallen statue.

I took refuge in writing poetry. Apart from keeping my mind off the possible death of my father, the finished poems were the only thing that seemed to draw my mother out of the narrow world she now inhabited. When she read them she'd manage a smile or give me a hug before fading into the twilight of her boozy ruminations. She'd lost so much weight she was now gaunt and hunched. Sometimes I'd sit at her bedside and pick up strand after strand of fallen hair from her pillowcase and sheet. She had to get up occasionally, however – the nights she had to work at the hotel, for example – and the several times she had to accompany my sister to court in Blacktown during the trial of the boys who'd raped her.

Sometime during the spring she began seeing other men. One was a jolly, overweight man nicknamed Whoopsie, who always bought me ice cream. Another was a grey-haired man with a handlebar moustache and eyebrows that joined in the middle. Another was a Lebanese mechanic in his late twenties. The three suitors were all customers of the bar where she pulled beer. At one point she was seeing all three of them at the same time and I wondered how she managed it in such a fragile physical condition. When she was at work my sister and I would privately discuss the virtues and deficits of each of her boyfriends and we both concluded that we liked Whoopsie the best. It wasn't just the free ice cream: he also seemed the least complicated of the three and we hoped she would stick with him.

An uneventful Christmas passed and I was acutely aware of how quickly things could change in the space of a single year. Twelve months before my mother and I had moved into the basement room with Gerry and Gene and everything had seemed so hopeful. Now, everything had unravelled again. The four boys who'd raped my sister in the back of a panel van were found *not guilty*. Gene had left. I still didn't know the whereabouts of my father.

Four days after Christmas, on my sister's fifteenth birthday, Lisa was entertaining a few of her friends in the living room when my mother staggered out of her bedroom and appeared in the doorway. Lisa and I knew she'd been drinking all day, which in itself was nothing unusual, but when she leaned against the wall and began doubling over and slurring her words, we knew something more serious was wrong. We both stood up and walked gingerly towards her, scared of what would happen next. Our mother straightened up then and in a halting voice confessed, *I've just taken all my pills at once. I think I'm going to die.*

6

Tchaikovsky's Piano Concerto Number One is playing as my mother and her boyfriend argue about money. They live here in this large, sunny room of a suburban boarding house and my sister and I share a small room across the hall. He is demanding that she hand over all her pension money. He eats chopped liver and lemon juice with his hands, and keeps yelling at her with his mouth full. When he swallows his voice grows louder than the music: Fuck you! You nothing bitch! I kill you!

I cower with my book on the couch, but my mother is standing her ground, smoking a cigarette and glaring at him in a way that seems to be daring him to try it. He jumps to his feet, picks up his plate and throws it against the wall, narrowly missing her. The pieces of meat, onion and juice slide to the floor. She doesn't move as he grabs her purse, and begins going through it. Finding nothing, he throws it down and charges onto the enclosed veranda, filled with junk, and returns with a can of petrol. He turns the music up as far as it will go, a deafening cacophony of chords, and begins to tip the petrol on the carpet, one of the armchairs, the table.

I jump up and ask, in an unsteady voice, What are you doing? *But he can't hear me over the loud music. My mother, white-faced, has already stubbed out her cigarette and has moved from the table to the open door. He splashes the bedspread, the curtains, a pair of my mother's high-heeled shoes. With the sly expression of a man who has just won a bet, he turns to face us both, puts down the can and pulls a lighter from his pocket. He flicks it with his thumb, lowers it, and the armchair is suddenly aflame and a line of orange fire is now frilling across the carpet and rising up before me.*

My sister and I carried our mother back to her room and sat her on the bed. Lisa then walked out the front door to call an ambulance from the public telephone across the street. Two medics arrived with a stretcher and carted our mother away, along with the empty prescription bottles. The next day we walked to St Vincent's Hospital and met one of her boyfriends, the young Lebanese one, and waited to see her. A doctor told us her stomach had been pumped and she was well enough to go home. The boyfriend collected her from the ward and she walked through the foyer towards us, steely-eyed, as if virtually nothing at all had happened, as if she'd just caught the wrong bus or had made a slight *faux pas* and didn't wish to discuss her error. As the boyfriend drove us home we did not raise the subject. She crawled back into bed with a brandy and milk and told us to turn out the light.

A few weeks later, I came home from school and was surprised to see the front door of our flat wide open, and then the young Lebanese boyfriend behind me, carrying an armful of clothes. I walked inside and was further surprised to find cardboard boxes in the hallway and in my mother's bedroom. *What's going on?* I asked, noticing a horrid framed picture of a bullfighter painted on imitation black velvet hanging on the lounge room wall.

She waited until he was back down the hall and out of earshot. *Oh, Hakkim's moving in for a while*, she declared airily. She must have detected my feelings of both disapproval and disbelief. *Don't worry*, she added. *It won't be for long.* I worried about how long *not long* would be, and if it would overlap with the day my father, if he were still alive, would return.

Hakkim had won her over with a few acts of simple kindness: a bunch of flowers, a new dress for me, a night out at the Texas Tavern. But I mistrusted this gift-giving because it implied that we would have to give something in return and I wasn't quite sure what that would be. We never saw Whoopsie or the man with the monobrow again. My mother had obviously made her choice.

He was a handsome man with fine brown hair, a tanned olive complexion, and green eyes flecked with gold. He wore fashionable men's clothing of the early 1970s: tight shirts, flared pants, shoes with inch-thick soles. He needed the extra inch because he was shorter than my mother and even though he was in his late twenties he looked much younger, as if he were perhaps my mother's dark-haired nephew. She was now forty-two but since her breakdown and attempted suicide she'd aged several years – her face was more lined, her shoulders more rounded.

He'd been in Australia for five years but still struggled with English. A simple conversation with Hakkim would sometimes result in his misunderstanding an innocent remark and interpreting it as a slight or even a criticism of him and it was then that his temper would flare. He'd only been living with us a week when he first smacked my mother around. I don't know what prompted it but I was shocked to see her running naked out of her bedroom, crying, a wound in the shape of an almond oozing blood above her eye.

He was contrite and apologetic after the first couple of times, begging her to forgive him. The third time, on the night of my eleventh birthday, he knocked her to the floor and when I tried to defend her he backhanded me so hard I went reeling across the room and hit my head against the wall.

His growing control over my mother was slow and insidious, like some cunning, ruthless disease. He demanded to know where she was at all times, who she'd been with, how much money she'd spent – despite it being her own. He still turned up at the Sliprail Bar after work and watched her every move, making sure she didn't chat to any of the other male customers for too long when she served them beer or gave them change. I knew this because of the arguments that would rage when they arrived home late at night, after my sister and I had gone to bed. When she was drunk she would stand up to him, call him *crazy*, and *an idiot*, and then it wouldn't be long before he'd be beating her up and she'd come howling into my room. I couldn't figure out why she allowed him to stay, but in all their brawls I never heard her tell him to leave or even threaten to call the police. A few months after her first suicide attempt she overdosed again on pills, and again my sister called an ambulance. The hospital pumped her stomach, and she was released the following day, just as she had been before.

Early one night when my mother was at work and Hakkim was no doubt keeping an eye on her, there was an unexpected knock on the door. My sister was busy painting her toenails so I jumped up and ran down the hall. When I opened the door I was shocked to see my father standing before me, holding a bottle of scotch, grinning widely, and then I was even more amazed to see he had his arm around a young woman, aged about twenty-five, who was also smiling warmly. She was petite and very attractive, with a heart-shaped face and wavy long blonde hair. And she was dressed impeccably: in a sea-green suit with cream trim, stockings and high-heeled shoes.

How's it going, beautiful? he announced, engulfing me in a cuddle. He kissed me a couple of times, but all I could do was look at the woman and think that my father had fared so much better than my mother in the love stakes.

You must be Mandy, the woman said, bowing a little and smiling again. *Your dad has told me all about you.*

This is Sue! Gerry declared. *She's English!* he boasted, as if being English were a very rare thing. *She's an air hostess! I met her on a plane back from London. I've been away to England! Did you know that?*

I shook my head, wondering why he'd gone overseas for six months and hadn't bothered to tell us. I opened the door further and let them in, and they swept merrily down the hall, arm-in-arm, as if arriving at a party.

They greeted my sister in a similar fashion. I realised then that they were tipsy and my father was almost manic in his attempt to seem joyful and optimistic. Perhaps he was nervous underneath all that bravado. He went to the kitchen and returned with some glasses. *Where's your mother?* he asked, pouring three scotches, the third one obviously intended for her.

My sister and I traded uneasy glances. *She's at work*, said Lisa. *She works at a pub.*

When'll she be back?

Lisa played with her hair. I could tell she was as terrified as I was that Hakkim would arrive home soon and not only make a scene, but would also beat our father to a pulp. *I don't know*, she lied in a wavering voice, *sometimes she gets home late.*

He asked her to put on some jazz, which she did, and then he asked her to turn it up. Gerry and Sue drank and smoked, told stories and laughed, and when a fast tune came on they jumped up and danced around the lounge room together while my sister and I sat on the couch and watched them, almost paralysed with anxiety, expecting our mother and Hakkim to arrive home at any moment and imagining the awful scene that would surely follow. And so it was with a certain amount of relief that, when the record finished, he asked us where our brother was now living. Gene had since moved to Glebe, into a house with some musicians. Lisa wrote the address on a slip of paper. Within moments of pocketing the address, my father and Sue were sweeping down the hallway and out the door with their bottle of scotch. They vanished as suddenly as they'd appeared, not even leaving a telephone number.

When Hakkim and my mother arrived home a quarter of an hour later, we waited until Hakkim went to the toilet before we told her about the visit. She didn't seem surprised to hear about the woman named Sue and merely urged us not to mention anything to Hakkim.

In his ongoing attempt to take full control of our lives, Hakkim decided to move my mother, sister, and me out of Kings Cross and into a boarding house miles away, in a southwestern suburb called Belmore. It was a place where we knew no one, but where he had several acquaintances. In fact, Belmore was so heavily populated by his fellow countrymen that it was nicknamed Little Lebanon. Most of the store signs along the main street were handpainted with the calligraphic curves and diamonds of Arabic, and there were many shopfronts that displayed cured meats, Turkish flat bread, and roosters hanging from large metal hooks. Most women on the streets wore heavy black gowns and wimples, and I found it unnerving to glimpse only their disembodied eyes staring out at me through the narrow slits of those funereal veils.

The day we shifted it was raining heavily. Hakkim had hired a truck for only three hours and by the time we'd removed all our belongings from the back of it, he announced that he had to return the vehicle. We'd managed well in the appointed amount of time, but the landlords weren't at home to present us with the keys and, while we waited for them to arrive, all our furniture was strewn throughout the back yard, sitting in the downpour. I lowered myself into one of the soggy armchairs, soaking wet, and allowed the rain to sweep across me, not caring anymore. Hakkim had already forbidden me from finishing my final year at Plunkett Street Primary and had forced my mother to transfer me to the school closest to where we would now live, which Mr Swords, my teacher, had advised her against. I, too, had fought hard against the move – argued, bawled, ranted at both her and Hakkim, assuring them I was old enough to travel back and forth by train each day to attend my beloved school. *And anyway*, I said, playing my final card, *next year I'll have to travel that far, when I take up my scholarship at Sydney Girls' High.*

Hakkim's eyes narrowed then and he shook his head. *No scholarship*, he said firmly. *No Sydney High*.

I glanced desperately at my mother, waiting for her protest, but she merely walked out of the room.

Belmore Public was a rather big, ordinary school with a fairly even number of migrant and Anglo-Saxon kids from lower middle-class families. They were not *disadvantaged* – like the ones at Plunkett Street – nor were they privileged, like the ones at Frenchs Forest. There were four classes in the sixth grade and I was placed in one of them. My teacher, Mr Bruce, was a freckle-faced man in his late twenties who wore belted shorts with a collar and tie. When he wanted to make a particular point he would sometimes write it on the blackboard upside down.

I was ready for the usual jibes about being *the new girl*, ready to eat my sandwiches alone at lunchtime and bid a hasty retreat to the library. But this mob surprised me when, after only a week or so, they voted me class captain. At first I thought it was a trick or a practical joke they were playing, or that being dubbed class captain was some kind of insult. But when Mr Bruce smiled, patted me on the shoulder and congratulated me, I realised it was some kind of authentic honour and could not believe my luck. Not only were the kids not being mean, at least half of them actually liked me.

My duties as captain were fairly slight: the biggest responsibility was making sure girls in my class didn't linger in the toilets after the bell rang, and if they did, I was to *report them* to Mr Bruce. But since I was one of the worst offenders of this rule, I never did any reporting at all, and by the third term of the year, when the next elections came around, I was voted out and replaced by another new girl who dutifully turned me in almost every week. It was then that I realised Mr Bruce might have rigged the votes every term – after all, he was the only one who tallied the secret ballots. Perhaps it was his way of making new students fit in and feel popular, and also a covert way of controlling his students.

Out of all my many teachers, it was Mr Bruce who grew the most exasperated with my talking and whispering in class. While Mr Swords had casually whacked me with a stick, without even raising an eyebrow, Mr Bruce lost his temper so badly that his face would ruddy into the colour of a pomegranate and, as he leaned forward and screamed at me to *shut up*, I would marvel at the way in which two serpentine blue veins never failed to pop out on either side of his head.

I learned, however, to be quiet at home. It did no good to inflame Hakkim's temper in any way, even accidentally. Most of the time I tried to avoid him. When he was in a bad mood I hid in the high branches of the backyard frangipani tree or underneath the house. But sometimes I think he grew lonely and would demand that I keep him company. He had no English-speaking friends that I knew of, and he didn't get along with the men at the Camperdown garage where he worked. He came from a Muslim family of fifteen children but, apart from his younger brother, they were all back in Tripoli. He didn't seem particularly close to any one person – even in Little Lebanon – and I wondered what he'd done with himself before he knew my mother. Sometimes he'd give me pocket money in exchange for English lessons. I concentrated on syntax and vocabulary, and tried to teach him one new word a day.

I was not remotely interested in cars but on the weekends he made me help him work on his Holden, passing him tools, holding wires, oiling the engine. One day he jacked up the vehicle and ordered me to change one of the tyres on my own, which I eventually managed to do, after wrestling and struggling with the weight of the replacement. That afternoon he also told me to connect two extension leads, but the cords were wet and when I pressed the fittings together a bolt of electricity forked through me so intensely I almost flew through the roof of the carport.

The only good thing about living at the boarding house was the two-year-old daughter of the young Lebanese couple who owned the place. I used to play with her out in the back yard and take her for walks. My mother got along exceptionally well with the girl's mother. In the large, communal kitchen at the end of the hall, the two would chat while they cooked and traded recipes. But not even all that bonhomie was enough to save us once Hakkim had set fire to the room in his attempt to cremate my mother alive. After the fire brigade arrived and put the blaze out, we were given three days' notice.

Hakkim and my mother found a cheap rental property in a nearby suburb called Kingsgrove. It was an old weatherboard house, the only one on a street of sturdy and expansive brick homes. There were two front bedrooms, one of which was claimed by my mother and Hakkim; the other went to my sister. I was allotted the one that adjoined the living room. It had no door and was merely curtained off with a pair of plaid drapes; three of the four fibro walls were covered with mould. Fortunately, I didn't have to change schools again because Hakkim allowed me to travel on two separate buses back to Belmore

Public, which usually took an hour and fifteen minutes. But I didn't mind too much because I now had a friend at the school – a real *best friend* – something I hadn't had in years. Her name was Joanne Hanby and she lived in a normal house with a normal family and she had a mother who worked in a retirement home and a father who drove a train.

My new friend and her family provided some respite from Hakkim's increasingly erratic behaviour. Some weekends I'd escape our house and go and stay at hers. Hakkim began to drink heavily and ordered us about like servants. My mother would have to keep his dinner hot until he came home drunk from the pub at night. He'd sit on the floor and she'd have to bow and serve him and if the food had cooled or dried since she'd cooked it, he'd smash the plate against the wall and order her to clean it up. Then she'd have to go into the kitchen and prepare an entirely new meal and the serving ritual would begin again.

After the incident with the fire, my mother was too scared to defy him about money. Each second Wednesday, he would arrive home early from work and confiscate her pension. He now forbade her to drink at home, unless he was drinking with her, and he thought depriving her of money was the one way he could enforce this rule. Whenever she had to buy anything, like food, she had to ask him the night before and, after purchasing whatever we needed, she'd have to list each item individually on a piece of paper, along with its price. If the amount she'd spent didn't exactly reconcile with the total amount on the piece of paper, he'd slap her around until she begged him to stop.

The biggest problem was that we could never anticipate what would set him off, even when he was sober: a turn of the head, an innocent comment, a sudden burst of laughter. One night when we were at a Chinese restaurant and were unable to finish our food I suggested that perhaps we would need a doggy bag. I saw his face suddenly cloud, his fists clench against the table. *You think I'm dog?!* he demanded.

No, I explained nervously. *It's just what you call it. Everyone does. You call me dog!*

My mother tried to intervene, but he told her to shut up.

No, it's called a doggy bag, I continued. *It's what you take your food home in.* But the more I tried to explain the angrier he became, and when we arrived home he knocked me to the floor and ordered me to bed.

His paranoia grew worse. Early one evening, my mother, Lisa and I came home from shopping and unpacked the groceries. We chatted to each other. My mother cooked dinner. Hakkim didn't arrive home after work and she kept his food warm in the usual way, between two plates placed on top of a simmering saucepan. We ate our meal and watched some television. I yawned and said I might soon go to bed. We had just finished discussing what kind of flowers we might plant in the front yard when we were astonished to see Hakkim rise up from behind an armchair angled against a corner of the lounge room, a sheepish expression on his face. He'd been cramped up behind the chair for hours, since before we'd arrived home with the shopping. When my mother asked him what on earth he'd been doing behind the chair all that time, he merely rubbed his eyes and said he'd fallen asleep. But the three of us knew he'd been hiding, obviously waiting for us to make some disparaging remark about him. I didn't want to think about what kind of punishment we would have suffered if we had; fortunately – and surprisingly – we hadn't mentioned him at all.

Hakkim wasn't the only person in the house who nursed a mercurial temper. One night when Lisa arrived home late and my mother demanded to know why, my sister replied happily that Gerry had come to see her at the hairdressing salon and had taken her out for a few drinks after work. *You've been seeing your father?!* my mother screamed, as if it were some deep betrayal. *How dare you see your father! He doesn't care about you. He doesn't give a damn about you!* My sister burst into tears and cried, *I don't give a fuck what you think*, and fled to her room. I was sitting on the couch while all this was happening. It was the first time either of us had sworn at our mother, and I was so shocked I didn't move for several minutes.

Not long after this incident, I was in bed one night when I overheard my mother talking to Hakkim. *Gerry came to see me today*, she said. *He wants a divorce. Sue wants him to marry her.* Hakkim thought this was a good idea and seemed quite happy as he ate his dinner.

On the weekends, in order to get away from Hakkim, my sister returned to the western suburbs, to the home and family of her best friend, Prue Crampton, while I retreated to Joanne Hanby's house, where we skateboarded and played with her dog and ignited our farts with matches. Joanne had already witnessed Hakkim's behaviour and knew he beat us regularly. She confided in her father, pleaded for him to intervene, but he told her there was nothing he could do, *unless he lays a finger on you*.

One Sunday afternoon in late winter, after spending the weekend at Joanne's, I arrived home to find our house surprisingly silent. Hakkim's car was not in the driveway and, as I walked down the hallway, it seemed that everyone was out. I put my bag in my room. In the kitchen, I was puzzled to see my mother's purse sitting on the counter, because she never left home without taking it. I ran to her room and pushed open the door to find her sprawled on the bed. I shook her, called her name, but I couldn't wake her. There was an empty bottle of scotch on the floor.

I darted back to the kitchen and checked the cabinet where she kept her medications: all five bottles were completely empty. There was a glass on the counter still holding the dregs of water.

We didn't have a telephone and the nearest public booth was several streets away. I took some change from my moneybox and ran as fast as I could. I made the call to summon an ambulance and ran home just as quickly. Since I'd seen this happen before I knew what to do, and gathered the empty bottles of sleeping pills and Valium so the doctors at the hospital would know exactly what drugs she'd taken. But I also knew it would be up to me to estimate how much was now in her bloodstream and, as I sat beside her limp body, reading the dates on the labels, I felt myself growing cold. I realised she'd had the prescriptions refilled only two days before, and had drunk down three months' worth of medication.

Hakkim pulled up just before the ambulance arrived, and after the officers took her away, we drove to the hospital in silence. I expected the nurses would merely pump her stomach and that she'd be discharged the following day – as had happened twice before – but by the time we'd parked the car and inquired at reception, she'd already been admitted to intensive care.

Before we were allowed to see her, a doctor appeared with her empty prescription bottles and began to question Hakkim, but Hakkim's comprehension of English was so limited that the doctor, frustrated, had no choice but to turn his attention to me. *Did she take the full contents of these bottles? Has she been drinking alcohol? Has she been depressed recently? Has she attempted suicide before?* To each question I nodded and said, *Yes,* and the doctor, exasperated by the answers, raked his hands through his curly black hair.

She's going to be all right, isn't she? I asked. *She's always been all right before.*

The doctor shook his head. *She's taken enough medication to kill an elephant.*

When we finally got to see her she was lying in a bed, a tube up her nose, another inserted into a vein in her wrist. When I took her hand it was so cold it sent a shiver through me. Her head was tilted to one side on the pillow, a bluish tinge rising through her face. Even so close to death she looked bitterly disappointed, as if the very relief she'd yearned for wasn't as good as she'd expected.

It was the first night of my life I did not sleep. I just lay in bed, worrying about what would happen if she died. My sister hadn't returned from Prue Crampton's house, as she always did on Sunday nights, and as yet had no idea our mother was in such a critical condition. The following morning, I didn't go to school, and accompanied Hakkim back to the hospital. She was in the same bed, still unconscious, and the doctor told us she'd made no progress.

I found a public telephone outside the ward and called the salon where my sister worked, but the French woman who owned the business told me, *Lisa did not come in to work today.*

Puzzled, I looked up the Cramptons' number in the phone book and asked Hakkim for another five cents. Prue's mother, Gladys, answered after just one ring and she seemed disappointed to hear it was only me on the line. *Lisa's not here. They've both disappeared.* When I asked where they'd gone she said she didn't know. *But their clothes are gone, and so are the suitcases.* I stood there, my grip tightening around the receiver, hardly believing what I was hearing, and Gladys had to explain it to me again, that Prue and my sister had run away and probably wouldn't be coming back any time soon.

But Mum's in hospital, I said, as if stating this fact could somehow bring them back. And then I asked Gladys if she thought we should call the police, but Gladys didn't think that was such a good idea. *They'll come back when they want to*, she said in a resigned voice, as if this kind of thing happened all the time. I could not imagine my sister ever wanting to come back to live in our house with Hakkim but I kept this opinion to myself.

I spent the day at my mother's bedside, watching the clear liquid from the IV bag slowly pulsing along an adjoining tube and into a vein in her hand. Hakkim, restless, paced in and out of the ward, disappearing to smoke in the garden or eat a hamburger or move the car from one parking spot to another. Sometimes he'd bail up a nurse and harangue her, demanding to know why they weren't doing more for my mother, and each in turn would explain, with growing impatience, *We've done all we can. Now it's up to her.*

We left late that afternoon and, on the way to the car, I spotted a stretch of clover on a nature strip. I dropped to my hands and knees, and began inspecting them one by one. I was convinced that if I could just find a stalk with the lucky four leaves, my mother would miraculously rise from her coma and live on for many years. But my search yielded only handfuls of the common variety, so I divided two and pressed them together. That night I cellotaped the four leaves to the wall above my bed, the two strips of tape forming a transparent cross. Even though I'd long since given up on God, I was hedging my bets: if the Irish amulet didn't work, perhaps the crucifix would, and I got down on my knees and prayed to the minuscule shrine above my bed.

When we entered the ward the following morning, however, she was still in a coma. It proved to me that there was no God in heaven. I sat on the chair beside her and held her hand, feeling the slight flutter of her pulse against my palm. The vigil, as usual, went on for hours, and during that time I thought about the various possible things that might happen to me after she died. I realised a child welfare agency would probably decide my fate. Perhaps I'd be placed with a relative, Auntie Joan, for example, or even my father and his girlfriend, though I didn't think the latter was very likely as I had no idea of his address. The one good thing would be that I would no longer have to live with Hakkim, because he was only my mother's boyfriend and I knew it would be illegal to grant him custody.

I was just beginning to think about the possibility of foster care, of living with a family I didn't yet know, of moving to another suburb and attending yet another school, when I glanced at my mother and thought I saw her head shift on the pillow. I held my breath, wondering if I'd imagined it, and after what seemed like a very long time, her lips parted slightly and then her eyes gradually opened, like the lids on an antique porcelain doll. I stood up and called for the nurse, who was wheeling a medicine tray across the ward. My mother frowned, her green eyes glazed, as if she were struggling to recognise me. Her right cheek twitched and then she looked down at the IV tube attached to her hand. The first thing she said was, *Get me a cigarette*.

As usual, there was a silent understanding between my mother and me that we would not discuss what she'd done to herself. I didn't have to ask her why, and she obviously didn't feel the need or desire to explain her actions in any way. I also sensed I wasn't allowed to tell anyone, especially my grandmother, because my mother always wanted to seem perfect in her eyes – the favourite child still straining to please. The doctors kept her under observation for another two days and, after she was released from hospital, our routines returned to their normal cycles, as if nothing unusual had happened. Even when I broke the news about Lisa running away with Prue Crampton, she seemed unaffected by the loss, as if she'd been expecting it or even envied my sister for having managed to escape.

For a few weeks Hakkim behaved himself, didn't drink too much or hit us. He found an abandoned black-and-white kitten at work, which was only about two weeks old, and brought her home and gave her to me to look after. I kept her wrapped in a woollen scarf, fed her milk through an eyedropper, and called her Mojo.

My world at this time mainly revolved around school, my homework, a swing, playing with my cat, and writing poetry. After school, I would crawl into my bed and scribble several stanzas. Then I would go out into the back yard and practise what I thought of as my Circus Routine. Hakkim had strung a doubled-knotted rope over a branch in a huge tree for me to play on, and I would climb up into its boughs and swing out, striking some dramatic pose, and pretend that hundreds of people were applauding me. Then I would leap from the rope onto the side of an old ten-gallon oil drum and, if I didn't slip off, I would roll the barrel along the grass by walking forward, then backward, struggling to keep my balance. I would rehearse this over and over, until it got dark, and my mother called me inside to have my dinner.

After my mother's most recent suicide attempt, I thought Hakkim had reformed and our lives were improving. But only about a month or so passed before I heard a fight erupting between them late one night, and the sound of shattering glass. I came home from school the next afternoon to find my mother sitting on her bed, drinking a beer. She had lots of makeup on but not enough to cover the bruise on her cheek and the cut on her forehead. I noticed she already had a bag packed and before I had a chance to say, *Hi*, she told me to go into my room, change out of my uniform, throw some clothes into my school case and to do it in a hurry. As I unbuttoned my blouse I remembered it was pension day and realised she wanted to flee the house before Hakkim arrived home from work and took the money from her.

Mojo was curled up on my bed, asleep. *Can I take the cat?* I called to her.

She appeared in the doorway, wearing her sunglasses even though it was cloudy outside. *No*, she said. *You can't take the cat. Now come on, for godsakes. It's getting late.*

She slammed the front door behind us, grabbed my free hand and we half ran down the street. I had no idea where we were going and when I asked her, she merely said, *You'll see*. It was already getting dark and I could tell she was hurrying so much because in all likelihood Hakkim would drive around the corner at any moment. We turned left into Shaw Street, which ran along the railway line, and I realised we were heading towards the station and were probably going to catch a train. I thought this was a good plan because within minutes we would be spirited out of Kingsgrove and far away from what would soon be Hakkim's hunt for us.

But just as we stepped off a kerb to cross the road, we saw his familiar white Holden about a block away, heading towards us. My mother doubled back and pulled me up the path and through the doors of the nearby Catholic church. I wasn't sure if he'd seen us or not, but my mother obviously wasn't taking any chances. We dropped to our knees and crawled along the floor, lying face-down beneath a pew near the altar. As he strode through the door, his footsteps sounded like the beats of an ominous drum, and we could hear him walking about the empty church, calling our names. I saw my mother raise a finger to her lips, urging me to be quiet, but she needn't have bothered because I was so scared I wouldn't even allow myself to exhale.

He stomped down the aisle and approached the pew under which we were hiding – so close I could even see the mud caked onto his work boots, but not close enough for him to look down and spot us. Finally, he backtracked, shuffled around the confessional box, and we heard him leave through a side door.

Within minutes we were sitting in a smoking carriage of an old red train rumbling out of Kingsgrove station. A sense of relief overcame me, as if we'd made a near-impossible escape from a high-security prison. While my mother smoked, I gazed out the window at the city's diamonds of electric light, and wondered again where we were going. I didn't want to seem as if I were pestering her so I waited until she'd had her third cigarette before asking her again.

We're going to stay at a hotel, she replied.

In town?

She nodded. *You'll like the place. It's called the People's Palace.*

The word *palace* stirred my imagination. I had visions of marble floors and chandeliers, thick velvet curtains and bellboys in red uniforms and caps. It would probably be even better than the Hydro Majestic. I wondered how my mother could afford for us to stay in a palace, but I knew there were lots of things she preferred not to tell me and I assumed she had some specific plan in place to get us through this period.

A cold wind cut through us as we alighted from the train at Central station. We walked along the platform, down the stairs and past the ticket collector. She led me into Belmore Park, where drunks sat amongst carpets of dead leaves, gulping from flagons of wine. A few dozed beneath crumpled pages of newsprint. We crossed Hay Street and my mother disappeared into a corner pub and emerged moments later with a bottle of brandy. She shoved it into her bag and then realised she'd forgotten something. *Oh*, she said, *you haven't had your dinner*. She popped into the milk bar next door and bought me a meat pie and a tiny container of tomato sauce.

We walked hand-in-hand up Pitt Street, past derelict stores and closed pawnshops with dusty windowpanes. Garbage bins overflowed. I could smell rancid meat. And then a row of steps appeared on our right and when I looked up to the top of them I saw a battered sign painted above the open doorway: *The People's Palace*.

The foyer walls were the colour of burnt eggs, stained by years of cigarette smoke. I looked down at the floor and the linoleum was so cracked I felt as if I were standing on an enormous map of some strange foreign country. At the desk, my mother asked for a room for one night and paid for it in cash. I was surprised to find she was intending to stay one night only and wondered what she had planned for the next day.

An ancient, groaning lift took us up to the fifth floor and we followed a row of identical doors down a long hallway. Our room was at the end. My mother unlocked the door and switched on the light. We found ourselves inside a small room with two single beds and a window that looked out onto a brick airwell. I sat down on one bed and ate my pie. My mother sat on the other and began drinking. After dinner, I went to find the communal bathroom, down several different hallways, and got lost.

By the time I found my way back to the room, my mother had gone through about a third of the brandy and was now squinting out the window at the brick wall, as if there were a set of directions printed on it in very small writing.

Are you all right? I asked.

She nodded, not taking her eyes away from the wall, and suggested that I turn out the light and crawl into the other bed, which I did.

There were two yellow rectangles glowing from the curtained windows on the other side of the airwell. They shone into our room and I could see my mother's profile clearly. I turned on my side and watched her continue to drink and smoke and stare at the wall. There was something peculiar about her behaviour – she seemed unusually withdrawn. I thought perhaps she was planning whatever it was we were going to do next. I didn't think we could go back to Auntie Joan's because Hakkim would surely find us there. I heard the clink of glass as she poured another drink and leaned back against the pillows.

Mum? I asked again. *Are you all right?*

She didn't answer for what seemed like a long time, but it was probably only ten or fifteen seconds.

Mandy, she announced, in a deadpan voice. *I'm going to die.*

I thought I'd misheard her. *What?*

I'm going to die tonight, she said matter-of-factly, as if she were telling me what time it was, or commenting on the weather.

My immediate thought was that she had overdosed again, probably while I'd been in the bathroom, and I crawled out of bed and found her handbag on the table. As I pulled out her four prescription bottles, I was relieved to hear the rattle of her pills inside them, and was glad she wouldn't be going back to hospital any time soon.

I sat on the side of her bed and put my arms around her. *You're not going to die, Mum. You're going to be all right.*

I am! she said, and then she began sobbing against my shoulder. *I know it. I'm going to die tonight.*

I hugged her tighter and began rocking her back and forth. I told myself she was just upset and had drunk too much and was unsure about the future, but as she continued to tremble and weep in my arms another thought occurred to me, that perhaps she'd figured out another way to end her life and had already set about doing it. Had she taken something else, apart from the brandy, that was already in her system? Or was she planning something more violent and dramatic, like jumping out of the window and falling five floors to the ground?

I wondered if I should go down to reception right then and ask the clerk to call an ambulance. But what would I tell him? I didn't have any real proof that my mother would kill herself, only a prediction, and a vague one at that.

Mum, you'll be OK, I said, trying to convince myself more than anything.

She pulled away from me and rested against the pillow again. She sipped her drink and lit another cigarette, obviously trying to calm herself down. *Go back to bed*, she said, *and get some sleep.*

I was reluctant to move. *Are you going to be all right?*

Go back to bed, she repeated. *I'm fine.*

I noticed that she was staring out the window again and wondered if this were a clue to her intentions. I stood up and crawled back into my own bed, but I couldn't take my eyes off her profile. I feared that she wanted me to be asleep so she could do to herself whatever it was that she was planning, without any interruptions. I grew even more panicky then. It was night and I knew no one in the city.

Mum, I asked, *do you know where Dad is? Do you know where he lives?* I knew it was a long shot, but I was becoming desperate for a solution.

She didn't answer right away, just took a long drag of her cigarette. *Go to sleep, love*, she said in a slurry voice. *It's getting late.*

The two yellow rectangles across the airwell suddenly vanished, but I could still see her head turned towards the brick wall. I lay there listening to the various hotel noises, the creaking floorboards and the groan of water moving through pipes, forcing myself to stay awake so I could stop her before she took all her pills or tried to jump out of the window. Finally, she extinguished her last cigarette and nodded off against the pillows. The night seemed dark and infinitely long, but I kept listening to the rise and fall of her breath, making sure it continued, until I heard pigeons cooing and saw the airwell gradually filling with early light.

For breakfast, she took me to a milk bar across the street and we sat at a laminex table. She was wearing thick makeup and had her sunglasses on. I was tired but relieved she was still alive, and while I ate toast and honey she sat opposite me, drinking tea and reading a newspaper. I wondered if she was looking for a job or a proper place for us to live, but before I had a chance to ask, she spread the entertainment section on the table and said, *How would you like to go and see a movie?*

I was not expecting this, and for this reason the question made me feel uneasy.

You pick one! she added, trying to sound bright. I wiped my hands on a serviette, turned the paper around and glanced at the advertisements. My mother usually took me to see musicals like *Funny Girl* or *Hello, Dolly!* but there was nothing like that being shown.

I don't know, I said. *There's not much on.*

Pick any one you like, she said again. *You choose.*

I read through the choices a second time and finally settled on a disaster movie, *The Towering Inferno*.

OK, she said. *The Towering Inferno it is.*

She paid the bill and we walked up to the Hoyts theatre in George Street, hurrying to make the ten twenty-five session. Once there, I ran to the Ladies. When I returned she was standing by the doors.

There you go, she said, handing me a ticket. *I'll meet you back here when it's over. It finishes at one o'clock.*

I looked at the ticket and then back at her. *But aren't you coming?*

She shook her head.

But I thought you wanted to see a movie, I said. *It was your idea.*

I've got things to do, she said, clasping her hands around the strap of her shoulder bag. *I'll be back here at one. Now run along*, she added, giving me a nudge, *or else you'll miss the start.*

I sat in the dark, almost empty cinema and tried to get interested in the drama of a burning skyscraper, of Steve McQueen battling walls of fire. And yet I couldn't shake the real-life drama of the past day and night. I was worried about what my mother was up to now that she had freed herself of me. When the building was finally saved and the credits began to roll, I was relieved. I bolted from my seat and returned to the glass doors where we'd arranged to meet. It was raining now and I stood outside under the awning, watching umbrellas bob up and down the street. I waited ten minutes, fifteen, my eyes straining to catch a glimpse of my mother turning a corner or crossing the road.

By the time the Town Hall clock had inched its way toward one thirty, I was convinced that her idea about seeing a movie had been a complete ruse. I was sure by now she was never coming back, that she'd either tried to kill herself again or had merely abandoned me for some other life, one that wasn't complicated by having a daughter.

While the umbrellas continued to bob down the street, I realised I had no money of my own and nowhere to go but back to the People's Palace, and I was just about to start bawling when my mother appeared, weaving between the cars as she tried to cross the road. As she approached I could see her hair had been flattened by the rain and when she was up close I smelled the scotch on her breath, heavy as cheap perfume.

Where've you been? I asked, as she took my hand.

Come on, she said. *I want you to meet someone.*

She led me back down the block and we crossed the road, and then we walked further down George Street until we came to a pub. I followed her into the public bar, filled with cigarette smoke and workmen drinking beer and listening to the races on the radio. There were the usual dartboards and signs advertising hamburgers and mixed grills. I trailed her as she walked along the bar to a round table wedged up near a window. A man older than my mother stood at it, wearing a blue singlet, shorts, and heavy work boots. He had a tattoo of an eagle on his arm and was drinking a schooner of beer.

Mandy, this is Bob, she said.

The man called Bob smiled, and as his mouth widened I could see the lines between his teeth were black from years of smoking. A few strands of ginger-coloured hair stuck out from both his nostrils. He said, *Hello*. I nodded back uncertainly.

My mother lay her hand on my shoulder. *Everything's going to be fine now, love. We're going to live with Bob.*

Bob lived in three small rooms in an old guest house in Lavender Bay. His kitchen was really just an old laundry outside on the back veranda, containing a bar fridge and an electric hotplate. There was a hole in the sink plugged with styrofoam.

My mother and Bob were quite tipsy by the time we put our bags by the fireplace. They planted themselves in the front room and, soon after, a mate of Bob's dropped around with a carton of beer and the three of them kept drinking throughout the afternoon and into the evening. As time went on she grew louder and more vivacious, and I found it hard to believe this was the same woman who, only eighteen hours ago, had sobbed that she was going to die. It was obvious from their banter that Bob and his friend were both attracted to her, though I was fairly sure Bob would be the one who'd eventually get her into bed. Fortunately, I fell asleep early in the next room, on a settee, exhausted from my vigil in the People's Palace.

The next morning, my mother rang Hakkim at work and told him she was leaving him for good, and that she wanted to come back to the house in order to collect her things. I was glad about this, because I wanted my cat, but I wondered how we'd fit all our furniture into Bob's three rooms.

I didn't think it was a good idea that we return to Kingsgrove unaccompanied by Bob, but that was what we did, because Bob was busy laying bricks on a city construction site. Hakkim was already at home when we arrived around lunchtime, glowering on the veranda, fists clenched. Once inside, he and my mother argued, he slapped her around, and within half an hour we were inside Hakkim's car, driving back to Lavender Bay to collect our belongings from Bob's flat.

The rest of our time in the Kingsgrove house did not get any better. My cat suddenly vanished and I suspected Hakkim had dumped her in order to punish me for something he imagined I'd done. This feeling was confirmed when he cut down my tree swing and took away my ten-gallon drum. I moved out of the mouldy third bedroom and into my sister's old room, but after I did so, Hakkim's younger brother, Nuri, moved into the one I'd just vacated. Nuri had no job and was broke and Hakkim insisted that he come and live with us. He had curly black hair and rounder features than his brother, but wore the same tight shirts and flared pants, and always had a thick gold chain around his neck.

Nuri was less volatile than Hakkim, in fact he was so indolent he sometimes seemed barely alive. He slept until about five o'clock every afternoon, at which time he'd rise, shower, and dress in one of his fashionable 1970s outfits. By this time, Hakkim would have arrived home from work and my mother would serve them their meals – Hakkim's dinner and Nuri's breakfast – which would be traditional Lebanese fare: lamb or liver cooked in onions and lemon juice, flat bread, vine leaves, baba ganouge, hommous. Then Nuri would rise from the table, a toothpick between his teeth, and go out for the evening to play cards and drink and do whatever else it was that kept him out all night.

Apart from cooking for Nuri, my mother was also forced to do his washing and ironing. She had to make his bed and ensure he had clean sheets and towels. Hakkim made her do all these things because that's what women in his culture did, without complaint, and without expecting any money or even thanks in return. Of course, my mother was not happy about this; in fact it sometimes enraged her, particularly since Nuri contributed nothing towards the rent, did not work, and stayed out all night, gambling and drinking. His presence in the house was the cause of many violent arguments between my mother and Hakkim, and sometimes I wished she'd stop resisting this arrangement because all it ever amounted to was her getting beaten up.

One afternoon I came home from school and was surprised to find that the curtains to Nuri's room were open and that he wasn't on the bed, asleep. And then I turned to find my mother sitting on the couch. I took one look at her flaring nostrils and tight mouth and knew she was furious. *The lazy bastard didn't come home last night*, she said, and dragged on her cigarette. By the singsong slur of her voice I could tell she'd been drinking, and knew there'd be hell to pay when Hakkim got home.

Christ! she announced, standing up, *I've had enough of this.* She rolled up the sleeves of her blouse. At first I thought this meant that we were running away again, but she surprised me by striding into Nuri's room. *Come on!* she said. *Give me a hand.* She grabbed a corner of Nuri's bed and pulled the entire mattress on its side. *Grab the other end*, she said. I was scared of the mood she was in, but I did as I was told. I gripped the nylon piping, heaving the weight up into the air. We carried the mattress into the living room, through the kitchen, down the back stairs, across the grass, until we reached the end of the back yard. She dumped her side just a few feet from the paling fence and I dropped mine, wondering what point my mother was trying to make – was it that Nuri should sleep outside now, instead of under our roof? I watched with unease as she disappeared into Hakkim's shed and returned with a full bottle of turpentine. She doused the mattress with the entire contents, told me to step back, and ignited it with a burning match.

We stood beneath the tree and watched the flames unfurl and spiral towards the sky. The chemicals in the material turned the fire into a brilliant violet inferno against the twilight, and under different circumstances it would have been something beautiful to behold, like midnight fireworks. But I knew that whatever fleeting pleasure my mother was now experiencing she would soon pay for a hundredfold. And I waited with growing dread as the blaze gradually reduced the mattress to a mound of smoking ash.

An hour later, when Hakkim arrived home with Nuri and realised what she'd done, he held her against the living room wall and backhanded her over and over, until she was screaming and howling, begging him to stop. And then he ordered her to get down on her knees and apologise to Nuri, which she did. As she was clambering to her feet, Hakkim demanded that she make up another bed out of cushions from the couch.

Nuri finally moved out of our house just before Christmas and I was relieved we wouldn't have him hanging around over the holidays. On Christmas Eve, my mother and Hakkim allowed me to see my major present, which was a blue bicycle with coloured streamers hanging from the handlebars. After I rode it happily up and down the street a few times, my mother called me inside and said we were all going for a drive. Half an hour later, we were pulling up outside the Hero of Waterloo, an old hotel in the historic district of The Rocks.

I followed my mother and Hakkim into the pub, which was overcrowded and smoky. There were framed oil paintings hanging from the sandstone walls. We wove our way through the people, until my mother paused, leaned over and kissed the cheek of a man who was sitting at the bar drinking a schooner of beer. And then I realised that man was my father. *Hello, Gerry*, she said. *I thought Mandy would like to see you on Christmas Eve.* He turned on his stool to face me, his face breaking into a grin, and he engulfed me in his arms, crying, *My beautiful girl!* and I hugged him back, thrilled to be back in his presence. Since his girlfriend, Sue, wasn't anywhere to be seen, I assumed she and my father were no longer together, that my mother knew this already, and that she would dump Hakkim immediately and my parents would resume their former relationship.

Gerry shook Hakkim's hand. *Whaddya drinking?* Hakkim said, *Beer*, and found a couple of stools for my mother and himself. I could tell he felt awkward in my father's presence, but was trying to appear cool. I held on to Gerry's hand while he ordered a round of drinks, feeling supremely happy, until I realised he was asking for five drinks – including a lemonade for me – and then I saw Sue shouldering her way through the crowd, making her way towards us. She greeted my mother, me and Hakkim, and sat herself on a stool at the bar. She had her blonde hair styled into loose curls, and she was wearing a silk blouse, a short dark blue skirt, stockings and high-heeled shoes. I felt sorry for my mother then, having to see a kind of version of herself, twenty years younger, now living with her husband and, once the divorce was finalised, planning to marry him.

Well, isn't this great? announced my father, after Hakkim had bought a second round of drinks. *Us all getting along together, without any hassles.* He raised his schooner, and the other three agreed and clinked glasses with each other.

My brother appeared out of the crowd, grabbed hold of me, and swung me in a circle. He joined the others at the bar, sat me on his knee, and began drinking. He no longer worked as a mechanic, he said, but was now driving a van for a carpet company. He explained he was living in a room upstairs, while my father and Sue shared a flat just around the corner. I eyed Hakkim carefully, wondering how he would react to all this conviviality, to the fact that he wasn't the centre of attention, but

Hakkim merely smiled and nodded and offered Gene a cigarette. It was obvious he was trying very hard to fit in and I almost admired him for his effort.

Round after round of drinks ensued. The air grew thick with cigarette smoke. Sue slipped her high heels off and sat in her stockinged feet. My mother relaxed and slowly became more certain and flirtatious with my father, recounting stories from *the old days*, when she used to sit on the back of his Manx-Norton motorbike as a teenager and they went speeding down highways and along bush tracks. My father and brother joined in with the boozy reminiscing and laughter, trading anecdotes about drinking in the beer garden of the Coogee Bay Hotel, about the annual Musicians' Picnic, about the time the bandleader, Jeff, operated the pedals and Gene manned the steering wheel when Gerry was too pissed to drive.

It wasn't long before they were all drunk and happy, spilling their drinks and dropping their cigarette ash onto their clothes. By this time, my mother had persuaded Gene to return with us to Kingsgrove that night, so we could celebrate Christmas together. Just before midnight, my father slipped off his stool and announced to everyone that he just had to *go up the road to see a guy*.

Can I come? I asked, taking his hand.

He shook his head. *But you can mind my seat. I'll be back in a minute.*

I nodded and clambered onto his stool. Sue disappeared with my father, and Gene, saying he needed a pee, headed in the opposite direction, on his way to the toilet.

Now that he was alone with us, Hakkim frowned and flicked dirty glances at my mother. He drained his drink and ordered another. He smoked his cigarette down to the filter, and kept drawing on it until he burned his fingers. *Your husband bastard*, he said finally. *You – slut . . . Gerry bastard. He come back, I kill him!* My mother and I were too stunned to say anything. Everyone in the pub was crying *Merry Christmas!* and hugging one another. A man in his twenties staggered towards me and, before I could stop him, pressed his lips against mine and stuck his tongue in my mouth. I reeled sideways and shoved him back. Hakkim was still muttering to himself, one fist clenched, and then he suddenly picked up an empty schooner, smashed the rim of it against the bar and, to my horror, began eating the broken shards. Blood pooled at the sides of his mouth as he bit into the base, chewing it hard, as if it were piece of tough meat. I tried to stop him but he pushed me away. *It taste good!* he cried. *It taste fucking good!*

Fortunately, one of the bar staff had alerted the manager of the pub, a burly man in his late thirties, who leaned across the bar and said to Hakkim gently, *Mate, we're closing up. It's time to go home.* And Hakkim miraculously nodded, put down the glass he was eating, wiped his mouth, and told me to go and find my brother.

Once the four of us were in the car, he began ranting again, about Gerry, about my mother being a slut, all the while struggling to steer the car in a straight line. On George Street, he nearly hit a couple crossing the road, and narrowly missed crashing into a double-parked car. *Fuck this country!* he screamed, suddenly stepping on the accelerator. Sitting in the back seat, I gripped my brother's hand, glad that he was beside me. *Fuck your husband! Fuck your kids!* And Gene was yelling at him to stop right now, that he wanted to get out. The car sped down Broadway in crazy S's as Hakkim whacked my mother a few times with his left hand. Car horns blared as my brother continued to plead for Hakkim to slow down, to stop.

Finally, Hakkim pulled over in front of a car dealership. Gene immediately opened the door, squeezed my hand and asked me, *Are you coming?* I glanced at my mother and, as much as I wanted to flee, I didn't want to abandon her when Hakkim was in this kind of mood. I glanced back at Gene and shook my head. He jumped out of the car, slammed the door and went running back down Broadway, into the darkness.

Hakkim hit the accelerator again and the Holden sped along the highway, sliding randomly in and out of lanes like a dodgem car. He continued to belt my mother as she cowered against the window, sobbing. The speedometer rose to seventy-five, eighty, eighty-five kilometres an hour, and when a woman began crossing the road at a set of lights ahead, he didn't slow down, but steered the car straight towards her, as if she were a target. I was glad to see her jump back before it was too late, and even more relieved to hear, coming up behind us, the howl of a police siren.

Hakkim finally pulled over again, and two policemen ordered him out of the car. My mother was crying, over and over, *He's got a knife!* Hakkim kept saying he wasn't drunk, that he didn't have a knife, that he didn't realise he'd been speeding. As he spoke, blood pooled from his mouth and ran down his chin. The officers forced a breathalyser on him, and finally found his knife hidden beneath the driver's seat. They ordered me and my mother out of the Holden, then locked Hakkim in the back of their paddy-wagon.

Can you give us a lift home? my mother asked, before they drove away. *My daughter and I don't have any money for a taxi.*

The officers shook their heads. *Sorry, lady*, said one of them. *That's not our job.*

The paddy-wagon sped off and we were left on the side of the highway. My mother was still drunk and I had no idea where we were. I put my arm around her waist to support her and we turned left and walked a few blocks along a suburban, tree-lined street, where houses were wreathed in Christmas decorations and strings of flashing lights. *Hang on, love*, said my mother. Suddenly she let go of me, sat down on the kerb, and vomited into the gutter. After she threw up a second time, she wiped her mouth, stood up unsteadily, and we continued along the street for a few more blocks, arm-in-arm, until we came to a huge sandstone church with a floodlit lawn. As soon as my mother glimpsed it, she hurried me forward, steered us along the path and up the few stairs to the arched wooden front doors. She took hold of the metal knocker and banged heavily. A dog, then two dogs, began barking from somewhere behind the church. We waited for a few minutes but no one appeared. She banged again, even louder than before, and the dogs continued barking raucously. Finally, we heard approaching footsteps, and then the click of a lock. The door creaked open and a man's pale, sleepy face appeared before us.

Father, my mother pleaded. *My daughter and I are lost. We've got no money* –

Do you know what time it is? the man said wearily.

I'm sorry, Father, she continued. *It's just that, if you could loan me five dollars so we can get home. I'll post it straight back next week.* She clasped her hands together, as if in prayer. *I'm a Catholic!* she added.

The man sighed and told us to wait. He closed the door,

locked it and, after about three or four minutes, we heard the footsteps again, the door unlatching, and then I saw a hand appear, holding out a five-dollar bill.

It wasn't long before I glimpsed a vacant taxi and hailed it down. My mother and I arrived home after 2 am and, as I crawled into my own bed, I was so exhausted I thought I could sleep until New Year.

Hakkim was released from the police lock-up and returned home on Christmas morning in a filthy mood. That afternoon, I was playing underneath the house and found an old tin container marked *Poison*. I unscrewed the lid and smelled the contents, and the fumes were so strong they made my eyes water. I wanted Hakkim to die, but there was obviously no way I could smuggle this kind of poison into his food without him detecting that something was amiss. But perhaps another kind of poison could be found, I reasoned, one that didn't smell so bad. And even if I were caught by the police, I knew I had a fair chance of getting off a murder charge because I was only a kid and he'd been abusing my mother and me for well over a year. The only worry with this plan was that, if Hakkim ever realised I'd put something in his food or drink, he'd definitely kill me first.

I dropped this plan when I began taking kung-fu lessons with my friend Joanne Hanby at the Belmore Police Boys' Club. I wanted to be able to defend myself against Hakkim, and kung-fu seemed a reasonable way in which to do it. The black belt master, Glen, was part Asian. He was handsome, had a taut, muscular body, and was probably in his late twenties. But the thing I admired about him the most was how his presence commanded the entire hall for the duration of the hour. When we joined, Joanne and I were the only girls in a class of twenty or so young men, and yet Glen treated us as he did any other students, demonstrating basic defence moves in a corner of the hall, patiently correcting our postures.

It felt good to sense my muscles lengthening, my body growing taut. Even though I was a good swimmer, I'd never enjoyed sports at school: I lacked the competitive drive required to help win softball and hockey games. I was the girl who invariably dropped the ball or tripped over at the worst possible moment, and hence I was always the last student to be selected for a team. But practising self-defence was a solitary exercise, and it wasn't so much about winning or losing as merely protecting myself.

One morning, about a month after I began the lessons, I awakened with stomach cramps and nausea, and my mother allowed me to stay home from school. We did not know what the problem was, and she wondered if I'd pushed myself too far during my stretching exercises the day before. Throughout the day, the pain rose and ebbed. I drank sweet tea and watched television. When we ran out of butter, I climbed onto my bicycle and rode to a corner store about eight blocks away. As the elderly Italian shopkeeper gave me my change I suddenly grew dizzy and coloured dots began moving in front of me like flies. Then I felt myself dropping down what seemed to be a very deep well and crashed backwards onto the floor.

I woke up in the arms of the shopkeeper, who was gently tapping my cheek while his wife waved a bottle of smelling salts below my nostrils. As they helped me to sit up, they explained that I had fainted, and then the wife disappeared and returned with a glass of water, which I drank. As I clambered to my feet, I thanked them for their kindness. They didn't want me to ride my bike home, but I insisted that I was fine – the trip back was mostly downhill anyway.

Later that afternoon, I went to the bathroom, and when I sat on the toilet I was shocked to find I was haemorrhaging. I leapt to the conclusion that I had some terminal illness and wondered how much longer I had to live. Terrified, I called to my mother, assuming she would summon an ambulance immediately and have me rushed to hospital. But when she glimpsed the blood running down my thighs, she merely threw her arms around me and kissed me on the head, as if I'd accomplished some rare and extraordinary feat. *Congratulations!* she announced. *Now you're a woman!*

In one way it was a relief not to be terminally ill, but I was still just as miserable. I'd had some dim understanding about what menstruation was, but it was a bit like the notion of having a car accident or being run over by a train: it was theoretically possible, but I presumed it would never happen to me. Up until that point, my mother had explained nothing about these monthly cycles, so that afternoon I was mortified to learn that I would have to wear an elastic belt around my hips to hold up the thick sanitary pad that was now wedged between my legs. By this time it was around 3 pm, and I was due at the Belmore Police Boys' Club at six. I worried that these extra items beneath my clothes would interfere with my technique.

How long is this thing going to last? I asked, fingering the elastic belt. *Will it be over by the time I take my kung-fu lesson?*

My mother snorted and shook her head. *It won't last five*

minutes, love. More like five days. You won't be doing any kung-fu tonight.

At the end of each lesson Joanne and I had to spar one another in front of the class, and I found this difficult, because she was my best friend and I didn't want to hurt her. Of course, the person I did want to hurt was Hakkim. I thought if I could just train and practise hard enough I would be able to defend myself and my mother against his attacks. Glen had told me I had very strong and flexible legs for someone my age, which gave me hope. After school, I would stand in the back yard, pivoting on one foot and kicking high into the air with the other.

One day Hakkim was amused to find me doing this and playfully challenged me to a fight. I agreed, and we faced each other, preparing for a mock duel. He managed to duck my first two blows, but as he was regaining his balance I raised my right foot and suddenly side-kicked him in the head, and he went reeling back against the tree trunk. He picked himself up and just stood there, wide-eyed, cradling his chin as if he had a toothache.

From that afternoon he forbade me to take any more lessons, his excuse being that the five-dollar weekly charge was too expensive.

Glen, however, didn't want me to stop: he thought Joanne and I had a lot of potential. Glen waived his fee for me, and encouraged me to keep attending. But I had only two more lessons before Hakkim finally put his foot down and told me I was never to return to the Police Boys' Club. To make his point clear he punched me to the bathroom floor – giving me a bloody nose – and pushed my mother's head through the kitchen window.

Those lessons may have stopped after only two months, but another form of education was just beginning. Kingsgrove High was a large institution with many buildings, an enormous playground and a sports oval. My friend Joanne now attended Wiley Park Girls' High because it was closer to her house. For a short while I befriended a girl named Leah, who talked constantly about sex and the hemline of her uniform, but after a few weeks she dropped me for a girl named Sandra who'd apparently already had sex *heaps of times*, and who wore the shortest skirts in the seventh grade. Another tentative friendship evolved with a chubby girl named Susan, until I invited her over to my place one Saturday afternoon and Hakkim, dressed in his overalls and covered with grease, blundered into my room, demanding to know where he'd left his masking tape. When he went back outside, Susan, obviously taken aback by his youth, his accent, his abrupt manner, asked, *Is that your father?*

No, I assured her. *My mum just lives with him.*

The following Monday Susan took me aside in the playground and explained that her mother wouldn't allow her to play with me anymore. It wasn't anything against me personally, she said, it was just that my mother was *living in sin*.

From then on I vowed that I would never bring a friend home again; in fact, I decided to refrain from discussing any aspect of my life outside the school. During the next year and a half, I never had sleep-overs at my place, my excuse being *my mother's very ill*. I brushed off guys who wanted to *go with me* because I was *already going with somebody else*. Any bruises that appeared on my neck or shoulders were explained away as *love bites* from a boy from my old school who was keen on me. I returned to the library during lunchtime breaks, read paperback novels and sometimes helped the librarian with the shelving.

One afternoon I was copying some information from the blackboard about the Renaissance when a student teacher entered the classroom and summoned me to see the principal. I assumed that I was in trouble, and as I climbed the stairs to her office I wondered what on earth I had done wrong: I didn't smoke; I didn't wear a short uniform; I always did my homework. I didn't even talk or laugh in class anymore.

She faced me sternly across her desk and told me to close the door, which I did.

Mandy, she said, *I've got something to ask you.*

I nodded, pinching a button on my uniform.

And I want you to tell me the truth, she added, clasping her hands together.

I nodded again, dreading the worst. I suspected she knew about my life at home and I would be obliged to tell her everything.

Mrs Macallow sighed and pursed her lips. *Do you have a sister?* she asked.

I wasn't expecting this question and took a little longer to answer than I should have. *Yes*, I replied.

My hesitation made the principal a little more suspicious. *How old is she?*

I thought for a moment. *Sixteen.*

And what does she look like?

Well – I said, wondering where on earth this line of questioning was going – *she, she's got long blonde hair. She's short . . . shorter than me. She's really pretty.*

The frown faded from Mrs Macallow's face. *All right*, she said,

I just wanted to check. Mandy, your sister's here to see you. She's waiting in the tea room down the hall.

Lisa wasn't in the tea room, but I eventually found her on a balcony adjoining the offices, leaning against a railing. It had been six months since I'd seen her. I noticed her hair was a little shorter and her skin was tanned, but apart from that she didn't appear very different for having spent so much time away. She seemed tense, yet when we embraced I could tell that she had missed me.

Prue and I hitched to Queensland, she explained. *I just couldn't stand it anymore.*

How did you know I was here? I asked, as I'd been in primary school when she'd left.

I knew you'd be in high school. It's the closest one to the house. She then went on to tell me why she'd stayed away for so long: she didn't want to be forced by the child welfare authorities to come back and live with Hakkim and my mother, and had waited until she'd turned sixteen before returning to Sydney. She'd enjoyed herself, she said, spending the summer months on a plantation, picking mangoes and bananas and living with Prue Crampton in a little workers' cottage.

I told my sister that nothing much had changed at home, except that on the weekend she'd run away our mother had tried to kill herself again, and this time had almost succeeded.

Lisa hung her head then and didn't seem to breathe for a long time. *I wanted to take you with me,* she said, *but you were just too young.*

I leaned on the railing and watched a group of pigeons pecking at a discarded packet of chips on the footpath below. *Have you seen Mum yet?* I asked. *Does she know you're back?*

Lisa shook her head. *But could you do me a favour?*

Sure, I said. *What?*

I want to come home. Can you ask her for me?

I wondered why she'd want to return to live under the same roof as Hakkim after having made such a great escape. Maybe she didn't have any money, I thought, or anywhere to live.

OK, I said. *I can do that.*

She told me I could ring her at Prue Crampton's house, where she was staying for the time being.

Before we said goodbye, she paused and ruffled my hair. *Hey*, she said, *what class did I just get you out of?*

History, I replied.

She rolled her eyes. *At least I've done something for you.*

I was about to tell her that history was one of my favourite subjects, but it didn't seem to be the right time.

As soon as I arrived home that afternoon, I sat down with my mother and told her everything. She listened and nodded, but did not seem overly concerned or surprised. It was as if I were telling her what the weather was like outside, or what I ate for lunch. I was startled by how detached she seemed. Over dinner, she raised the subject with Hakkim, and when she asked him if it would be all right for Lisa to move back in, the smile that widened across his face left me cold. *No*, he said triumphantly, *she run away. She no come back here.*

And that was the end of the discussion. I rang my sister the following day and told her the verdict. Lisa, however, didn't seem particularly unsettled by the news. A few days later she and Prue Crampton registered for the dole and moved to Katoomba, two hours west of Sydney, where they rented a cheap cottage on the main street. And even though my sister and I had fought and argued all our lives, I missed her keenly, and wished she were only a few feet away, in the bedroom next door, brushing her hair, or painting her nails, or even yelling at me to be quiet.

7

It is after midnight and my mother and I are in our pyjamas, rushing along a highway through the rain. The baby is in her arms, wrapped in a woollen blanket. My slippers are soaking wet and I can already feel a bruise swelling my right cheek. Occasionally, a car speeds past, tyres hissing against the wet road, but no one stops for us.

The baby starts crying. We cross another street, running into the glare of a flashing orange traffic light. We have no spare nappies, no change of clothes, no food. We don't even have twenty cents between us, and I doubt we will get very far. A taxi appears in the distance, its vacant sign glowing white through the darkness. My mother hurries to the kerb, raises her arm and flags it down.

She opens the door to the back seat. Get in, *she says to me, and I do as I am told, while she clambers into the front seat with the baby.*

I don't have any money, she says to the driver. But I want you to take me somewhere.

The driver glances at the baby, then into the rear-vision mirror, at me. The windscreen wipers slap back and forth. He slips the taxi into gear, hits the accelerator, and we go speeding into the night.

*

One afternoon, not long after I began high school, I came home to find my mother sitting on the couch, knitting a white booty. I thought this was strange and when I asked her why she was doing it, she merely looked away and replied, *It's for one of your dolls*.

I found this answer a little disturbing as I hadn't played with dolls for many years and the two I still owned were not in need of any footwear. Throughout that month the steel knitting needles continued to click, the constant rhythm producing bonnets, shawls, tiny jackets in either pale lemon or ivory, all intricately patterned and ribboned with pale satin.

The idea that my mother could be pregnant to Hakkim filled me with dread. It was entirely possible that they would even get married – and then we'd never be able to escape him. I grew more tense with every item she knitted, as if each one were further confirmation of this awful possibility. When my sister visited one weekend I confided in her, and Lisa comforted me with the notion that Mum was merely going mad. She explained that it was quite common for women in their mid-forties to experience what doctors called *phantom pregnancies*: their periods become irregular, their hormones go wild and, in an attempt to recapture their passing youth, they imagine they are pregnant. Lisa was quite confident about her diagnosis: she'd read an article about it in *Woman's Day*. I was relieved by her certainty.

But not even a week passed before I overheard a discussion between my mother and Hakkim about *the baby*. I was in my room, standing by the door, my ear pressed against the keyhole. They were talking about the possibility of moving house *before the baby is born*. They didn't want to put *the baby* in the mouldy third bedroom, where it might develop a disease. I found it hard to believe my mother was going through with the pregnancy and couldn't understand why she wasn't having it terminated. Perhaps she thought a child would make their relationship better, or somehow calm Hakkim down, but I found this hard to imagine and spent a restless night in bed, thinking about the consequences.

There was a good side to my mother being pregnant: she stopped drinking, and it was the first time I'd seen her sober for any extended period of time. The anxieties and disappointments of the past few years slowly faded from her face, her natural beauty returned, and a pink blush flowered through her skin. Her nature softened, too, and she was as gentle and angelic as a sylph, cuddling up with me in the afternoons, reading books and sharing lollies. I wanted her to be pregnant forever.

Hakkim, however, was not so contented. He was drinking heavily and came to the unlikely conclusion that the child had not been fathered by him. He kept ranting about the fact that he'd come home one night and seen a man hiding in the bushes, a man who'd obviously been having sex with my mother and who must have made her pregnant. Each evening, when he came home drunk after work, we'd have to go over the night in question, and each time I'd have to tell him, again and again, that I'd been in the back yard with my mother the entire afternoon, and that there'd been no man in the bushes or anywhere else, that he must have imagined it all.

Once I'd convinced him of this notion, however, he'd move on to his second theory: my mother fell pregnant the night we stayed at Lavender Bay, to the bricklayer, Bob, whom she'd met in the pub. And it was then that I would have to lie to him: *I was there the whole time, Hakkim. They never had sex.* I didn't feel bad about doing this because I knew the man from Lavender Bay could not have impregnated my mother: the dates were completely wrong. But I sensed that logic and reasoning would not have persuaded Hakkim and that it was best to keep it simple and deny everything.

His paranoia grew so bad he refused to buy anything for the child: no clothes, toys, nappies or bottles. He would not even allow my mother to see a doctor for prenatal care, and it was she who had to sit down by herself and calculate the due date. He forbade her to make a booking at a hospital, lest he be landed with a bill for the birth of another man's child. *If baby no look like me*, he often said, *you know I'm going to kill it.*

My mother was into her sixth month of pregnancy when we moved once again, to the adjoining suburb of Bexley. Because she couldn't lift anything, Hakkim and I had to shift all the furniture ourselves. The new house was a brick bungalow with three bedrooms. There was a garage out the back where Hakkim could repair the second-hand cars he bought cheaply at auctions. This kept him busy on weekends, but not busy enough to distract him from his growing obsession about the paternity of the unborn child.

At night, when he'd slap my mother around, I feared that she would miscarry and I'd leap between them, offering him my face, my shoulders, my arms. Once, I ran across the street to the church and begged the priest to call the police, but he shook his head and closed the door, not wanting to get involved.

My mother's stomach grew larger, and when she was sitting down she could balance a teacup and saucer on top of it, as if it were a tray. The due date she'd calculated – 10 August – came and went. Two weeks later, she still hadn't gone into labour. For

Hakkim, the wait was excruciating, and he reacted as if my mother were deliberately prolonging the pregnancy in an attempt to further upset him. *What have you got in there?* he'd demand, pointing to her stomach. *A dozen bottles of beer?* By late August he'd convinced himself that my mother wasn't pregnant at all, that she merely had some severe disease or cyst that made her stomach swell.

The September school holidays came, and I spent most of my time in my room, writing stories and poems, and stashing all the pages into a hole in my mattress. At night, I'd turn the light off and scribble under the blankets by torchlight, so Hakkim would assume I was asleep and wouldn't barge in and disturb me. But some nights, when he was drunk, even that didn't deter him: the door would crash open, the light would go on, and he'd be pulling me out of bed, demanding that I confirm some minor detail about the night he supposedly saw the man in the bushes, or the time my mother and I spent at the flat of the Lavender Bay bricklayer.

One Saturday afternoon my sister visited us. She was now living by herself in a room in an old Mount Druitt guest house because she'd been forbidden by court order to associate with Prue Crampton. In Katoomba, the two of them had been arrested for breaking and entering, and had been lucky to escape a fine or detention. The judge had concluded that they were a bad influence on one another – and were never to meet again – but my sister told me privately that she and Prue still saw one another all the time and the judge could *go stuff himself*.

I thought this would be the most surprising news that my sister would deliver that day, but in the kitchen, while we were washing up, I was startled to hear her announce to my mother and me that my brother, now twenty-one, had recently married.

What? said my mother, dropping a plate back into the soapy water.

Last weekend, said Lisa, *in a registry office. There were four guests. I was the only relative.*

My mother squeezed the small of her back and sat down in a nearby chair. I couldn't imagine my brother being married: I'd never known him to even have a girlfriend.

Where was Gerry? asked my mother. *Why wasn't he there?*

Well, this is the funny thing, said Lisa, nervously lighting a cigarette. *You're not going to believe this, but Gene married Sue.*

My mother, too startled to say anything, just wiped her hands on a tea towel.

I gazed intently at my mother, confused. *But I thought she was going to marry Dad*, I said. *That's why you two had to get a divorce.*

My mother, still dazed, shook her head. *Our lawyer went bankrupt and shot through to Queensland. The divorce never happened.*

Later that week, when Joanne Hanby's family invited me to go on a short holiday with them, I gladly accepted, and spent three days in a caravan on the coast. Joanne and I swam, fished and collected shells, and while we did this I processed this new information: my brother was now married to my father's girlfriend, to the woman who had broken up the relationship between my parents, and the person who would have been my stepmother was now my sister-in-law.

After Lisa had told us about the wedding between Gene and Sue, our mother lit a cigarette and made a confession of her own, finally explaining to us what had really happened between her and Gerry back in Kings Cross. Not long after we had moved to the apartment on Springfield Avenue, when she and Gene had made the surprise visit to Wollongong on the night of her and Gerry's twenty-third wedding anniversary, she knew something was wrong when Gerry virtually ignored her all evening. During his breaks he didn't come near her, but merely made a beeline towards the bar. It was when my mother noticed the young blonde cocktail waitress who always served him drinks that she realised the extent of the problem.

But Dad told us Sue was an airline hostess, I said, *that he'd met her when he went away to England.*

My mother shook her head. *He never went to England. She was a married barmaid from Wollongong. They just pissed off together on a tour through Queensland. She even left her two kids behind.* My mother paused and dragged on a cigarette. *Well, Sue always wanted to be a Sayer*, she added, shaking her head. *At least she got what she wanted.*

As I walked along the beach with Joanne, I tried to figure out why my father had lied, why my mother had kept so much from us, and came to the conclusion that maintaining a long silence or telling a fib can occasionally seem like the right thing to do – or at least the easiest way to get through an awkward time in your life. And as I strolled, other things from the past began to make sense: my mother's first two suicide attempts, not long after Gerry's departure, and the way she had so easily allowed Hakkim into our lives.

On our second day in the caravan, Joanne and I woke before

dawn and I witnessed my first sunrise, a tangerine sliver against the horizon. On our third and last night, I could not sleep, and merely thrashed around in my narrow bed. In the early hours of the morning, however, when I looked out at the moon glowing yellow through the trees, I understood why I was so restless: my mother was now giving birth, and I was not there to see it.

When I arrived home that afternoon, Hakkim was sitting on the veranda, waiting for me. As I walked through the front gate I eyed his face, trying to judge the mood he was in. He didn't seem particularly happy or angry, just slightly tense as he sat with his shoulders hunched, smoking. *Your mother have boy*, he said matter-of-factly. As I walked onto the veranda I could see how tired he was, and thought perhaps any joy he still felt was tempered by exhaustion.

He drove me to Crown Street Women's Hospital. I saw my mother first. She was lying in a bed in a public ward, receiving a blood transfusion. It had been a difficult labour, complicated by the fact that she'd had no prenatal care, no obstetrician, and no booking at a hospital. She told me it had been *a breech birth*, explaining the baby had not been in the proper position and had come out feet-first, ripping my mother's insides in the process. *I've lost a lot of blood*, she said, *but I'm all right now. Everything's going to be fine*. It occurred to me that the last time she'd been in hospital she'd been so close to death. It seemed almost impossible that, only a year later, she'd just given birth to another human being.

A nurse walked into the ward carrying a tiny white bundle. At first I thought it was just a bedsheet or a set of pillowcases, but then she lowered the bundle into my arms and I saw myself looking down into the newborn's face: honey-coloured skin, a crown of dark brown hair, a tiny wrinkle on his brow. To my great relief, he looked exactly like his father.

While my mother and the baby remained in hospital that week, Hakkim's behaviour grew even more erratic. At night, as I was preparing for bed, he'd come into my room, wanting to kiss me goodnight, and suddenly he'd be throwing me down on the bed and pushing his tongue into my mouth. When I tried to beat him off, he'd pin my arms down and cry, *Give me your tongue*. But I preferred to be slapped than raped by him and always resisted. Finally, he'd give up, perhaps out of a sense of guilt, and walk away.

After we collected my mother and the baby from the hospital, we had to go shopping. Hakkim must have realised the baby looked like him, because he consented to pay for a dozen nappies, four singlets, three pairs of plastic pants and two bottles. He refused, however, to shell out any money for a bassinet until he received the results of a paternity test, which he wanted to take before the month was out. Instead, he bought a yellow plastic laundry basket and put a pillow inside it, saying, *Baby sleep in this*.

My mother and the baby had been home only two nights when Hakkim told her to get dressed so they could go out to a local club. Since she was breastfeeding and still weak from the birth, she said she didn't think this was a good idea. But Hakkim became insistent and would not stop ranting until my mother expressed some milk into a bottle, put on some makeup, and slipped into a black evening gown.

We'll be home soon, she assured me as they walked out the front door.

I liked being left with the baby all to myself, and sat for a long time just watching him sleep. When he woke up I changed his nappy and marvelled at how, only days before, this tiny, kicking creature had been inside my mother's body. I warmed his milk and fed him and after that I just sat on the bed and cuddled him.

But as the hours passed he grew hungry again and began to cry. Tears trembled down his cheeks as I tried to pacify him with a dummy. I rocked him back and forth, pacing up and down the room. He spat the dummy out regularly and one time cupped his mouth around my left nipple and tried to suck some milk through the cotton of my pyjamas.

By the time Hakkim and my mother arrived home the baby was hysterical – red-faced, kicking and howling. My mother made a beeline for the bedroom, unzipped her dress immediately and put the baby to her breast. And then Hakkim staggered into the room, screaming his old complaint, that the child wasn't his, that he was going to do something about it. He wrenched him from my mother's arms, yelling, *You no mine! You no mine!* And before we could stop him he threw the baby across the room. Fortunately, the little bundle landed on the bed and as I dived for him I could tell he was completely unharmed.

The next morning I was woken by Hakkim, who was pulling me out of bed. *Get up*, he ordered. *We go get test*. It was not even eight o'clock and I told him no doctors' surgeries would be open at this time of the day.

I walked into the main bedroom to check on the baby and my mother. She was lying against the pillows of her bed, her face grey-blue as a slab of ice. And then I looked down to see, scattered across the carpet, what seemed like large red chunks of chopped liver and strings of clotted blood. My immediate thought was that this was all that was left of the baby after

Hakkim had carved him up. Panicking, I ran across the room to the laundry basket, and was relieved to find him safely inside it, his large blue eyes crusted with sleep as he gazed back up at me.

Mandy, my mother said, *I'm haemorrhaging. I've got to get back to hospital.*

Hakkim appeared in the doorway. *No*, he said, lighting a cigarette. *We go get test.*

I looked down again at all the blood, at the clots as large as a fist, and could not believe it had all come from inside my mother.

Help me up, she said. When she threw back the bedclothes I saw the sheets, too, were stained red.

We go get test, Hakkim said again impatiently, *to see if baby mine.*

I ignored him and helped my mother to her feet. She put an arm around my shoulder as we headed for the bathroom, but she only took two steps before her knees buckled and I looked down to see more liver-like chunks dropping out of her and onto the floor. I guided her back to the bed. Hakkim grew more irate about his need for the paternity test. I tried to reason with him, but it was like trying to communicate with someone whose language I didn't speak, or a demanding two-year-old on the verge of a tantrum.

If we don't get her to hospital, I said finally, *she's going to die. She's going to bleed to death.*

He looked down at the floor, at all the blood clots strewn across the carpet, as if he hadn't even noticed them before. He took a long drag on his cigarette and let the smoke escape from his nostrils. *Clean up mess*, he finally said. *I warm up car.*

While my mother rested, I kneeled and lifted the larger clots onto pieces of newspaper spread out on the floor, then wrapped them in parcels. After I threw these into the garbage bin, I sponged up what I could of the blood. I cleaned my mother and helped her into a fresh nightie. Hakkim and I supported her as we walked her to the car. I returned to the house, grabbed a few clean nappies and picked up the baby from his basket.

In the back seat of the car, I held the child close to me. We sped along the highway, back to Crown Street Women's Hospital, as Hakkim continued muttering to himself.

My mother and the baby were readmitted immediately. Again, she was close to death, having lost so many litres of blood. A nurse finally explained to me that what she'd been haemorrhaging was the afterbirth, which hadn't been properly removed and weighed after the umbilical cord was cut. My mother and the child remained in the maternity ward for a further four days. While she was there, Hakkim resumed his nocturnal visits to my bedroom, and I continued to fight him off, repulsed by the crazy look in his eyes, and his beery, tobacco breath.

It was during this difficult month that something miraculous happened, something that would change me, however slightly, forever. I was doing my usual lunchtime mooning around the high school library, looking for something interesting to read, when I stumbled upon a journal propped face-out on a revolving stand. It was called *New Poetry*, and on the cover was a black-and-white reproduction of a Pre-Raphaelite woman with thick, wavy hair and wearing a flowing gown. Curious, I picked it up and thumbed through it. Some pages were illustrated with only swirling, calligraphic brushstrokes. I found their brevity and simplicity intriguing. Then there were the poems themselves. I was surprised to find they addressed subjects I'd never thought worthy of writing about before: being a housewife, for example, or hating your husband. And some of the poems were so dense I didn't understand them at all, which excited me. Even though they were hard to understand, for some inexplicable reason I knew they were good. But the most thrilling aspect of these new poems was the fact that they *didn't rhyme*. I decided immediately that this was the way I wished to write poetry from now on.

When my mother and the baby were discharged from the hospital and came home, I wrote a little poem for the child in free verse. I read it to him once, when no one else was around, as he lay in his laundry basket. I also began a novel, about a girl wrongly committed to a lunatic asylum, and how she makes her escape. Writing became my own escape. In an imaginary world I could make anything possible if I could just find exactly the right words.

Meanwhile, my mother and Hakkim fought constantly over the right name for the baby. Hakkim wanted to call him 'Omar Mohammed'. My mother, however, didn't think he should have a foreign-sounding name and was insisting on 'Jason Luke'. Hakkim argued that if the child was indeed his, then the boy should have a name that reflected his father's Muslim background. My mother pointed out, again and again, that the child would be growing up in a non-Muslim culture, and should therefore have a name that was Anglo-Saxon. Personally, I didn't care one way or the other, although I liked the name 'Omar' because it was simple and unusual, and because I thought the Egyptian film actor, Omar Sharif, was handsome. The rows between Hakkim and my mother went on for days, and the only times the house was quiet was after he lost his temper and hit her. Of course, he finally got his way, as he always did, and I thought it was a shame that my mother had gone through all that grief for nothing. On the last legal day for registering the baby's birth – four weeks after he'd been born – he was named Omar Mohammed.

I thought things would settle down after Hakkim's victory, but his unhappiness became even more complicated. My mother's arguments about the child growing up in an Anglo-Saxon culture must have rattled him deeply, because only days after registering the birth he announced to the two of us that he planned to take the baby back to Lebanon and have his own mother raise him as a good Muslim boy. It was late one night, after he'd come home drunk. He called my mother *a pisspot* and *a slut*, and said she wasn't worthy of rearing his son. Then he demanded that she bring him a bucket of boiling water, which she did. This in itself was nothing unusual, as he often liked to soak his feet when he came home from work. But when she placed the steaming bucket on the living room floor, he didn't roll up his trousers, but merely took one last drag on his cigarette and butted it out.

Now, he said, *go and get baby*. My mother and I exchanged looks. Her face blanched and she began to tremble. And then I realised that I, too, was shaking as I imagined what Hakkim would do next.

Go and get baby, Hakkim repeated, dipping the tip of his finger in the boiling water. My mother gazed at the steaming water and, before I could stop her, she picked up a broom and began swinging at him, but Hakkim ducked twice, and rammed her against the wall. *You're not going to kill my child*, she cried as he yanked the broom from her hands and punched her to the floor. I grabbed hold of one arm and tried to restrain him but he elbowed me back and hit me in the face. My mother was still screaming as he grabbed her by the hair and dragged her out of the living room and down the length of the hallway.

When he finally let go, she staggered to her feet, ran into the bedroom and snatched the baby from the laundry basket. *Come on*, she yelled to me as she charged out the front door, and I rushed out behind her, into the rain, still wearing my pyjamas and slippers.

The taxi driver was a kind and patient man who drove around Sydney, looking for a women's refuge my mother could only identify as Elsie's. She'd read an article about the refuge in the *Women's Weekly*, but the address hadn't been published, my mother said, because the women and children who stayed there were being sheltered from violent husbands. All she knew was that the refuge was somewhere in the inner-city suburb of Glebe. The driver stopped at petrol stations, motels, late-night cafes, crawling out into the rain, asking people if they knew of such a place. Finally, he pulled up at the Glebe police station and got the address from a night desk clerk.

The refuge was a yellow Victorian mansion on Derwent Street. Two women on duty paid our taxi fare and ushered us into the house. It was after one in the morning. The women sat us in the front room and made us tea and my mother and I explained to them what had happened to us that night. It was only then, in the light of a desk lamp, that I could see the bald patches on my mother's head, as big as fifty-cent pieces, where Hakkim had pulled her hair out by the roots.

Don't worry, said one of the women, Dot, who was plump and grandmotherly. *We'll look after you.* I noticed she smelled of talcum powder as she stroked my hair. The other one made us more tea and provided disposable nappies for the baby. The refuge was so full that night there were no spare beds, but Dot and the second woman, Fran, dragged a mattress up three flights of stairs to an attic that was now used as a sewing room.

My mother and I settled down on the mattress with the baby between us. The relief that overcame me was as strong as a tranquilliser, and yet I still found it hard to believe we'd finally escaped and were far away from Hakkim. But even so, I was unable to sleep and merely lay for hours, gazing up at the gables of the attic roof and the triangular shapes made by the moonlight.

The next morning, we had breakfast in the huge kitchen downstairs, and then introduced ourselves to the two new women on duty. One, Mary, was young, dark-haired and olive-skinned. The second one, Steve, was plump, had cropped blonde hair and was wearing overalls. We discussed with them our immediate problems, which were lack of money and clothes. Steve made a note in the logbook, then unlocked the petty cash box and handed my mother a twenty-dollar bill. *Come on*, said Mary, *follow me*. Still wearing our pyjamas, we followed Mary out to her parked station wagon, and she drove us around the corner and down Glebe Point Road. She pulled up in front of a small unopen store, also called Elsie's. As we climbed out of her car, Mary explained the business was an opportunity shop run by *the collective* to create revenue for the refuge. She unlocked the door and we walked inside. Mary gestured to all the clothes hanging on racks, the shoes, belts, underwear and socks. *OK, girls*, she said, *pick out anything you like*. An hour later, my mother, the baby and I returned to the refuge with an entirely new wardrobe.

Living at Elsie's was like an extended holiday after the tension and anxiety of the past few years. There was a well-stocked kitchen and we were invited to help ourselves to food any time we wished. A large living room boasted a 24-inch TV. The front office held shelves of books and magazines. After a few nights, my mother and I were moved to our own small private room on the first floor with a wardrobe and dresser and a set of bunk beds. My mother and the baby slept on the lower tier and I slept on the top. Floss, now seventy, visited us once, curious to see her new grandchild. She and my mother didn't talk much about Hakkim and focused instead on the baby.

There were about twelve other women staying at Elsie's, and at least twice as many children. In the afternoons, some of the older kids and I would loll about on the couches in the living room, trading stories: *Your father pushed you down the stairs – that's nothin'. I was in the car with my dad one night and he put his foot on the pedal and drove it right into the kitchen.*

During our first week there, Mary interviewed my mother and me about Hakkim and wrote our answers out on a photocopied form. I remember one of the questions clearly: *Was your husband abused physically as a child?* And my mother, downcast, nodded and replied: *His mother used to whip him.*

Mary noted her answer on the form, ticking a small box. *That's the only common denominator between abusive men*, she said. *As boys they were abused themselves.*

We stayed at the refuge for six weeks. During that time, the workers at the refuge helped my mother negotiate with the social welfare office so she could have her pension cheque redirected to Elsie's quickly and confidentially. And while we waited for that to happen, my mother allowed me to do whatever I wished: I could eat peanut butter sandwiches between meals, watch television until 5 am, take the baby to the park. And sometimes I did absolutely nothing at all, just lay on the top bunk bed and stared at the paint peeling off the ceiling. I was happy I didn't have to start another school right away, but by the fifth week of our stay at Elsie's, the workers explained to me that, by law, they were obliged to make me do so. They enrolled me in Petersham Girls' High, which was a ten-minute bus ride away.

On my first day there, I realised quickly that teenage girls were even meaner when boys weren't around. In the playground I was taunted about my lack of a school uniform, my flat chest, my braided hair. I reacted in the only way I knew how: in my classes, when questions were posed, I repeatedly raised my hand and provided the answers. By the second day, I had transformed myself into a teachers' pet, which of course riled the girls who hated me. At lunchtime, two of them even threatened to knock out my teeth if I didn't shut up in class. Their anger gave me a huge amount of pleasure. At the end of the third day, however, I returned to the refuge to find out that my mother had signed a lease on a flat for us to live in, and I was relieved I wouldn't have to return to Petersham Girls' High.

Our new home was an old Art-Deco apartment just two streets away from Bondi Beach. My mother and the baby shared the one bedroom and I slept on a narrow enclosed veranda. You had to walk through my mother's bedroom to get to my room, and through my room to get to the bathroom, but I didn't care: we were safe and finally on our own, and I liked the wooden picture rails that lined the living room wall. A fund from the refuge helped us pay our bond and the first two weeks' rent, and again the Smith Family helped with furnishing the flat. Finally, the baby got his bassinet, a white wicker one on a stand and with a veil. Once we were settled, my mother changed my brother's name by deed poll to Jason Luke Sayer.

By the time my mother told me about the letter she'd written she'd already posted it. I asked her why she'd bothered, and she told me she'd felt the need to explain to Hakkim why she'd left and why she was never coming back. I didn't think this was worth doing and said so. After the way he'd treated us, I felt he didn't need or deserve an explanation.

Don't worry, replied my mother, *I didn't write our address on the back of the envelope. I'm not THAT silly.*

My new school was on top of a hill, overlooking the sea. Fortunately, I was able to stall the date of my first day there because I began to suffer from headaches so severe that I was unable to bend over or move suddenly. The doctor we visited said it was probably an allergic reaction caused by something in or around our new apartment. I spent several days in bed, watching television and eating bowls of my mother's vegetable soup. By the beginning of our second week in Bondi, the pain began to fade as mysteriously as it had arrived, and I was obliged to begin my first day at Dover Heights Girls' High.

It was the biggest school I had ever attended and during the trawls between one building and another I would often get lost and arrive late for my next class. I realised quickly that I could not pull any of my smarty-pants routines with these students: most of them were well-educated and knew their various subjects far better than I. The eighth grade curriculum was of a higher standard than my last two schools and I found myself struggling to adapt to it, especially since I was joining the classes towards the end of the school year, in late October.

On my first day, walking into the science room, I was relieved to run into two of my old friends from Plunkett Street, Fatima and Rita, whom I hadn't seen for two years. It was the one good moment in an otherwise complicated and depressing day, and I immediately assumed that we three could suddenly pick up where we'd left off, that we could be as close and happy together as we had been under the tutelage of Mr Swords. But by the end of the lesson I knew I was naive to have thought such a thing: they each had another tight-knit set of friends and didn't need the company of someone from primary school. Rita paid me little attention and, during an experiment, when I spilled water all over my uniform, Fatima joined a few girls who were snickering and calling me a dickhead.

The good thing about living in Bondi was that we were so close to the beach. After school, I took my brother for long walks in his pram along the Esplanade. I spent my weekends swimming in the surf, returning home only to eat the lunches my mother had prepared. *You're going to be so healthy by the end of summer*, she'd say, serving me a plate of salad. She herself would not eat with me, but would sit in the back yard, quietly sipping a cold beer. After clearing my plate, I could always tell she wanted me to stay and keep her company, but I found it boring hanging around the flat, especially on sunny days; the lure of the beach was too strong. *Why don't you come with me?* I'd say. *Come and have a swim!* But she'd merely shake her head and make some excuse: the baby needs a nap, or she was going to wash her hair. Now that we were away from Hakkim and had settled into a better life, I wondered why she seemed so distant and unhappy. There was no one taking all her money from her, no one ordering her around and beating her constantly. We had a nice new home, a beach at our doorstep, yet she seemed even more depressed than when we'd lived with Hakkim, and I could only attribute her behaviour to loneliness.

This was confirmed when she began dressing up every night after dinner and going out to the Hakoah Club – a block away from our flat – while I stayed at home and looked after the baby. Each time I saw her taking the rollers out of her hair and applying lipstick, I grew uneasy, as if an accident were about to happen. I knew what she was doing: the elaborate makeup, the backless dresses, the high heels she wore were an unequivocal announcement that she was looking for a man. I was surprised she was so keen to find another boyfriend after having just narrowly escaped the last one.

A week went by, then two. She continued her nightly pilgrimage to the Hakoah Club, and when she returned I was always relieved to hear, from my bed on the veranda, that she was walking through the front door alone.

By the end of our third week in the new flat, however, I was sitting in the living room, only about an hour after my mother had left, when I heard two sets of footsteps coming up the path. Puzzled, I stood up to turn the television down. The key went into the lock, the door swung open. I turned around to see my mother walking through the door, and what I saw next seemed impossible. I took a couple of steps forward, squinting into the darkness outside. Behind her was Hakkim, hands in his pockets, grinning sheepishly. He walked up the steps and into the apartment. *Hello, Mandy*, he said, and leaned down to kiss me. I ducked his mouth and backed away against the wall. *What's he doing here?* I asked. But my mother merely walked into the kitchen.

I come see baby, said Hakkim. *I come take you home.*

My mother said very little as I argued with Hakkim that night. The talk went on for hours, circling around the same points like a current. Hakkim was unusually contrite, saying how sorry he was, that he'd never beat us again. I demanded to know how he'd found us, and Hakkim explained that he'd discovered a clue to our whereabouts from the letter my mother had written him. Even though there'd been no return address, the postmark on the envelope had read *Bondi Beach*, and for the past three weeks he'd devoted all his spare time to walking up and down the beach and trawling the shopping centre, looking for us. When that turned up nothing, he said, he'd had an even better idea: *I know you mother like drink, and I think, look in pub, look in club!* And then he announced, rather proudly, that the Hakoah Club was the first place he'd searched – and that is where he found her, sitting up at the bar, drinking a scotch and dry.

He promised us a colour television set. He said he'd stop hurting us. He pleaded, saying he loved his son and wanted to look after him. My mother seemed to have been convinced by this performance, but I thought it was just an act, and told him so, and it felt good to be able to be defiant towards Hakkim without fearing that I would be beaten. But I was also trying to goad him back to his true nature, to make his temper snap, so my mother could see that nothing had really changed and that we should get him out of our flat before it was too late.

But it was already too late. By midnight, I could tell by the glazed look in her eyes that she was already defeated. She took him to bed. The next day Hakkim arrived with a truck and began packing our belongings and loading them up.

I re-enrolled at Kingsgrove High. I was back in the same classes, with the same teachers. I was also back with the same circle of students, and there were a few deeply awkward moments when they demanded to know why I'd suddenly disappeared for ten weeks without telling anyone, and why I was now back at school again, as if nothing had ever happened. I thought about explaining to them that I'd had some kind of disease, that I'd been hospitalised, but it seemed implausible and too much of a fib, so I merely explained that *my parents separated*, and now they were *back together again*. This was sort of the truth and allowed me to say it with some conviction, enough to appease their curiosity and for them not to want to ask me any more questions.

For the first time in my life, I floundered in some of my classes. I'd missed out on two and a half months of the school's curriculum and, even though I did well enough in my favourite subjects, I struggled through mathematics and science. I tried to catch up, did my homework religiously as soon as I arrived home from school, but I'd obviously missed some important lessons. At the end of the year I failed my first exam by one point and I was devastated. I felt stupid and a failure and if I had only just answered one more question correctly I would have passed and everything would have seemed so much better.

Life improved at home for a little while. Hakkim kept his word and bought a colour television, which he set up in a corner of the living room. He didn't drink heavily, didn't carry on about the baby not being his. On Sundays we went on drives together, picnicked on the beach, went fishing. He allowed my mother to buy other items for the baby, like jumpsuits and rattles. The school year ended; Christmas was coming. I helped Hakkim decorate our tree. But sometime just before New Year he cracked. He and my mother went out to an RSL club one night while I stayed home and looked after the baby. They returned home after midnight, drunk and yelling at one another. He was accusing her of flirting with another man, and she kept repeating, *I just said hello to him. I just nodded and said hello.*

You fuck him, screamed Hakkim. *You fuck him before. He father of baby!* And then he began hitting her across the face until she ran into their bedroom, sobbing.

Three weeks later we were back at Elsie's. My mother had a black eye and my neck and shoulders were bruised. The workers there were not surprised to see us return and welcomed us into the refuge, almost as if they'd been expecting us. It was the height of summer – the school holidays – and the refuge was empty of residents except for my mother, me and the baby.

Only a few days passed before it was the beginning of the Australia Day long weekend, and the remaining workers at the refuge were all going away to a festival in the country. *Are you sure you'll be all right on your own?* they asked my mother. *You sure you won't get scared?* She assured them that she'd be fine, that she knew how to lock all the doors at night and that she'd write down any phone messages in the office logbook.

So you're going to a festival? I heard her say suggestively to Mary and Steve. Mary nodded and said she was taking her three-year-old daughter, Rona, as well. *Oh, that's nice*, my mother continued. *You know, Mandy doesn't want to be cooped up inside all weekend. Why don't you take her along, too?*

Mary and Steve glanced at me. I was ambivalent about going because I didn't know them very well, but I also didn't want to offend them. Finally, I nodded back, and my mother said, *Fine, love. Go up and pack some clothes.* As I climbed the stairs to our room, I couldn't figure out if she was just trying to do me a good turn, get me out of the refuge and allow me to have some fun, or if, for some reason, she was trying to get rid of me.

The only festivals I'd ever heard of were music festivals like Woodstock, and as I sat in the back seat of Mary's car, I wondered if there'd be large stages, rock groups and people wearing hippie gear. And then I remembered there was another kind of festival, like the ones celebrating Chinese New Year, with marching bands and floats and twirling acrobats. We drove for about an hour and a half, to thick bushland on the outskirts of Sydney, but when Mary pulled up at a campsite, I saw no stages or bands or parades through the fading twilight. I shouldered my bag and followed Steve, Mary and Rona along a path and into a large weatherboard hall. It was filled with about two hundred women, who were sitting at trestle tables, talking. Many of them were topless, their breasts swaying languidly as they laughed or smoked. Others wore bib-and-brace overalls with nothing underneath. At first, I wondered if it were a nudist colony, but then I noticed that some of the women had their arms around each other and a couple in the corner were tongue-kissing. My mother had packed me off to a lesbian festival, I realised, and now I was stuck there without escape for the next three days.

Mary then nudged me, and told me we had to register. There

were large forms tacked to the wall and I mimicked her and wrote my name, age and my address (Elsie's). I left the *Occupation* part blank, but as I looked along the column I was shocked to see how many women had written *Teacher*. Well over half the women in the hall, I realised, taught in the public system, and I was amazed that, in all the schools I'd attended over the years, I'd never noticed even one lesbian.

Mary and Steve led me through the hall, past trestle tables being laid with a buffet dinner, and into a narrow adjoining dormitory with a row of flyscreen windows and five bunk beds. I was given the top bunk closest to the door, the others claiming beds further down the room. I then followed them back out into the hall, where we joined a queue for the buffet.

Eating spaghetti bolognese at one of the tables, I felt painfully self-conscious. As I glanced around the packed hall I realised there was no one there my age. The oldest kid was probably only six or seven – a naked girl with a big butterfly drawn on her stomach – and the youngest adult was a topless woman in her early twenties with a crew-cut and a right breast that was larger than her left one. And then I was astounded to see Dot, the plump, grandmotherly woman who'd comforted me and my mother when we'd first arrived at Elsie's, the woman who'd made us tea, who'd stroked my hair. She was now standing in the buffet line, wearing a pair of overalls, smiling and waving at me. So Dot was a lesbian too? But Dot had five kids. Dot baked raisin scones. Dot crocheted. I'd never really thought about what a lesbian was supposed to do or look like, but I certainly never imagined they taught in public schools, had an interest in baking, had children.

I went to bed straight after dinner, feeling more confused than ever, and fell asleep to the buzz of mosquitoes and the strumming of guitars.

The following morning was bright and hot and, after breakfast, Mary and Steve invited me to come down to the river with them and Rona for a swim. *But I haven't got a swimming costume*, I said. *Don't worry*, replied Mary, *you can go in the nuddy*. I thought she was joking – no decent person actually swam naked in public – and assumed I could bathe in my underwear.

Outside the hall there was a grassy clearing dotted with tents and, as we wove between them, I noticed, through the open flies, entwined legs, escaping laughter, the wagging tail of a dog, the bell of a saxophone. Past the clearing we joined a dirt path that snaked down steeply through thick bushland and as I inhaled the scent of eucalypts and heard the cries of a currawong, I realised it was the first time in many weeks that I felt myself relaxing. We climbed down some rocks and passed a shallow cave, and then a waterfall appeared before us, iridescent in the sunlight.

As we neared the river, however, I began to tense again. About a dozen naked women were sunning themselves on a large, flat rock, and a few others were frolicking in the water. When we reached the rock, Mary and Steve unfurled their towels and stripped off immediately, and then Mary helped Rona unbutton her blue dress, while I stood there awkwardly, not knowing what to do.

Don't be shy, said Mary, as Rona ran off to play. *Come in for a swim.*

I eyed the bevelled surface of the river, the fronds of the willow tree overhanging the water. I was sweating from the walk and wanted desperately to peel off my clothes and plunge into the currents. My breasts were just beginning to emerge, and I had only a few wiry pubic hairs between my legs. I no longer looked like Rona, but I certainly didn't resemble anyone else at the riverside. Besides, all these women were lesbians, and if I took off my clothes maybe one of them would fall in love with me.

No, I replied, *I don't feel like it*. And I merely removed my shoes and dangled my feet into the shallows.

After about half an hour, I left Mary, Steve and Rona, and walked back to the campsite by myself. Even though the surroundings were idyllic, I had never felt more alone. I worried about what I would do with myself for the rest of the three days: there were no books around, no television, and not only did I not know anyone very well, I didn't want to. When I reached the campsite, I sat on a low stone ledge and leaned over to tie my shoelace. There were some women playing volleyball to my left; to my right, a table had been set up and someone was lying naked, face-down, while a woman, massaged her back. I was just looping the bow on my lace when I heard a familiar voice: *God, love! What are YOU doing here?*

I straightened up to find my Auntie Joan standing before me, wearing jeans and a blue singlet. Her hair had been cropped short and she was no longer wearing her cat's-eye glasses, but a modern rectangular pair with silver rims. I was so shocked to see her I didn't know how to answer. The last time I had stayed with her she'd been having an affair with an overweight married man called Brian, whose wife wouldn't grant him a divorce.

Joan sat down and gave me a kiss and a cuddle. *Is your mum here?* she asked.

I shook my head, and then explained that she and I had recently left Hakkim again and were staying at Elsie's, that the women from the refuge had brought me along with them to the festival.

Hey, Joan, I asked, after a suitable interval, *what happened to Brian?*

Heart attack, she said. *Died two years ago. And guess what?* she added, taking my hand. *My name's not Joan anymore. I've changed it to 'Shannon'*.

Having my aunt at the festival made it a little easier for me over the next couple of days, though sometimes I would merely observe her from a distance, watching the way she ate her lunch or played cards or hugged an old friend. I was trying to see any difference between my old aunt who was a widow with three children and this new one who now had a lover named Ruby. I noticed she cut her sandwiches the same way – in fours; she still had a slight facial twitch and smoked Escort cigarettes. She talked about my cousins and my grandmother with ease. Apart from her clothes, hair and glasses, I couldn't see much difference, which is probably why I accidentally kept calling her 'Joan' that weekend, and she kept correcting me with 'Shannon'.

My mother's demeanour had not changed in the slightest by the time I was dropped off at Elsie's on Monday afternoon: she was sipping a brandy and milk in our room and smoking nervously. As soon as I saw her hunched shoulders I knew that something was wrong. Her bag was packed and the baby's nappies were folded inside a cardboard box.

Get your things, she said. *He's waiting for us.*

I glanced at the baby sleeping on the bed, and wondered what she was talking about.

On Saturday I took the baby for a walk, she explained. *Hakkim jumped out of his car. He cornered me in a laneway and pulled a knife.*

She drained her glass and dragged on her cigarette. *If we don't go back he said he's going to cut the baby's throat.*

We were back in the house at Bexley that night. The baby was returned to his veiled bassinet, 'Love, American Style' was on the colour television, and my mother cooked rissoles and chips for dinner. She'd left a note for the workers at the refuge, explaining what had happened, along with the keys to the front door.

I couldn't figure out how he'd found her, since the address of Elsie's was supposed to be a secret. Days later, my mother finally admitted that when Hakkim had tracked her down to the Hakoah Club in Bondi, he'd demanded to know where we'd gone the night we'd run off in the rain.

I didn't tell him the address, she hastened to add. *Just that we went to a refuge in Glebe.*

It had only taken Hakkim two days of stalking Glebe's main street before he spotted a tall blonde woman pushing a baby's pram.

The positive aspect of that escape from Hakkim was that it had been during the Christmas holidays and I hadn't had to change schools. I'd also had the unusual experience of having attended a lesbian festival, and had found out my aunt was gay. All this I kept to myself when I returned to Kingsgrove High the following week, and when any of the other students asked me what I'd done over the break, I just shrugged my shoulders and said, *Nothing much.*

We finally broke free of him about four weeks later, on pension day. My mother let me have a day off school and we went window-shopping in Hurstville. Hakkim had been as erratic as ever and, depending on his mood, each night he'd threaten either to kill the baby, or to take him back to Lebanon and have him raised by his mother as a strict Muslim. I was so nervous I'd developed ulcers inside my mouth, and a facial tic that made me squint repeatedly. That pension day – a Wednesday – my mother and I were looking through clothes in a Salvation Army shop, and I came across a suede knee-length skirt, which I held up against myself in front of a mirror.

Do you want it? my mother asked.

I said I liked it, but it cost two dollars.

So you do want it? she persisted, feeling in her bag for her purse.

I told her if she spent two dollars on a skirt for me, Hakkim would hit the roof when he found out, tell her she'd wasted money. What I was implying was that she'd probably cop a belting over the purchase, and it wasn't worth the trouble.

As I dropped the skirt back into a bin, her face suddenly clouded and she pursed her lips. *I'm buying the skirt*, she announced, pulling it back out. *It's my money. I can do what I want.*

By the time we arrived home, she was in a tense, frantic mood, similar to the one she was in the day she'd set fire to Nuri's mattress. She'd bought three large bottles of beer and, after she'd put the baby down for a nap, she retired to her bedroom with them, while I sat in the living room, dreading the sound of Hakkim's car in the driveway. Not only would he beat her for buying the skirt, he'd also punish her for buying and drinking beer.

However, she'd only been in her bedroom for about half an

hour when she stormed through the kitchen, down the hallway, and out the front door, leaving it wide open. I had no idea where she was going, or why, but about five minutes later, she strode back in and paused in the living room.

OK, love. I've called a taxi. Go into your room and grab anything you want to take. You've got five minutes.

Then she took a pad and pen off the mantelpiece and, in capital letters, scrawled, GONE FOR GOOD.

8

I am lying on a bed inside a dormitory of an Adelaide women's refuge. It is sometime before dawn and I can hear my baby brother howling from his cot. The dormitory is lined with four bunks. Even though my brother keeps crying, nobody stirs. My mother's unconscious because yesterday she began drinking again.

It is February and it is so hot the tar on the footpath outside has melted. There is only one air-conditioned room in the refuge – the television room down the hall. The woman who sleeps in the bunk next to mine has bad acne and lives on onion sandwiches. There's an unstable young lesbian in an adjoining room who flashes her breasts whenever she's in the kitchen. A pretty blonde girl, my age, is secretly in love with a local Aboriginal boy, whom she meets behind the back fence in the afternoons. She continues to do this in spite of the fact that her mother, married three times, called her a little slut *and forbade her to mix with* a nigger. *Two middle-aged women share a small back room. Their window, facing the back yard, is always open because, mostly at night, men slip through it and pay them for sex, without the workers at the refuge ever knowing.*

My brother continues to howl and I finally crawl out of bed and pick him up. I pace the room, rocking him, trying to settle him down. I pat his back, stroke his hair. I wish he would shut up because in three hours I will have to get dressed and go to school. I push a dummy into his mouth but he spits it out, screaming even louder. Suddenly, I find myself shaking him, shaking him so hard his tiny head lolls back and forth like a rag doll splitting at the seams.

With only five minutes to collect whatever belongings I wanted to take on our next journey, I ran into my room, trying not to panic. I pulled a sheet from my bed and spread it across the floor. After flinging open the wardrobe, I pulled clothes from their hangers randomly, throwing them onto the sheet, along with handfuls of underwear, socks, and several pairs of shoes. A few books went onto the pile, including my volume of *New Poetry*, the bracelet and choker my father had given me, the eight-inch portable cassette player I'd received for Christmas, my tapes, and a few knick-knacks from my bedside table. I drew the four corners of the sheet together and knotted them like a swag, hoisted it over my shoulder, and ran outside. My mother was already on the footpath, dropping a couple of bags she'd packed.

Stay here and wait for the taxi, she said. *If Hakkim pulls up, run in and tell me.* She raced back into the house while I guarded our few possessions. I was too nervous to sit down and kept my eyes trained on the corner of our street. I only wished my mother had decided to do this half an hour earlier, before Hakkim was due home to confiscate the money from her pension cheque. I hugged myself and shifted my weight from one leg to the other.

My mother strode back out the front door, lugging a few more bags. She dumped them beside the others and disappeared again. Finally she returned, pushing the baby in his red-and-white collapsible stroller. We waited on the kerb for several more minutes. *What taxi company did you call?* I asked, fearing that it would arrive too late. She told me the name and I went sprinting across the road, to the telephone box a block away. I called them, complaining about how long we had been waiting. By the time I was crossing our street again, a yellow cab was turning the corner and heading towards my mother.

We did not return to Elsie's because Hakkim would obviously look for us there and drag us back home again. When my mother had rung the refuge earlier, the workers on duty had advised her to go straight to Dot's house in Petersham, where we could stay in secrecy until a more permanent plan of action was figured out. It was only when we were on the highway that I realised I'd left all my poetry and story manuscripts behind – about four years of writing – hidden in a hole in my mattress.

As our taxi pulled up in front of an old, narrow terrace, I had never been more glad to see Dot's plump face. She helped us in with our luggage and gave us a small room in which one of her kids usually slept. A couple of hours later, at six o'clock, a weekly meeting of refuge workers was convened in Dot's living room, which my mother and I attended. After discussing general matters like funding, cleaning rosters and proper garbage disposal, the subject turned to my mother, brother and me, and what was to be done with us. Since Hakkim had tracked us down twice in four months, all the workers were in agreement about the fact that we would need to move interstate as quickly and as secretly as possible.

What state would you like to live in? asked Steve. *Take your pick.*

My mother thought for a moment. *Well, I like warm weather. I've always wanted to live in Queensland.*

What about Brisbane, then? asked Mary. *We've got places in Brisbane.*

My mother thought some more and finally shook her head. *Hakkim knows I like warm weather. If he thought I was interstate, that's the first place he'd look.*

We all sat in silence for a while, musing over the options.

Well, you've got to go somewhere he'd never dream you'd go, said Steve. *I for one think Adelaide's the best city. South Australia has the best social welfare system in the country – and you're going to need all the services you can get now that you're on your own.*

Forty-eight hours later, we were inside a sleeping carriage of the Southern Aurora as it pulled out of Central station. Mary, Steve and Dot had seen us off, with lots of hugs and good wishes. They'd purchased our tickets out of a special fund established by the refuge workers, and had given us spending money. Even though I was relieved to be escaping Hakkim, I was sad to see the last of those three women, who had been kinder and more thoughtful than anyone I had ever met. As the train rumbled through the twilight, past the shadows of old industrial buildings, I was conscious of the fact that they had probably saved our lives.

I had never travelled on an overnight train before and I liked the idea that I would sleep on a bed, five feet off the floor, that had to be pulled out from the wall, while my mother and the baby would share the lower bunk. But the biggest novelty of all was an adjoining cubicle – with a sink and flushing toilet – that was so small it seemed like a bathroom for elves.

My mother and the baby fell asleep early, but I was too excited to lie down, and stayed awake for hours, gazing out into the darkness as we sped along ridges and up hills, past small, remote towns, and through rural train stations with peculiar names like *Yerrinbool, Binalong, Uranquinty,* and *Table Top*. Every now and then I imagined Hakkim driving around the streets of Glebe, circling the block of the refuge, looking for us. Once the train pulled out of Albury and we crossed the state line into Victoria, I climbed the ladder to my bed and soon fell asleep to the rhythm of the wheels on the tracks.

The next morning, as we pulled in to Spencer Street station, I noticed immediately that Melbourne was cooler and somehow darker than Sydney. The sky seemed closer to the earth. When I stepped onto the platform I immediately recognised the woman who was to meet us by her short dark hair, her khaki overalls and boots. Once she glimpsed my mother and the baby she smiled, came forward and introduced herself as Jo. She helped us carry our luggage back to her car, and then drove us to a two-storey mansion on Beaconsfield Parade, Middle Park, which directly overlooked St Kilda bay. Steve, Mary and Dot had planned everything well: we were to stay at this refuge for the next two nights, to rest and recuperate, before taking the final leg of our journey to Adelaide.

After we'd settled into a dormitory on the second floor, I soon realised that this refuge was far less carefree than Elsie's – in fact it didn't even have a woman's name attached to it, but was merely called the Middle Park Refuge. There were no naked toddlers running about with chocolate smeared over their torsos, no books and toys strewn across the living room carpet, no smell of burnt toast and soiled nappies. There was even a cooking roster on the fridge, stating the times that individual women could have the kitchen all to themselves. Each room was clean and neat and, even though I was glad to be there, I missed the anarchy of Elsie's.

That afternoon, in the living room, another worker introduced herself to my mother and me, but she was much younger than Jo – perhaps in her early twenties – and smoked roll-your-own cigarettes without a filter. She had short dark hair that feathered her face, and a yellowish pallor that made her seem as if she were recovering from an illness, lending her a sensitive, slightly tortured air, which suited her perfectly. Her vowels sounded a little English. *It's a pity you're not staying in Melbourne*, she said, dragging on her rollie from a corner of her mouth. *There's this great school up the road. It's a free school.*

Free? I asked, confused. *What, like it doesn't cost any money?*

No – she smiled and shook her head – *there are no rules. You don't have to take any classes you don't like. You don't wear a uniform. There aren't even any exams!*

Intrigued, I asked her more questions about the school, and Maeve told me it was an experiment funded by the state education department, the most radical of its kind in Australia. There were no traditional grades as such; instead, each student was encouraged to *learn at their own pace*. There were no tests at the end of the year because *learning shouldn't be about competition*. The students ran the school along with the teachers by openly debating and voting on issues in a weekly general meeting.

I went there for three years and had a ball!

I stuck my hands in my pockets and gazed at her, wishing that I was staying in Melbourne, too.

Two nights later, Maeve drove us back to Spencer Street station in her mother's car, a big old 1940s Rover with a plastic daisy stuck onto the front end of the bonnet. *You'll like Adelaide*, she said brightly, as we sped along the tram tracks of St Kilda Road.

How many times have you been there? I asked.

Maeve shrugged. *So many times I can't remember. My best friend lives there.*

Before she waved us off on the platform, she pressed the telephone number of her friend into my hand. *Call her when you get there*, she said, smiling. *You'll really like her.*

As the train pulled out of the station, I was sorry to see the back of Maeve O'Hara's head disappearing into the crowd. She was young, yet curiously worldly and, even after such a short period of time, I found myself wanting to be like her, or wanting at least to be around somebody like her, who was so different from my mother and anyone else I'd ever met.

Later, my mother allowed me to eat alone in the buffet car and, as country towns flickered by, I ate tepid tomato soup and sipped tea. Halfway through my second cup I paused and pulled from my pocket the piece of folded paper with the phone number on it. There, above the seven digits, was scrawled the name *Maeve*.

We were met at the station in Adelaide by a woman wearing jeans – not overalls – and a T-shirt proclaiming, *A woman needs a man like a fish needs a bicycle*. Her blonde hair was cropped into a crew-cut and she wore thick glasses without any rims. As Lee helped us with our bags I was overwhelmed by the change in temperature. *God, it's hot*, I said, squinting against the glare.

Lee nodded. *Heatwave*, she said. *The worst one we've had in years.*

The refuge was a sprawling 1930s brick home with a wide veranda that overlooked the traffic of Prospect Road. The front door opened into a long hallway, with bedrooms on either side, that led through to a huge living room. An adjoining kitchen was on the left and a television room on the right. It was smaller than the two previous refuges, and was only one storey, but it seemed to hold as many – if not more – women and children as the others. Throughout our first afternoon, half-dressed, snotty-nosed kids ran through the house, yelling and slamming doors; ashtrays brimmed with butts and bread crusts; and a plump blonde English woman sat down across from me and ate three onion sandwiches in a row. Older children always seemed to be ducking in and out of the kitchen, and then disappearing into the air-conditioned TV room. Naomi's was as messy and chaotic as Elsie's – perhaps even more so.

The refuge was so full we had to share a dormitory with two other women and four kids. I didn't care – I was reassured by the fact that my mother hadn't had a drink since the day we'd left Sydney, and I was relieved to be away from Hakkim. Lying in my bunk bed that first night, I became more and more astonished by the fact that I would never again have to hear the click of his key in the front door late at night, or the sound of his staccato voice: *Give me your tongue, You fuckin' slut, Clean up mess, I kill baby.*

Narlsworth High was a big school with a mixture of early twentieth century redbrick buildings and squat contemporary portable classrooms. I enrolled with two other girls from the refuge. On our first day, we each wore a school uniform that my mother had made on an old Singer sewing machine at the refuge. These students and teachers seemed friendly enough and I didn't experience the usual taunting. During my first English class, however, we were being instructed on the term *dialect*. My teacher pointed to me and asked me to stand up.

Say pool, Mandy, she said.

Pool, I repeated. All the kids in the class suddenly burst into laughter. I glanced about, wondering what was so funny.

The teacher stifled a smile. *OK, Mandy. Say school.*

School, I said. The students laughed harder, and it was only when I heard a boy nearby imitating me that I realised how different I sounded to them. The teacher and the Adelaide kids pronounced it as the English would: *schoorl, poorl*, which sounded posh and highly educated, while I pronounced it nasally, *schewl, pewl*, which seemed working class by comparison.

See? said the teacher happily. *Mandy speaks STRINE. Does anyone know what Strine is?*

The other students glanced about, shrugging, and then they all stared at me, assuming that I would know the answer, since I was the one who spoke it.

Embarrassed, I sat down. The teacher wrote STRINE on the blackboard. *Strine is slang for Australian*, she explained. *You know, as in I speak AUSTRINE. Mandy speaks Austrine because she is from Sydney. In Sydney, everyone talks like her. In Brisbane, they speak even worse!*

In spite of this first humiliating lesson, I slipped easily into the curriculum of the new school. There was one class, however, that I completely loathed. My brief time staying in the refuges, reading about and overhearing feminist rhetoric, was already beginning to have an effect on me. During my first week at Narlsworth I fell into a heated argument with a teacher about a particular school policy: *All girls are required to take home economics as an elective.*

But I want to take woodwork, I said.

The teacher shook her head. *You're a girl. Home economics is compulsory.*

But it's an elective. How can an elective be compulsory?

You'll need to know how to cook, to look after a house and raise a family.

I want to study woodwork.

Only boys are allowed to do woodwork.

I folded my arms angrily. *That's sexist!*

Now listen, young lady, said the teacher, *don't get dirty-mouthed with me.*

Our first assignment in home economics was to draw a detailed diagram of the house we each lived in, indicating the various rooms, the place where our mothers *kept the linen*, where *the glassware was stored*, and where the family dined. After hearing this, I decided to try and get out of this class in another way and, as the other girls began scribbling away madly, I walked up to the teacher and explained, in a low voice, that I did not have a home. I had come from Sydney two weeks ago and now lived in a women's refuge.

The teacher smiled and patted me on the head. *That's all right, dear. Just draw a diagram of your refuge.*

I returned to my seat, further disgruntled, until an idea popped into my head. I picked up my pencil and began sketching the proportions of Naomi's, the several dormitories, the hallway, the kitchen. After completing the blueprint I began filling in the details with arrows and explanations. *Lila sleeps in this bunk – she lives on onion sandwiches. In this bunk sleeps a lesbian who is also a schizophrenic. Here we eat dinner, usually sitting on the floor. This back room is reserved for two prostitutes who live with us – the men climb in and out through the window at night.*

When my workbook was handed back during the next home ec class, the teacher's only comment, written in neat copperplate, was *Mandy, I wish you would take this class SERIOUSLY*.

The other two girls who lived at the refuge were more interested in a neighbouring Aboriginal boy than they were in hanging out with me. After school they'd meet him behind the back fence and smoke cigarettes. He was keen on the blonde girl, Sylvia, and boasted that he'd kissed her several times. Sylvia told me the most handsome boy in the ninth grade, Shane – tall, tanned and fair-haired – was keen on me. I was flattered but wary. I stayed away from Shane because I didn't want him to know where I lived or anything personal about me. He probably wouldn't like me if he knew anything more and – even worse – would spread all my secrets around the school.

Instead, I found the piece of paper Maeve O'Hara had given me and rang her best friend, also called Maeve. She seemed friendly on the phone and invited me to a rally she was organising in Rundle Street Mall. The following Saturday morning I turned up at the rally, along with my baby brother in a stroller and my mother, who had nothing else to do. There were hundreds of women shouting slogans and carrying placards: *I am not a baby-making machine; Women's Right to Choose; Legal Abortion on Demand*. My mother and I hovered at the edge of the crowd. There were the usual women with crew-cuts and wearing overalls, and I remember wondering why so many lesbians tried so hard to look like men when they were supposed to be in love with women. And as I was thinking this a woman, well over six feet tall, with cropped brown hair, wearing a leather jacket, jeans and army boots came walking towards me, carrying a megaphone. *You must be Mandy*, she said, holding out her hand. *I'm Maeve – the one you called*. I held out my hand, a little disappointed: so Maeve O'Hara's best friend was a lesbian, and probably her lover, which meant Maeve O'Hara was a lesbian too.

After six weeks at Naomi's, my mother was still waiting for her pension cheques to be transferred to South Australia. The workers at the refuge had already put our names down for public housing and, until they both came through, there was nothing to do but wait.

My mother began hitting the bottle again. I didn't blame her – she didn't have much to occupy herself every day. She was hundreds of miles away from the city she once called home and, when she thought about her own future, she probably didn't see a whole lot there. It started off with just a few beers in the afternoon. I could always tell when she'd been drinking because, when I walked into the dormitory after school, there'd be a cream bun waiting for me on my dresser. If the treat was even more elaborate – say, a chocolate eclair, or a slice of cheesecake – I knew she'd been drinking more than beer and had probably moved on to brandy. I kept my eye on her because I'd seen her in these kinds of moods before, back in Bondi, for example, when she became lonely and more withdrawn. I was alerted to the possibility that she could do something unpredictable, something that could sabotage the progress we'd already made. At least we were in Adelaide, I thought, which seemed to me to be a long way from trouble.

The only real problem for me was that I did not like Adelaide very much. Apart from feeling isolated, like my mother, I found the heat unbearable. And there was a uniformity to the city that I found disconcerting – all the parks and churches looked similarly pristine, the stores in town sold the one type of bland clothes, each blade of grass on every suburban lawn seemed to be exactly the same height. I looked for something different – a Chinese district, a poor section, even a slum, perhaps – but all I could find were more churches and parks and more bends in the Torrens River.

One morning my mother shook me awake, crying, *Mandy, there's something wrong with the baby*. I rubbed my eyes and crawled out of bed. He was lying in his cot, sweaty, red-faced and bawling. *I felt his forehead*, she said, *he's burning up!* I touched his forehead too: she was right, he did have a temperature, and I thought about the way I'd treated him a few hours earlier, when he woke me up and wouldn't stop crying and I lost my temper and shook him. I wondered if shaking a baby could somehow cause a fever and began to be consumed by guilt.

My mother packed me off to school. When I arrived home that afternoon, she was trying to control the baby's temperature by keeping him in the air-conditioned room. We took turns feeding and nursing him throughout the evening. By the next morning, he was even worse, crying and refusing his bottle. We took him to the hospital and within an hour he'd been diagnosed with acute pneumonia and was rushed into intensive care. The doctors placed him inside a humidicrib, fed him a drip and oxygen. My mother and I were told that he was in a critical condition: *The truth is, he might not make it*. I gazed at his tiny body curled up inside the plastic capsule and suddenly felt dizzy, as if I might faint. I wanted to ask if shaking a baby could cause pneumonia, but I didn't want to give too much away.

Doctor, I asked, *what brought it on?*

He nervously clicked his biro. *Heatwave*, he said. *The sudden change in temperature.*

That week, I spent a lot of the time at the hospital, in the paediatric unit. He was still in a humidicrib and my mother would only leave his side to eat or smoke outside. She forgot about her bigger problems – like where we were going to live and what she was going to do with the rest of her life – and merely concentrated on the one problem in front of her, assisting the nurses when they changed him or fed him antibiotics. There were a lot of other sick babies in the unit, far worse off than my brother. Two premature twin girls were born no bigger than my hand and, as they writhed in their humidicrib like beached fish, the nurse told me they would probably die because their lungs were underdeveloped. There was also a six-month-old boy who had some kind of disease that made his entire body balloon with fluid, until he was swollen into a big bluish ball; it seemed that, with just one touch, he would burst.

My mother refused to return to the refuge and slept in a chair by the humidicrib. Occasionally, I felt as if Hakkim were cursing us from afar, as if he were keeping his promise to *kill the baby* if we ever ran away again. Five days into my brother's hospitalisation, the tiny twin girls died, just hours apart. The day following their deaths, the boy with the fluid problem was drained for the third time and was shifted into another ward. The day after that, my brother's fever finally broke, he began feeding again, and he was allowed to return to his cot at the refuge.

Now that our immediate crisis had passed, I felt I had to take control of our situation. We'd been in Adelaide more than ten weeks, my mother's pension had been successfully transferred, but we had yet to make a firm plan about where we were going to live. Like me, my mother hadn't formed a friendship with anyone in particular, and I had the feeling she was as uncomfortable in Adelaide as I was. The only person I'd felt any sort of connection with since we'd left Sydney was Maeve O'Hara, and she lived in Melbourne. Also, I couldn't stop thinking about that free school she'd told me about, the one she'd attended, the light-hearted atmosphere of the place and her colourful descriptions of the teachers. And I kept hearing her voice in my head: *Too bad you're not staying in Melbourne!*

When I broached the subject with my mother and raised the possibility of relocating to Melbourne so I could attend the free school, I was astonished when she took a sip of her beer and said, *OK, I'll discuss it with the girls in the office.*

9

I press the cardboard stencil against the billboard that advertises cigarettes. It is past midnight and the street is quiet and deserted. When I centre the cardboard properly, my teacher raises the can and sprays red paint against it. I pull the stencil away and we both stand back, admiring it – Free Abortion on Demand – right across a packet of Benson & Hedges. The stencil was my idea. I made it at school this afternoon, because writing graffiti takes too long and increases our chances of getting caught.

I press the stencil against the billboard again; my teacher begins to spray once more, when a paddy-wagon suddenly swings around the corner. Before we have a chance to jump in my teacher's car, two cops leap onto the footpath and are upon us. Do you know defacing public property is a serious offence? asks one, his hand resting on his holster. The other one has already pulled out an official notepad and is writing the date at the top.

He asks for our names, addresses, dates of birth. My teacher gives the correct information and I do too. I am only fourteen and afraid that if the police figure out I'm breaking the law with my teacher, she will get into trouble and possibly lose her job.

The second cop hands us duplicates of our booking forms. You'll receive a summons to court through the mail, *he says*. And if we catch you two spraying any more graffiti tonight, we'll throw you both in the lock-up.

The men get back into the paddy-wagon and drive away. We climb into my teacher's car. I rest the stencil on my lap while my teacher starts the engine.

OK, *she says*, let's do it again! But this time we'll go to South Melbourne.

Beachside Free School wasn't even housed in a proper building – just a large old church hall and a 1920s rectory. On my first day, I entered the church hall to find a third of it filled with tables and chairs, where about a dozen kids were smoking and drinking coffee. A couple of long-haired boys were playing guitar and singing on a stage at the other end of the hall. A few barefoot girls were sitting on the floor, holding a litter of newborn kittens. And, over in the corner, another couple of girls were performing some kind of folk dance, but it wasn't choreographed to the music being played. Everywhere I looked there were handmade clay pots brimming with cigarette butts.

Near the main door was a large timetable stuck to the wall, indicating the times and rooms of the classes being offered. I figured the classes must be very small because most of the students seemed to be hanging out in the hall, having fun. I looked over the timetable carefully, and was intrigued by the range of subjects: photography, Indian studies, psychology, politics, film studies, senior English, maths, creative writing, painting, sculpture, science, music theory, instrumental music, cooking, weaving, drama and dance. During my interview with the school coordinator, Leon (the word *principal* wasn't used at the school because it implied authoritarianism), had explained that I wasn't obliged to take any classes at all, and encouraged me to arrange my own timetable, based on what I enjoyed or was curious about learning. This concept seemed entirely sensible to me and, having loathed the conventions of each new school I'd had to attend throughout my life, that morning I could feel years of accumulated tension in my shoulders beginning to melt.

For my first class I chose senior English, which I noted was being held in the Fantasy Room. The door was painted apple-green. I pushed it open to find a group of students squashed around a table in a room that was probably only about 10×10 metres. There was a bearded teenager standing in a corner, reading a poem in free verse.

I noticed the four walls were covered in a mural of elves, fairies, goblins and leprechauns, some sitting on polka-dotted mushrooms, others dancing around a pond – the same apple-green paint dominating the background. I found a stool in the corner and sat down. I realised the students in this class were much older than me. Three of the five males had beards. All of the girls had breasts. One of them was dressed in a pink 1940s dress, a string of pearls around her neck; another was wearing an army jacket; another wore a pillbox hat with a veil which she had to lift every time she dragged on her fragrant cigarette. Everyone was focused intently on the student reading the poem and once I stopped admiring my new surroundings I concentrated on the poem too, and began to appreciate its cadences. The lines reminded me of the free verse I had read in *New Poetry*.

When the student finished reading, a woman with long fair hair stood up and opened a window. She didn't seem that much older than anyone else – perhaps in her early twenties – but she was dressed more moderately, in jeans and a long navy-blue cardigan. And she was so tall – probably around six feet – that she hunched a little in a way that made me think she'd always been self-conscious about her height. Still, I wasn't sure who she was until she turned to the class and announced, *Well, let's discuss Allen Ginsberg*.

Through Grace I was introduced to a wide range of writers in those first few weeks of attending the Free School: from Kerouac to Edna O'Brien to Colette. She loaned me her own books to take back to the refuge to read on weekends. In my politics class we discussed the Communist Manifesto and Dostoyevsky's *Crime and Punishment*. In psychology we read about social phobias and Freud's theory of hysteria. I also took mathematics, creative writing, poetry, Indian studies and photography, and soon found myself busier than I'd been in years.

I was glad to be back living at the Melbourne refuge, where my mother, the baby and I were eventually given our own room on the ground floor. It was the most privacy we'd had since we'd lived at Bondi and, since the place wasn't full, it was almost like staying at a private guest house with all expenses paid. Jo and Maeve O'Hara had helped my mother apply for a Housing Commission flat, and we were on the emergency list, but until that came through we could do nothing but remain at the refuge. Maeve worked there several times a week and, when she did, I would hang around the office and chat to her about the school and what I was studying at the moment. And she'd tell me about her years there – about the time she and her friends caused an explosion in the kitchen, or the day a kid slipped some LSD into the lunchtime soup – puffing on her rollie and sipping strong tea. *Is Simon still there?* she once asked. I nodded and told her that he'd invited me to join a new class he'd soon be starting, which he called an encounter group. Maeve frowned then and shook her head. *Simon always was a little weird*.

I'd been at the new school for about two months when all the teachers and students went away on a school camp to Wilson's Promontory. Before embarking on the trip, a general meeting was held and Lucy, a drama and science teacher, gave us a lecture on sexually transmitted diseases and contraception. Lucy was a petite woman with dyed blonde hair. In her late thirties, she always wore tight-fitting clothes that showcased her voluminous breasts. She distributed boxes of condoms and told us to use them if we were going to have sex during the camp, and demonstrated how to do so by unrolling one onto a cucumber purchased earlier for that day's lunch salad. *If you run out, just come and ask me for more*, Lucy announced, dragging on her Menthol cigarette. *More condoms or more cucumbers?* I joked, which made her laugh through a blue arabesque of smoke.

I spent my time during the three-day camp swimming, walking and reading, but everywhere I went I encountered students having sex, not only in the dormitories we shared, but also in the communal bathrooms, on the sand dunes, in the bushes. During the second day, the boy who slept on the lower tier of my bunk bed made an overture towards me, touching my hair, my neck, but I still did not want anyone close to me, and the thought of him kissing and possibly penetrating me filled me with horror. I backed out of the room as soon as I could.

I walked down to the beach, where I found an enormous grid carved into the sand and two groups of students – mostly naked – standing within separate squares, facing one another, using their bodies as chess pieces.

A few weeks later, Simon, the history and politics teacher, kept his word and began his new encounter group class, which met in his rather large corner room of the old church rectory. About seven students attended the first class, and I wondered if Simon had personally invited the three other girls, as he had me. One, Vera, was thin and about a year older than me, a chain-smoker in tight jeans and with bad posture. The other, Willa, was about sixteen; she had long light brown hair and was very overweight. The fourth, Raeleen, was almost nineteen. She had short frizzy hair and pale, acne-scarred skin. She took most of the classes that Simon taught and, under his supervision, had read a huge number of works by Marx.

After our first meeting I came away with only a hazy idea of what we would be studying in this class. It had something to do with spirituality, and something to do with *getting in touch with our true feelings*. One of the selected texts for the class was Krishnamurti, which I purchased and began reading. After that initial meeting, however, Raeleen dropped out. And then Simon suggested we meet in a less formal environment, so the following week we had our class in the apartment of one of the male students, who lived there with his brother for free because his parents were rich and had bought it for them. The class involved sitting on the floor in a circle and *communicating with one another.* 'Trust exercises' involved pairing off, facing each other, and trying to mirror one another's movements.

I found Simon a gentle and attentive teacher, and when he

asked me for my opinions or ideas on certain subjects, he seemed genuinely interested, listening to me carefully and never interrupting. Occasionally, he would repeat what I'd said, but more eloquently, as if I'd uttered something special and unique, and this of course made me feel special and unique, as if the roles had been reversed and it was I who was now teaching him.

One afternoon when we were walking back from the rich student's apartment, he handed me an envelope and whispered, *Read it later*. After we arrived at school, I fled to the library room. I opened the envelope, unfolded the leaves of paper, and began reading. There, in blue ink, in the fluid, copperplate handwriting that had critiqued my essay on Dostoyevsky, was a solemn declaration of love. He described radiant skin, a heart-shaped face, how he couldn't stop thinking about me. For a moment I wondered if he'd given the letter to the wrong girl, until he mentioned the *understated simplicity* of the gold bangle I always wore. I was so astonished that I immediately needed to have a wee. The most attention I'd ever received from anyone was from the boy at camp, and being told by a girl in the school playground that *Shane wants to go with you*. The tribute to me went on for six pages, and I was overwhelmed and flattered. Simon knew about my background, that I lived in a refuge, and he didn't seem to care. I folded the letter and hid it in my pocket, realising there were several problems with this sudden outburst of affection: I was fourteen years old, Simon was thirty-nine. Apart from being my teacher, he was also married and had a three-year-old son.

I kept the letter hidden in a coat pocket hanging in my wardrobe at the refuge. Whenever I felt lonely or depressed

I would pull it out and reread it, marvelling that a grown, educated man could feel so strongly about me. And rereading the words made me feel as if I were much less plain and boring than I thought I was, and it wasn't long before the letter and the teacher who'd written it became a highlight of my life, like a particularly happy birthday party, or having a song written for my ears only.

We never discussed the letter, well, not immediately, anyway. We just traded knowing smiles in class and when passing one another in the hall. Then, a couple of weeks later, Simon suggested our encounter group go on *a field trip* to his country property at Daylesford. He'd recently purchased fifty-two hectares there and the property was *completely wild*. We'd camp for several days and learn to survive using our own wits. Everyone in the class was enthusiastic about the trip and it was promptly approved by the school coordinator.

Simon's land was about two hours north of Melbourne, and he drove us there in the school's white minibus. Since the start of the encounter group, I had become friends with the two other girls in it – skinny Vera and fat Willa – and had even begun to hang out with them on weekends, listening to records and going to the movies. I could tell that both of them were infatuated with Simon, the way they'd quote him all the time and speculate on the state of his relationship with his wife. Willa seemed to know Simon better than Vera and I did, and often assumed a superior and knowing air whenever the subject of his personal life came up. At these times Willa assured us that his marriage was on the rocks, and that Simon had been thinking about *getting a divorce* for some time, which of course assuaged any feelings of guilt we each experienced for having a crush on him. And as the minibus sped through the bush towards Daylesford, I didn't even mind that Vera and Willa had fallen for Simon – in fact I sometimes felt sorry for them, because I was the one who'd received a six-page letter of admiration and devotion, and I knew that he loved me only.

His property was about six miles out of Daylesford, dotted with eucalypts and manna gums. Once through the gate, we wove along bush tracks, passing several ravines, and drove up a steep incline. When we reached the top of the hill, Simon pulled up in a clearing, where a large tent and brick barbecue stood, as if waiting for us. The view was breathtaking, a green sweep of valley and undulating streams.

We pitched two more tents – Simon's and the rich kid's – and as the sun set we collected firewood and began preparing dinner. After a meal of chops and sausages, I noticed Willa unrolling her sleeping bag inside Simon's tent. The main tent was also used for food and tool storage and only had enough room to sleep three people. Two could fit in the rich kid's tent. As I watched Willa fluff her pillow, Simon leaned over and said to me, *Why don't you sleep in my tent tonight?*

I shook my head. *Willa's sleeping there.*

Simon smiled. *There's room for one more. Come on.* He stood up, grabbed his own sleeping bag, and unrolled it down one side of his tent, opposite Willa. And then he smoothed my sleeping bag down beside his, placing pillows beneath the hoods.

After that, we all sat around the fire for hours, toasting bread and trading stories. Simon told us he had inherited the property and that he wanted to become a part-time farmer. There was a cottage on the land that the three couples shared on weekends and holidays. I found it hard to picture Simon as a farmer – he seemed so urban with his thick glasses, knitted vests, and volumes of Marxist theory.

We all retired to bed at about the same time. Vera was the only girl to go into the main tent, along with the food, equipment, and two boys, and I felt a little sorry for her. Lying inside my sleeping bag, sandwiched between Simon on my right and Willa on my left, I wondered if I should have insisted on going into the main tent, too. Willa wriggled around for a while; an owl hooted; I could hear a small animal moving through the bushes, the rustle of leaves and branches. My face was still hot from the fire and I stretched my arms out and lay them on top of the sleeping bag. I'd never been camping before and I found the ground hard and lumpy. I closed my eyes and tried to drift off to sleep, but the words Simon had written to me in his letter kept repeating themselves in my mind. By now I almost knew the contents word-for-word, and wondered if he'd orchestrated this entire trip just so that he could sleep beside me. I thought it was sad that he was so unhappy in his marriage, and decided any problems they were experiencing must be the fault of his wife, because Simon was such a kind, gentle man, and I could not imagine him intentionally doing anything very wrong.

I was just beginning to nod off to sleep when I felt a hand moving up my arm, over my elbow. As I opened my eyes, I felt fingers through my hair, against my face. Then the hand slipped down inside my pyjama top and held the slight mound of my left breast. I could feel Simon's breath in my ear as he slowly unzipped his sleeping bag. I wondered what he would do next and worried that Willa would wake up. He took hold of my wrist and guided my hand down his body, over the T-shirt he was wearing. I could hear his breathing growing more shallow as I touched his ribcage, his stomach. Then he wrapped my fingers around his hard cock, squeezed and let go. Confused, I wasn't sure what to do next. I'd never touched a cock before, but I was fairly certain, with Willa only an inch away, that he wasn't going to try to have sex with me. Within seconds, his hand was around mine again, and he began jerking it up and down the shaft of his cock, faster and faster until, after about thirty seconds, a fountain of hot, sticky fluid burst forth, spraying my face, my hair, my fingers. He must have sensed my shock because he whispered in my ear, *It's semen.*

As we settled back into our respective sleeping bags, I heard Willa sigh heavily and turn over. I wiped my face with the back of my clean hand.

The next day I felt a little unsure of myself, embarrassed that I had not known what to do with an erect penis and that I'd been repelled by his sperm on my cheek. I also felt awkward around Willa, who'd had to lie there beside me, listening to me masturbating the man with whom she was so obviously in love. As we all bushwalked and picnicked and swam in a stream, she seemed a little downcast and I tried to avoid her as much as possible. I noticed Simon's behaviour was no different towards me or anyone else in the group as he pointed out particular flowers and trees and announced their Latin names.

Later that night, after dinner, he sat by the fire next to Vera and asked her if she'd like to swap with me and sleep in his tent that night, along with Willa. I saw a smile flash across her face and she nodded and said, *OK.* At around 11 pm, after we'd swapped the sleeping bags, I lay in the dark, inside the storage tent, listening to the wind whistle through the trees. I wondered if I would still be lying beside Simon right now if I'd been better at providing him with the pleasure he desired. Now, Vera probably had her fingers around his cock and, since she was older than me, would probably know what to do.

In the week following the camp at Daylesford, my mother, the baby and I finally moved out of the refuge and into a home of our own. The six-flat apartment block in North Fitzroy was owned by the Housing Commission but, as a consequence of a long bureaucratic bungle, had been sitting empty for two years. The workers at the refuge, exasperated by the commission's inefficiency, by how homeless women and children were made to wait months for 'emergency accommodation', had broken into the building the year before, turned the utilities on, and moved in mothers and kids from the refuge while they waited for the applications to be processed. Now, it was used as a kind of halfway house between the refuge and official housing.

Maeve explained it wasn't really 'squatting' as such, because all the tenants paid a nominal rent into a fund held by the refuge to cover ongoing legal costs. She helped us move into the three-bedroom ground-floor flat in Holden Street, which overlooked a tidy lawn. I'd seen a lot of public housing in my life and was relieved to find it wasn't in one of the high-rise blocks or, even worse, in some flat, remote suburb. We were now only seconds away from a shopping centre, a tram line, and minutes from the city. Our apartment even had a balcony. The most important feature of living on Holden Street, however, was that there was no Hakkim. My mother and I had spent three months living in the Adelaide refuge and another three living in the one in

Melbourne, and were secure in the knowledge that he could never track us down after such a long period and over so many state lines.

Unfortunately, the woman who lived across the landing from us was not so safe or lucky. Clare was an overweight Mormon with seven children under twelve, all of whom were squeezed into the three-bedroom flat. Even though she'd been bashed repeatedly by her equally religious husband, she and her kids still practised their faith staunchly: there was no television or radio in the flat, no alcohol, no music. The only comfort or distraction Clare allowed herself was food, in which she freely indulged. And, in midwinter, when the trouble started, she ate even more than ever.

It began with the delivery of a pizza she hadn't ordered. At first she thought it was just one of the neighbouring kids playing a joke on her because she was fat. But the next day, sirens were suddenly blaring, an ambulance arrived, and paramedics began bashing on her door, demanding to know the whereabouts of an alleged heart-attack victim. A few hours later, it was the police investigating a reported shooting. The following morning a tow truck pulled up with a driver demanding directions to a three-car pile-up. Unordered groceries were delivered; a representative from Natural Gas appeared, needing to investigate a potentially lethal leak, and tradesmen turned up to fix plumbing and electricity that were operating perfectly.

Poor Clare was beside herself by now, and eating more than ever. And then, late one Tuesday afternoon, in an extraordinary feat of timing, four fire engines, two ambulances, two pizza boys, a police car and a truant officer pulled up all at the same time and began hammering on her door. The front lawn was awash with flashing lights, fire hoses, stretchers, and inquisitive neighbours. A timid Clare, wearing her pink dressing gown, finally opened the door. *I'm so sorry*, she explained, her voice wavering. *It's my husband. He's torturing me from a distance.*

Soon after that incident, Clare and her kids were moved out of the flat by the refuge workers to a secret location. It seemed strange to me that a man so deeply religious could behave in such a way towards his wife and children, and I began to think about how violence and madness seemed to be a fairly democratic affliction, a kind of illness that could strike anyone. During my time in the refuges I'd seen battered wives and children whose husbands were French atheists, Greek Orthodox, Aboriginal, Italian Catholics, and English Protestants. I'd seen a woman who was married to a Victorian Member of Parliament with her arm in a cast and a black eye. I'd seen the wives and kids of schoolteachers and bricklayers, accountants and conmen – their experiences had not been so different from my own and my mother's. And I realised I could not rightly attribute Hakkim's behaviour to the fact that he was an immigrant, that he'd grown up as a Muslim and struggled to fit into an entirely new culture. It seemed now much more complicated and messier than that. For the past year I'd been surrounded by battered wives and children and was beginning to conclude that I could safely bet on the idea that some men were just total bastards and I'd do well to stay clear of them.

This feeling was deepened on our next school camp, which was in the Grampians, a small mountain range, a few hours northwest of Melbourne. The students were housed in dormitories while the teachers slept in individual cabins. There was a large hall where we ate and watched films that Grace projected at night. On our second morning, Simon sat opposite me at breakfast and we chatted for a while. We had not been intimate since that night in his tent and, even though I still attended his classes, I hadn't sought his company outside of that context. This was mainly because I felt that what we had done together wasn't right, and I was still embarrassed about Willa.

He asked me to join him on a walk after breakfast, down to a place near the river. I explained I had already agreed to go on a half-day hike with Grace and a few others. *But I've got to talk to you*, he said, lowering his voice. *I really must see you today. It can't wait.* I stopped eating my toast, wondering what on earth could be so urgent. *All right*, I said finally, and stood up to tell Grace I'd changed my mind about the hike.

As we strolled down a bush track, he linked his arm in mine, and named the various trees and flowers we passed, as if he were conducting a private botany lesson for my benefit only, which made me feel even more confused. Then we came to a log that had fallen across the river, the other end supported by a small island of rocks. He unlinked his arm and began to walk out across the water, signalling to me to follow him, which I did. When we were about halfway across the river, he sat on the log and I sat beside him, still perplexed.

Simon took my hand in his and said the past weeks had been an agony for him, that every time he saw me he was filled with love, a kind of love he'd never experienced before, and he couldn't stop thinking about me. Again, I was flattered, but slightly puzzled, finding it hard to figure out what a man pushing forty could see in a girl like me. I was not particularly pretty; I was beginning to put on weight; and I didn't agree with all the communist theory he taught in his political science class.

I looked up to see Grace and a few others hiking along a steep track on the other side of the river. When I saw her glance down at Simon, taking in the way he was holding my hand, I felt so embarrassed I wanted to flee. I realised I wanted to be on that half-day hike with Grace, rather than sitting around idly, listening to Simon's declarations and wondering if they were true.

After Grace and the others had rounded a bend in the track and disappeared, I scrambled to my feet and said I had to go. Simon stood up and followed me along the log to the riverbank. As we walked back to camp, he took my hand again and asked me if I would come and see him that night in his cabin, after the film was shown. I tried to come up with an excuse, but my head was throbbing and I couldn't think of a convincing lie. Finally, I said I'd think about it, and ran off to join a volleyball game.

All throughout the screening of *The Man Who Fell to Earth*, Simon and I sat on opposite sides of the hall. I'd thought about his invitation throughout the day and during dinner, vacillating over whether I would accept it or not. I often liked the attention Simon gave me; it made me feel attractive and special, but there was something unsettling about his behaviour – too intense, too urgent – and I was wary of getting closer to him. When the film ended, I slipped out the door without saying goodbye and went to my own dormitory. As I lay in my bunk, I decided I'd probably made the right decision. But I did not sleep well because I still wasn't completely sure.

When I woke at dawn the next morning, I needed desperately to pee. I made a beeline for the toilet block and I glimpsed a tired and bedraggled Vera creeping out the door of Simon's private cabin. Her hair was messy and she was shivering as she hurried down the track towards the student dorm. I wondered how many love letters he'd written her, how many times he'd declared his devotion, and whether, during the night, she'd given him more than a hand job.

Later that week, back at school, Willa sat Vera and me down and told us Simon's latest news: *His wife's three months pregnant.* I could tell by her downcast eyes that Willa was disappointed, that she'd believed the rumours about him being so unhappily married, about him planning to divorce his wife. But if Willa seemed disappointed, the look on Vera's face revealed that she was absolutely stunned – wide-eyed and suddenly pale as a peeled cucumber. Her hands were trembling as she lit a cigarette. It made me wonder if Simon said the same things to all girls, if he recycled his declarations of love and obsession as many times as his yellowing lecture notes.

Well, I said finally, *I guess he won't be getting divorced now.*

Willa shook her head dolefully. *Imagine how Raeleen feels.*

I thought of the white-faced, frizzy-haired nineteen-year-old who was a whiz at Marxist theory, the one who'd dropped out of our encounter group after the first meeting. *What?* I asked. *He's not on with her, is he?*

Willa nodded and lowered her voice. *For over four years.*

There were several advantages to living in our new flat, and one of them was that Maeve O'Hara lived within walking distance and would often drop in for a cup of tea. While she was visiting one night she led me to the telephone box directly outside our apartment and showed me how to make free interstate phone calls. It involved sticking the end of an unbent paper clip into the mouthpiece whilst pressing the other end of it against a metal part of the phone during a particular time in the dialling process. Since Maeve's lover lived in Adelaide, a couple of times a week she'd walk up to this public box with her paperclip and chat for as long as she wished.

I was beginning to live in a kind of awe of Maeve O'Hara: she'd introduced me to this fascinating school; she was partly responsible for us being able to live in our new apartment, and now she was instructing me on how to rip off Telecom and make free interstate phone calls. She was also an accomplished painter and sculptor. I wanted to be her best friend, but she already had scads of those and I was fairly sure she didn't want a fourteen-year-old following her around. Curiously, my mother was also drawn to her, despite their age difference. When my mother decided to have my brother christened in the Fitzroy Catholic Church, she asked Maeve to be his godmother. Since we didn't know any men, she asked a neighbour, Glenda, to be the godfather. Not remotely religious or even feminine, Maeve agonised over what to wear to such a ceremony. Finally, she turned up to the church in the finest clothes she could bear to wear: a bomber jacket and a pair of new white jeans. She'd also done something with her hair: a #2 crew-cut.

Not long after that, we received a week-long visit from my older brother, now twenty-two, and Sue, his wife. Gene arrived wearing a tie and three-piece suit. Sue was dressed in a prim, knee-length floral dress with pearl buttons. I was surprised by how conservative they both looked; the last time I'd seen Sue, she'd been wearing a mini-skirt, drinking double bourbons, and had been my father's lover. The last time I'd seen my brother, he was drunk on beer, the arse was falling out of his jeans, and he was sporting a goatee beard. Now, they were both sitting on our couch, sipping tea and telling my mother and me they had given up drinking and smoking. Then they announced their big news: they had recently become Jehovah's Witnesses. Gene opened his briefcase and began passing around booklets entitled *The Truth* as he quoted a passage from the Bible.

My mother seemed nonplussed by this turn of events and, for the rest of their stay, gave them her room and allowed them to sleep in her double bed, which I thought was fairly generous, considering that Sue had stolen her husband, then married her son, and was now trying to convert her to a religion that did not even permit blood transfusions. I was glad when they finally left, carting away their Bibles and pamphlets. I felt I no longer knew my brother and realised I liked him better when he wore jeans and drank beer.

I began to attach myself to people outside my family, people I admired, like Maeve O'Hara, and my English teacher, Grace, who lived only a few blocks away from our new flat. Grace began giving me lifts to and from school in her old, beat-up grey Austin, the passenger door of which flew open every time she turned left too quickly. During those drives I became more and more familiar with her – and she with me – and sometimes on the way home from school we'd stop off for coffee in a Lygon Street cafe and then peruse Readings, the local bookstore. Other times, we'd go back to her place for tea. She lived in a converted stable in the back yard of a prominent Labor politician. She slept in the downstairs bedroom and her sister, Trish, a university student, had the one upstairs. Grace's boyfriend, Ryan, a bass player and also a teacher, stayed over at her place most nights, even though he had a flat of his own.

The first time I met Trish she was sitting at the kitchen table, reading the *Age*. When Grace introduced me, Trish lowered the newspaper, scowling, and said in a deadpan voice, *Hello*, then raised the paper again. She had long, ethereal blonde hair and flawless white skin and I thought it was a shame that someone who looked so serenely and naturally beautiful should have such a sour personality. At first I thought she just didn't like me, but Grace later explained I wasn't to take Trish's behaviour personally. *She can't stand Ryan. She doesn't like me. She wouldn't like you because you're a friend of mine.*

I thought about this and nodded to myself. *So, what's she studying at uni?*

Grace smiled. *Psychology.*

Over the following months, Grace gradually adopted me. At first I thought it was because she felt protective: I'd been living in refuges for months and was now squatting in a Housing Commission flat with my mother. I'd also been one of Simon's targets and one day she let me know that she knew this: *At the camp, when I saw you two sitting on a log together, I thought, what's she doing hanging out with HIM?* Perhaps her attention had started off as a form of protection, but as the weeks drifted by I felt it beginning to grow into something far more unconventional.

Grace was curious about the refuge I'd lived in and wanted to volunteer to help out. One afternoon I introduced her to Maeve and Jo and, after several cups of tea, Grace decided she'd exhibit films on Thursday nights in the living room. Since she showed a rented film every Thursday afternoon at the school, it would cost nothing but her time to bring the projector and the movie down afterwards in order to provide a little entertainment for the residents. I accompanied her during these showings and, for the first couple of weeks, the plan worked out well, with three or four women sitting in the flickering light of the projector between feeding kids and changing nappies. But by the end of the month it became clear to us both that our volunteer efforts were being wasted at the refuge: the women were much more interested in watching 'The Price Is Right' on TV than sitting through Hitchcock's *Vertigo*.

After the film nights flopped, Maeve suggested we could do other things to help the feminist cause: for example, there were several Action Meetings at the Women's Liberation Centre in the city that we could join. We visited the centre after school one day, a large office near Chinatown wallpapered with political posters, and joined up for two meetings: the 'Right to Work', and the 'Right to Choose' campaigns, which met on Tuesday and Thursday nights respectively. By this time, Grace had become even more interested in the women's movement – she now wanted to start a women's studies course at school – and occasionally I wondered if she'd been drawn to me because she was intrigued by this culture and because I happened to know so many feminists and lesbians.

At school, the proposed women's studies course whipped up a heated controversy because Grace insisted it would be for female students only. At the weekly general meeting, the issue was hotly debated, with most boys and several girls arguing that the proposal was unnecessarily prejudiced and the program should not be adopted. Even Simon railed against it, saying the school would be practising sexism.

Well, why don't you go off and have a class for girls only? I said. *That'd suit you down to the ground.*

It gave me pleasure to see his face suddenly redden, to see him glance about at the other students and teachers and finally retreat into a corner. Eventually, the issue was put to a vote and the segregated class was passed by two hands only.

At the beginning of our first class a seventeen-year-old boy turned up wearing a dress and makeup, and Grace good-naturedly allowed him to stay. But he never returned for the second class, probably because no one had made a fuss about him being there. During those first months we read through and discussed a wide range of subjects: the suffragette movement, the definition of rape, the history of women in the workforce, wage imbalances, women's health, and sexism within the trade union movement. We also read novels by prominent feminists, Kate Millett's *Sita*, for example, and Rita Mae Brown's *Rubyfruit Jungle*. As the weeks went on, the reading became more radical, and the more I read the more affected I became by the stories, the statistics, the history.

Twice a week Grace and I attended the Right to Work and Right to Choose meetings at the Women's Liberation Centre. We helped organise rallies, handed out pamphlets. On Saturday mornings, we operated a stall on Smith Street, Collingwood, handing out information about contraception, terminations, women's employment and social welfare. Soon, Grace and I were wearing overalls too, or were swaggering about in old-fashioned men's suits we'd bought at St Vincent de Paul's. When we weren't attending meetings, Grace would pick me up and take me to the theatre, to a concert, or to see the latest French films. Through her, I learned about Truffaut, Bertolucci, Fellini and a lot of other things: commedia dell'arte, for example, and existentialism. Then I learned about modern dancers like Isadora Duncan and Martha Graham, and a multitude of writers, including Shakespeare, Oscar Wilde and Chaucer.

I was shocked when I found out that Grace was only twenty-four and already knew so much about art, literature and history. She was a vegetarian, so I became one too. Grace was interested in herbal remedies, so I began studying them too. When I realised she was learning the flute I vowed I would save up enough money so I could learn to play it as well. I imprinted myself upon her like a duckling does its mother. When she took me to a women's dance in south Carlton, I gulped straight Pernod from a bottle, just as she did. By the end of the night, I was swaying in her arms, too drunk to stand up alone.

After six months of squatting in Holden Street, my mother finally made it to the top of the emergency housing list, and we moved to a permanent home of our own in Carlton. The new flat was of exactly the same proportions as the old one: three bedrooms, a balcony – even the heater was in the same place. Cosmopolitan Lygon Street was just a few blocks away with its bookstores, cafes and pool joints. The Exhibition Gardens and the Pram Factory theatre were around the corner, and the city was only a fifteen-minute walk away. It had been over a year since my mother and I had fled Hakkim – and Sydney – and I was relieved that our long journey had finally come to an end.

About a fortnight after we moved in, I noticed a large platter of fruit, arranged by my mother, crowning the dining room table. She herself never ate fruit and my brother – now sixteen months old – ate only the odd mashed banana or peach. *I know you like fruit*, my mother said – *eat up!* Yes, I did enjoy an occasional apple or pear, but there was no way I could get through such an enormous display of produce on my own.

After about a week, she began giving the many remaining pieces away to neighbouring kids, and to the Polish woman who lived upstairs and who had a teenage son named Marco. But only a day or so passed before I came home from school and found another platter – even bigger than the first one – set in the centre of the table.

Why'd you buy so much fruit again? I called from the dining room. *You know I can't eat it all.*

It's good for you, she said, *eat up.*

I pulled a plum from the platter and walked into the living room. There, sitting cross-legged on the couch, munching on a nectarine, was the teenage Polish boy from upstairs.

Mandy, you remember Marco. My mother was sitting in her chair, smoking and drinking moselle. I glanced at Marco, at his pasty skin, his cheeks pockmarked with acne scars, the heavy gold chain around his neck. When Marco nodded in my direction he spilled some juice onto the crotch of his black polyester pants. I'd met him the day we'd moved in and had disliked him instantly because he'd skited to me about attending a local college, even though he was only seventeen. *What are you studying?* I'd asked. *Graphic design*, he'd replied boastfully, as if it were as complex as brain surgery or genetic science. *I'm near the top of my class.*

My mother, however, thought he was *a very nice boy*, and continued to invite him in occasionally for more fruit and cups of tea. For a while, I thought the platters were for Marco's benefit, that it was an excuse to have him visit and keep my mother company. One night, however, after I'd arrived home from having coffee with Grace, my mother announced that next Saturday afternoon Marco was going to take me *out on a date*.

What do you mean – a date?

Well, he likes ice skating, and I know you like ice skating. So I asked him to take you along with him on the weekend.

While my mother poured herself another glass of moselle, I stood stock-still by the heater, stunned. *You've got to be joking.*

He's very intelligent, Mandy. He's already attending university.

He goes to a college two nights a week, studying graphic design!

Now don't embarrass me like this. He's already agreed to take you out. It's all arranged. And anyway, she added, *it won't do you any harm to start mixing with people your own age.*

I fled to my room and slammed the door. Obviously, she was concerned about how rapidly I was changing: the feminist meetings I was now attending, the overalls I now wore, the books I read, and all the time I spent with my English teacher. I realised I must have seemed so unlike the average teenage girl who read *Dolly* magazine, wore too much makeup, and snuck out at night to smoke cigarettes and meet boys. I suspected my mother would have preferred this sort of behaviour.

The following Saturday afternoon, I thought a lot about what I would wear on my date with Marco, and finally dressed myself in gumboots, bib and brace overalls and, to look even more stupid, a girl's brown felt school hat that was a little too small for my head.

You're not going out like that, are you? asked my mother.

I was pleased to hear the incredulous tone of her voice. *Sure*, I replied, and slipped out the door before she made me change. I met Marco downstairs. He looked me up and down and grunted a hello. We caught a tram to St Kilda, sitting mostly in silence. Once we were inside the ice skating rink, Marco left me lacing my boots and met up with his own friends down near the toilets. I skated for about ten minutes, but Marco kept his distance from me. I was happy gliding around the ice on my own: the afternoon was unfolding just as I had planned. When I was confident Marco knew that it wouldn't work out between us two, I skated up to him, said I wasn't feeling well, and shook his hand goodbye.

What are you doing home? my mother called from the living room as I closed the front door behind me. I was startled to see yet another platter of fruit on the dining room table, along with several toffee apples.

He wanted to hang out with his own friends. He didn't want me tagging along. I took off my hat and walked into the living room. There, sitting on the couch, drinking a beer, was a bulky man in his mid-sixties with reddish, leathery skin and eyebrows so thick they turned up at the sides like a spit-curled moustache.

Mandy, this is Herb.

He jumped off the couch and his big, calloused hand encompassed mine. *G'day!* he bellowed. I noticed he had a hearing aid and wondered if he should turn it up. He was wearing long-sleeved blue overalls and boots and exuded a strange scent, like stale orange peel.

Herb's the one who's been giving us all the fruit, said my mother, draining her own beer. *He works in the grocery store up the road.*

I was ambivalent about my mother having another boyfriend. We had just settled into a new and better life and I didn't want it to change too much. But my mother later assured me, *He's just a friend.* She said it several times, maybe one time too many.

During the day, Herb drove trucks for Fairfax, delivering newspapers. At night and on weekends he cleaned the grocery store. He was sitting in his parked truck when he'd first spotted my mother – still blonde then – as she'd walked past on her way to the shops. He'd leaned out and called to her and she of course stopped and began chatting to him.

I wouldn't sleep with him, my mother often said. *Anyway, he's married.* Even so, Herb began dropping in several times a week, always with a six-pack of beer and more fruit than we could eat in a month.

It wasn't until Maeve O'Hara told me she was going overseas that I realised I had a crush on her. I'd had many friends come and go throughout my life and had grown accustomed to goodbyes, but few separations had made me panicky and tearful, as if I were losing someone deeply loved. This was a surprise for me to realise – that I was attracted to a woman, a woman who was my mother's friend, my brother's godmother. When she said she'd be gone *indefinitely*, I stopped breathing for what seemed like a long time and felt a dull pain in my gut, as if I'd been winded.

After Maeve left for England, I drifted away from my friends at school, especially Willa and Vera. They were both obviously still in love with Simon and took most of the classes he offered. The more I stood back and withdrew from them, the more conservative Willa and Vera seemed to me: they might have known the Communist Manifesto back-to-front, but around Simon they behaved like two passive, giggling girls who had never quite enjoyed enough attention from their father. I was glad I was no longer one of those girls, and dropped out of the encounter group and Simon's politics course.

My only real friend now was Grace and, when I was not with

her, or in one of her classes, I spent a lot of time in the school's darkroom, developing black-and-white photographs. Sometimes I'd write poetry or articles for the school magazine, or work in the herb garden we'd planted outside the rectory. I kept myself so busy, even at home, that there was not much time to feel lonely. But some weekends, when Grace went away to visit her parents, or was busy with her boyfriend, Ryan, an awful feeling of melancholia and boredom would overcome me and I'd fantasise about jumping off the roof of our building or throwing myself in front of a tram. It was at these times I would put my brother in his stroller and walk him up to the park, around the streets of Carlton, until I was exhausted and my legs were sore.

Grace knew how poor my mother and I were, so she soon got me a job, looking after the pre-school children of the Labor politician who owned the stable she lived in. It was one full day a week – and the school's coordinator gave me permission to take every Thursday off from school. The young, pretty wife of the politician had once been a successful journalist before she'd had children, and she now wanted to spend most of each Thursday locked in her study as she tried to write a book. The children – aged two and four – were cute and fairly easy to look after. I made two dollars an hour and calculated that I would have to baby-sit about one hundred and thirty hours in order to buy the new Suzuki flute I wished to own, instead of borrowing Grace's every week for my music lesson. I kept my savings in a bag under my bed and, usually every fortnight, in the days before my mother's pension cheque was due, she'd borrow five or ten dollars in order to tide her over.

Fortunately, after the failed date with Marco, she no longer tried to set me up with boys or with people my own age. But she was still fairly disapproving of the ways in which I was changing and often let me know it. When I became a vegetarian she threatened to take me to see a psychiatrist; when I toyed with the idea of shaving my head, she responded, deadly serious, that if I went through with my plan she would throw me off the balcony. But her biggest complaint was that I studied too many subjects at school and spent so little time with her.

Some of what she was complaining about was true. I was gradually drawing away from her through various pursuits. Reading, writing poetry, playing the flute and taking photographs allowed me to escape my mother's expectations. Like most teenagers, I was consciously setting myself apart from her. I no longer wanted to sit beside her at night, watching the 'Don Lane Show', while she smoked and drank beer. She must have sensed my withdrawal and was understandably upset. And after all we'd been through together, I thought it was a shame that, now we were settled, we weren't getting along for the first time in our lives. Occasionally, when she was drunk, she'd make loud, sarcastic remarks: *What? You think you can be a genius at EVERYTHING? You think you're so bloody clever, don't you?* Sometimes, when I was very quiet and didn't speak much, she'd accuse me of being *on drugs*. But the more I denied these accusations the more convinced she was that I was high, and I learned not to react to them. Other times, her natural generosity would surface, like the afternoon she bought me a second-hand black-and-white waistcoat as a surprise, or the day I confessed to her that Grace and I had been booked for writing pro-abortion graffiti. I thought she'd be upset, but she just shrugged and said, *Oh well. Bad luck*. It was often hard to predict what was going to set her off.

I attempted a reconciliation the week The Daly Wilson Big Band came to play in Melbourne. My father had taught the drummer, Warren Daly, when we'd lived in Stanmore. I had heard his records and loved each one and thought the concert might cheer my mother up, reconnect her with her past and Gerry. I could only afford the cheapest tickets. My mother drank too much before we caught a tram into town. In the foyer of the Dallas Brookes Hall she bailed up an usher and announced that she was the wife of the great drummer Gerry Sayer and pressed an envelope into the man's hand. She demanded that the usher let Warren know she was in the audience. *And give him my note*, she added. *It's very important*. She was unsteady on her feet, so I took her by the arm, guided her upstairs and into her seat. The curtain went up and the band began. I'm sure she was expecting the drummer to announce between tunes her presence in the audience, entreating her to come backstage after the show. But no such announcement was made and I heard her muttering to herself about the stupid usher who couldn't follow her simple instruction. I was so embarrassed I decided I would never take her out again.

I began to travel at any opportunity. During the school holidays, Grace and Ryan rented a coastal holiday house in Lorne and invited me and a couple of other friends to stay with them over the break. We swam naked in the ocean, bushwalked, prepared fabulous meals, read and played cards. I realised the further away I was from my mother the better I felt about myself. These periods forced me to communicate with other people and sometimes eased the heavy depression that was becoming a fact of my life. Once, I glimpsed Herb the fruit man kissing my mother in the kitchen and seeing this made me retreat even further. I knew she was probably trying to cope with loneliness, but I didn't think Herb was going to be much help to her.

At the end of my second year at the free school, Grace and Ryan were going off on a holiday on their own, and the six-week break yawned ahead of me like an impending gaol sentence. I dreaded the boredom and isolation, and wondered what I'd do with myself at home with my mother and without the distraction of schoolwork. So when Jo from the refuge and our neighbour, Glenda, mentioned to me that they were travelling to Sydney to attend a women's festival for a few days, I asked if I could come along. We drove up in Jo's car in thirteen hours and, when the Holden lurched down a bush track and pulled up beside an old weatherboard hall, I had a curious sense of deja vu. It was the same track, the same hall I'd encountered two years earlier, when I had inadvertently found myself amongst a horde of lesbians for three days. But this time it was different: I had chosen to come. That night I slept in a large tent with Jo, Glenda and Glenda's five-year-old daughter, Marcel. The following day, I peeled off my clothes and swam naked in the river, along with everyone else. Marcel was splashing about and laughing raucously. The sun shimmered across the surface of the water and, as I floated on my back, past the women sunbathing on the rock, I felt glad that I was no longer that self-conscious, judgemental girl of two years before, hiding behind trees as I watched women kiss.

10

I am sitting on the back of a utility truck, surrounded by drums, cymbals and boxes. The sun is setting as the truck pulls away from the kerb and heads down the road. Wedged between my feet is a large pot of half-cooked pumpkin soup and I am scared it will tip over before we find another place to live.

I am back in Sydney briefly, staying with my father. He has just been evicted from his large, sunny room with harbour views. In fact he was given only two hours to pack up all his stuff and get out. My father acts as if he doesn't care at all, as if he's happy at this sudden turn of events. I, however, feel guilty, and am scared that by nightfall we still won't have found another place to live and will end up sleeping in either the truck or the park.

My father's friend, Rich, turns several corners and drives us to the end of Argyle Street in The Rocks, where nineteenth century terraces overlook a row of ancient trees. He pulls up and my father and I climb out of the ute. We start at the west end of the terraces and work our way east, knocking on door after door, asking each landlady, Have you got a room for rent? *But each one shakes her head.*

We turn the corner and head down Lower Fort Street. We ask at the Hero of Waterloo Hotel, but the publican tells us he no longer rents rooms. We cross the road, heading towards the harbour, and a cold wind suddenly gusts up from the wharves.

The three-day women's festival was a carnival of music, swimming, singing and laughter. I frolicked naked beneath waterfalls, bushwalked, played table-tennis and nude volleyball. I looked for my aunt, but she was nowhere in sight, and I wondered if she'd gone straight again or just had something better to do that weekend. I did, however, see a few women from Elsie's, including Mary and Steve, and they were happy to know that my mother, brother and I were now safely settled in Melbourne.

At night I shared a flagon of wine with Glenda, an olive-skinned woman in her early thirties with long dark hair. As far as I knew, she wasn't a lesbian, but she did wander about topless and allowed her daughter to colour her breasts with face paint. I found the more I drank with Glenda, the more vivacious I became. The wine made me feel happier, prettier, and much more articulate. It drained away my natural reserve and allowed me to talk not only to people I knew, but also to complete strangers. It even allowed me to converse freely with Maeve O'Hara, who was back from England and camping at the festival with her new lover, Minnie. Of course, the next day I couldn't remember much about what I'd said the night before, but that was not the point. I'd finally found an antidote to my chronic shyness.

Buoyed by this discovery, on our third and last night I suggested to Glenda and Jo that we make a detour on our way back to Melbourne and spend the following day in Sydney, which was only an hour-long drive east from the camp. Glenda was enthusiastic about the idea, but Jo was reluctant as she had to be home for work by Wednesday. Within minutes, however, a compromise was realised: Jo would drop us off at Liverpool station in the morning, and then continue on to Melbourne with Glenda's daughter, Marcel, who wanted to return so she could visit her aunt.

Glenda didn't know Sydney very well, so I led the way. Shouldering our backpacks, we hopped off the train at Central station, found the booking office, and made two economy class reservations on the *Spirit of Progress*, which was leaving Sydney for Melbourne at eight o'clock that night. It had been two years since I'd been in my home town and I was glad to be back, without the pressure of having to live with Hakkim. I led Glenda through the city, heading towards The Rocks. I did not know for sure if my father still lived there, but I felt myself being drawn to the area where I'd last seen him.

I knew the only place I'd find him would be in a pub. As we passed the Fortune of War on George Street, I glanced into the bar, but there were only a few old boozers bowed over middies of beer. Further along was the Orient Hotel, a large, nineteenth century building on a corner opposite the overseas passenger terminal, but looking through the window I found that it, too, was virtually empty. Even though Glenda was enjoying the walk – the quaint sandstone shops and houses, the tree-lined footpaths – I felt I had to confess the real reason I'd suggested we spend the day in Sydney: I had not seen my father for three years and wanted to find him again.

Glenda smiled. *That's OK. So we're on a bit of an adventure!*

The Observer had merely a few maritime workers sitting up at the bar, eating counter lunches. Further up the hill, the green-tiled Mercantile contained only a group of Japanese tourists, drinking middies and taking photos of one another. Still we pressed on, up the hill, beneath the Harbour Bridge and into Lower Fort Street, where there was a row of large, nineteenth century houses. We turned left and popped our heads into the Harbour View Hotel, on the corner of Cumberland Street. Apart from a couple of wharfies playing pool, the pub was virtually empty. By this time I was hot and tired and suggested to Glenda we go into the pub and have a cold beer. *Let's just go down here*, she said, pointing along the street.

We passed houses with peeling paint and stone doorsteps worn smooth, then crossed the road. At an old corner shop I paused and glanced across the street to yet another pub. It was three storeys high, built of large sandstone blocks, and as I gazed at its long windows I experienced a quiver of recognition. Painted on the sign hanging over the door was *The Hero of Waterloo Hotel*. It was the same pub in which I'd last seen my father, when he'd disappeared with his lover, Sue, while I sat minding his stool, watching Hakkim eating glass and calling my mother a slut.

We crossed the road and walked through the open door. Initially, I saw nothing because my eyes were adjusting from the bright sunlight. Within moments, however, I could see paintings on the wall, along with the wooden pews below them, a few old boozers sipping shandies, and a short, middle-aged woman making change at the till. I gazed down the length of the bar. At the end of it there was a man sitting on his own, sipping a schooner of beer. As I walked through the pub I noticed he was wearing thick yellow glasses, a blue-and-white striped shirt. And then I realised there was something strange about him: he had absolutely no hair.

I hurried past the drinkers. The man glanced up and straightened on his stool. A grin broke across his face and he leapt to his feet. *Hey,* he cried, *here's my girl!* I threw my arms around him and pressed my face against his chest, inhaling his familiar scent. He kissed my hair, my forehead, my lips, and for the first time in years I felt the simple pleasure of being loved. Everyone in the bar was staring at us as he twirled me around and around, both of us laughing giddily.

Glenda came up behind us and I introduced her, explaining we'd just been at a women's festival about thirty miles away.

How'd you know where I was? he asked, signalling to the barmaid.

Well, I replied, *this was the last place I saw you.*

No doubt about you! He shook his head. *I always reckoned you should be a private detective.*

He pulled up two more stools and we sat down at the bar, and it felt odd to be doing this without my mother there as well. In the past it had always been her and Gerry who'd cosied up together in pubs and beer gardens, growing more affectionate with every glass they emptied. For a moment, I felt slightly guilty, as if I were sitting on her throne.

Hey, I said, *what happened to your hair?*

My father shook a Camel plain from its packet and lit it up. *I'm acting in a movie!* he announced. *It's called 'The Last Straw'. Got a pretty big part, too. I play a jazz drummer who's also a big-time drug dealer – the role was made for me! When I was offered the part, the director told me I'd also get to drive a late-model convertible*

Porsche in the movie. But he added that there was only one catch, and I was thinking that maybe I'd have to get a tattoo or have sex with a man or something. He said, You have to shave your head. And I said, Mate, is that all? To get to drive a late-model Porsche I'll shave my balls as well!

We all burst into laughter and I was happy to find my father was as irreverent as ever. While he told anecdotes about the film I enjoyed watching his hands draw circles in the air, as if he were conducting his own story, how he'd mimic the director, the cameraman, the cockney makeup girl – all through the nasal filter of his harelip. *I get to drive the Porsche around, even when we're not shooting. And get this: I get to do a whole drum solo – you know, in a nightclub with a big band, a full five minutes. I'm gunna do my ol' Gene Krupa routine!*

I had never seen his old Gene Krupa routine but I pretended that I had. For the first time I realised he had the enthusiasm and exuberance of a child, like a boy who'd just discovered snow or who had never seen the ocean before.

So how long're you in town for? You know I've got a gig tomorrow night!

I slumped on my stool a little, already anticipating the life I was returning to in Melbourne. *We're going back on the train tonight.*

I could see he, too, was disappointed. He threaded his fingers through mine. *Ah well, next time you come up you'll have to stay longer.* He squeezed my hand tightly and I could tell that he meant what he said.

Beers were thumped down in front of us on the bar. My father made a toast – *To us!* – and we all clinked glasses, and I was reminded of that first beer I'd had with him when I was three years old – my brother, sister and I sitting in our wet bathers, basking in the sun on the steps of the Coogee Bay Hotel. Back then, I thought nothing could shake such pure happiness.

So Gene marrying Sue, I said, *that must have been a bit of a shock.*

My father gulped his beer and shook his head. *I'll tell you what, Gene did me a favour.* He pulled another cigarette from its pack. *She was driving me bloody mad. I told her when we first got together, there're only two rules: no getting married, and no bloody kids.* He lit the cigarette and dragged the ashtray closer. *She was OK about it at first – I mean, she was already married to a bloke in Wollongong, and'd had a couple of kids with him. But after a few years she started to change, and kept harping that she wanted a baby before she was thirty.* He rolled his eyes. *I said, Sue, I've been through all that – and I'm not going through it again. All I am is a jazz muso. I'm not made for all that stuff. So you know what she started doing?*

I shook my head.

She'd stop taking her pills for a while, hoping to fall pregnant, y'know, like accidentally on purpose. When I found the packet with all the pills she hadn't taken I nearly shit myself. After that, I'd have to force her to take one every night.

Glenda, intrigued, rested one elbow on the bar. *But how did she go from being with you to ending up with your son?*

Gerry explained that, for the first few years, Sue loathed Gene. She and my father were living in a comfortable apartment in The Rocks, while my brother stayed in a pub around the corner. Whenever Gerry invited him over for dinner, Sue would fume. She was always complaining about his dirty clothes, his bad table manners, and the rough way he talked. By this time my brother was hanging out with a bad crowd, always drunk, missing work, living on fish and chips. In fact, my father had been so worried about Gene that he took a lease on a four-bedroom house in Kirribilli so they could all live together and have home-cooked meals and Gene could have some stability in his life. Sue, apparently, had baulked at the plan, but my father had won out in the end.

After they all moved in, Gene settled down, eating well, not drinking so much, and going to work every day. Six months later, however, my father got a job playing drums in a band on a cruise ship and left them in the house alone. When he returned twelve weeks later, he found Gene in his bed with Sue, both sleeping soundly.

So I say to myself, fair enough, and put all of my gear into Gene's room before they even woke up.

I was amazed by his composure. *But weren't you pissed off? I mean, it must have been a shock.*

Gerry shrugged. *Nah, not really. As I said, he did me a favour. After that, I went up to the Cross and found 'em a cheap flat to live in. I even gave 'em my portable television!*

I asked him about their sudden conversion to Jehovah's Witnessing, and how it fitted into the story.

Oh, that, he replied, shaking his head. *Well, you know, Sue tried getting me into all that stuff, too – she grew up with it, her parents are strict JWs – but I wouldn't have a bar of it.*

But Sue's kind of wild, I said. *I mean, she never seemed like the religious type to me.*

My father snorted. *I don't reckon she's into it that much, it's just her way of controlling Gene. Y'know, to keep him out of the pub and on the straight and narrow. He doesn't even play the drums anymore – too busy at Bible study.*

I couldn't help but laugh. The story was so incongruous. It made me wonder if I'd ever really known my brother or if he'd changed so radically he was now unrecognisable. My father, however, was exactly the same: telling stories and jokes, mimicking other people. Occasionally, he'd touch my hair or face and announce, *Geez, you're beautiful!* as if he'd just met me for the first time.

He continued to entertain us with anecdotes from his past, like the day the clutch on his truck failed and he drove backwards from Sydney to Katoomba, and the time he was touring with Frank Sinatra, when he and Frank jumped into a Brisbane taxi and demanded to be driven seventy miles south to the beaches of the Gold Coast. *When the driver refused to take us that far, Frank said, listen, son, if you don't drive us down there I'll buy the bloody taxi company and sack you!*

And then there was the time I was touring with Little Richard, who was holding up the bus because he was still in his hotel room. I was sent to look for him. So I go up and knock on his door and when there's no answer I open it and go inside. And there he is, standing there having a wank! And get this: after he finished, he got down on his knees and begged God to forgive him!

As the afternoon wore on, I grew light and effusive, as if all the problems of the past few years were dissolving. Whenever one of my father's friends walked past on their way to the toilet, he'd stop and proudly introduce me to them. *This is my daughter!* he'd boast, squeezing my hand.

Glenda and I stayed drinking with him until about seven fifteen, when we reluctantly prepared to leave for Central station.

One for the road! my father insisted. Glenda and I glanced at one another and grinned. *One for the road!* we echoed.

I returned to school feeling more optimistic. Food tasted better, jokes were funnier. Even though the time I'd spent with my father had been brief – only four or five hours – it had been enough to temporarily relieve my melancholia. Within a month, however, my elation began to fade, as if I'd been drunk for four weeks, but had suddenly run out of alcohol. Even though I approached my schoolwork with the same amount of concentration as before, I was growing increasingly dissatisfied with one aspect of my life: the burden of my virginity. It was as if I were constantly carting around a heavy, embarrassing sign that announced to the world that nobody loved or desired me.

Meanwhile, sex was all around me. Sometimes when I was out with Grace and her friends – all of whom were in their late twenties or older – I'd tense and begin to flush whenever the subject of sex came up, like the times they'd sit around trading stories about the best or worst root they'd ever had. I'd laugh, nod, shake my head at appropriate moments, pretending to identify with their anecdotes, then excuse myself and go to the bathroom before my turn came around.

The married music teacher who'd been on a holiday in Greenland described to me and Grace, in great detail, an affair she'd had with an Eskimo there (*We had sex for nine hours straight!*). The crafts and cooking teacher, Molly, had split up with her husband and was now in love with a woman. Ursula, the art teacher, confessed to me once that she didn't know the identity of her daughter's father because the month she fell pregnant she'd been involved with three different men. The daughter, now thirteen, also attended our school. Martine – a short, round-faced, pretty girl who looked no older than ten – was now quite openly having an affair with Simon; her mother, apparently, didn't seem to mind.

And then there was the trouble with Grace. A few weeks into the first term of 1979, she found out her sister and her boyfriend had been fucking one another for the past two years. This news came as a great shock to her, especially since her sister had never seemed to like Ryan much. The other surprise was that it had been taking place for so long and in the same small stable in which the three of them had been living.

Not only was I surrounded by people who were either talking about or having sex, so much of it was adulterous and illicit, and I wondered if these complications made the experience more pleasurable. I didn't want to sleep with any one person in particular, I just had an abiding need to be desired. I didn't necessarily want to *do it*, but I wanted to *have done it*, to have this mystery removed from my life.

The other problem was that I was far too shy and inexperienced to ever reveal my true feelings to the two people with whom I was infatuated. Maeve O'Hara was now living in a Carlton terrace with her new lover, Minnie, and was busy finishing her degree in painting. I didn't see her often. One morning when my mother and I dropped around to her place unannounced to visit, she answered the door wrapped in a towel, her face creased with sleep, and I was embarrassed to realise we'd accidentally woken her up. Of course, I had a much more intimate friendship with Grace, and when she broke up with Ryan and moved out of the stable, we grew even closer. She shifted into a shared terrace house in Clifton Hill, and we sometimes slept naked in the double bed. She had a long, smooth, tanned body, but I could not imagine myself touching it because I was certain she had no interest in mine.

I was rescued from this dilemma by an overweight blonde girl who began attending our school in autumn of that year. Silver was nineteen years old, wore vintage dresses with ugg boots, and exuded an air of experience and confidence as she worked in the herb garden or spun raw wool or read poetry aloud in the school hall. She joined our women's studies class and one day presented a seminar on Kate Millett. Over coffee in the hall, she chatted freely about her former boyfriends and girlfriends – of which she'd obviously had many – and to me she seemed much older than her age, as if she were in her late twenties.

One day after we'd worked in the garden together, she invited me over to her place for dinner. She shared a house with two other people. When I arrived, however, no one was home but Silver. She lit a fire in the living room, then served miso soup with seaweed and brown rice. After that, we sat on the floor by the fire and Silver rolled some marijuana into a joint and lit it up.

I'd never even had a cigarette before and when I took my first drag I accidentally swallowed a mouthful of smoke. I spluttered and coughed and felt dizzy for a moment but when I finally burped the smoke came up and I blew it out. I made a second attempt, then a third, trying to stifle more coughs and seem as if I'd smoked marijuana every day of my life. The joint went back and forth between us and for what seemed like a long time I felt nothing at all and secretly cursed myself for my inexperience. Then Silver threw the butt into the fire and as I watched it burn

I felt the carpet beneath me begin to undulate, as if I were sitting on the surface of an ocean. The flames seemed suddenly hotter and bigger and I could feel sweat dripping out of every pore in my body. Then Silver grabbed my shoulders, pushed me down onto the floor and put her mouth on mine.

I'd been half expecting this, but now that it was happening I was already feeling uncertain. She kissed me on the neck, shoulders, face, but as she pressed herself against me I felt suffocated by her bulk, as if her large breasts and rolls of flesh could easily devour me. A brief thought flashed through my mind: I could pull away now, stand up and walk out the door and leave Silver behind, but I quickly dismissed this possibility because the floor was still undulating and my feet now seemed a long way away from the rest of my body; in fact, I could no longer feel them at all. And even though I wasn't really attracted to Silver, she was obviously attracted to me, and that in itself was not a bad thing.

She helped me upstairs and took me to bed. She pulled my clothes off and then peeled off her own dress. Naked beneath her eiderdown, her hands were all over me, and it felt as if hundreds of crabs were scuttling across my body. Then she grabbed my wrist and dragged it down over her stomach, pushing my hand into the warm, wet folds between her legs. When my fingers found her cunt I was astonished by how big it was: she could easily take in my entire hand, and as I moved it in and out of her, I once again began to feel as if I were being swallowed up, as if she were consuming me.

When I woke up early the next morning my first thought was to flee. Silver had her arm draped across my stomach and was snoring softly, her fair hair splayed over the pillow. I lifted her arm and slipped out from beneath it, then eased myself from the mattress without waking her up. My clothes were scattered all over the floor and as I pulled them on I could hear a woman's voice on the radio from the house next door, singing 'It's Too Late'. I felt a little haunted about getting so high and losing control and then I remembered the sensation of my hand inside Silver's cunt and wanted to collapse with embarrassment. As I was doing up my shirt buttons, she stirred and told me to come back to bed.

I've got to get to work, I said truthfully. I rushed out of the room without saying goodbye and, as I walked down the stairs on my way to my baby-sitting job, I felt confused. The very experience I'd presumed would make me happy and complete had left me feeling sour and somehow soiled, and I carried this sense around with me for the rest of the day, the entire weekend, and on into the following month.

Silver sometimes accused me of being *aloof* and *nonchalant*, which was probably true, since I sometimes found myself avoiding her. Part of the problem was that she was just too overweight and, even though we remained friends, it was with a fair amount of relief that I found out two months later that she'd fallen for a university student. In the meantime, I wasn't too keen on any more sexual experimentation, ambivalent about allowing anyone else to get so close to me for a while.

It was not long after this that I received my first letter from my father. In it, he mentioned several times how much he loved and thought about me. I realised the handwriting wasn't his, but the words certainly were – I recognised the cadences and turns of phrase and realised he must have dictated the letter to a friend. It was better than a gift, these two foolscap pages, something I'd been waiting to receive since I was eight years old, when my parents had first split up and I began writing letters to him that my mother never posted.

I wrote back, and this time I mailed the letter myself, asking him if I could come and visit him during the next school holidays. Another letter came back immediately: *Of course you can!* I saved my money, packed my bags and, five weeks later, was back in Sydney.

He was now living in a pub, the Glenmore, which was just up the road from the Hero of Waterloo. I'd told him I'd arrive sometime around three o'clock on Sunday afternoon, but was running late. When I found the pub it was closed and all the doors were firmly locked. I banged on the doors, but no one answered. I checked the address again and walked up and down the block. The street was empty, the sun was beginning to set, and I had exactly twenty-six dollars in my pocket. I balled my hand into a fist and began banging on the door again, and kept on hammering until I heard the creak of a loose floorboard and the door finally opened slightly to reveal the head of a pinch-faced, bald man.

Yeah?

I'm looking for my dad, I said. *His name's Gerry.*

The man looked me up and down and frowned. *I don't know if he's home.*

Can you check? I asked. *He's expecting me. I'm supposed to be staying with him.*

The man sighed, as if I'd just interrupted some vitally important business. *All right*, he conceded. *You might as well come in.* He pulled back the door and allowed me into a hallway.

You can wait in there, he said, nodding to a dimly lit dining room. I carried my bags through and sat down at a table. After a few minutes, the man returned. *I banged on his door. No answer.* He seemed slightly pleased by this fact, as if he were somehow superior to my father.

I glanced about the dining room, trying to think of something to do or say. *Is it all right if I wait here?* I asked. *At least until he gets back?*

The man hitched up his trousers. *Right-o*, he said. *Just don't make any noise.*

I wondered what noise he thought I could possibly make on my own in a closed and empty pub.

As night fell, I sat there reading Helen Garner's *Monkey Grip*. About an hour later, the old man shambled back into the room. *He's still not home?* And when I looked up and shook my head, he sighed again with indignation, marched up the stairs, and banged on my father's door once more. This happened several times as the evening wore on and, by eight o'clock, the man was beside himself with frustration, as if my father's absence were inconveniencing him rather than me. By this time he'd corralled another man into the pursuit of my father, a long-term resident who also lived upstairs.

Let's break his door down, said the old man, *and see if he's inside.*

I tried to talk them out of this idea, but they wouldn't listen. I followed them up the stairs and down the hall. The younger man took a deep breath and threw his weight against the door, and then the older man did the same.

Suddenly, the door swung open and the two men threw themselves into nothing but air and then crashed into my father, who was wearing only his underpants, looking sleepy and confused. *What's all the fuss about, fellas?* he said. *I was just taking a nap.*

He quickly got rid of the men, bundled me into his room and

slammed the door. He threw his arms around me. *Sorry, love. I was expecting you earlier. When you didn't turn up I thought I'd have a lie-down. Look! I bought us some wine!* He picked up a bottle of Mateus Rose and within minutes we were sitting at his table, drinking and eating pistachio nuts and listening to the Oscar Peterson Trio, the same tape he'd often played when we all lived together in the basement room up at the Cross, before everything and our lives fell apart.

When I accidentally dropped a pistachio shell on the carpet and apologised, picking it up, he said, *Don't worry about it*, and deliberately tossed a shell over his shoulder, as if we were in a park. We started on a second bottle of wine and soon were sitting on the floor, surrounded by a moat of pistachio shells, flicking them onto the carpet like balls of snot and enjoying the mess we were making.

You know, he said, *I used to come out to Kingsgrove, when you lived with Hakkim. But your mother wouldn't let me see you. You'd always be at school or some bloody thing.*

My mother had never mentioned his visits and I told him so. *I thought you didn't want to see me*, I confessed.

He took my face in his hands and looked into my eyes. *All the time I was away, I never stopped thinking about you. I never stopped thinking about my girl.*

Even through his thick glasses, I could see his eyes growing moist, and knew it wasn't just the booze talking. It had never occurred to me that my father might have yearned for me over the years, that something could be missing from his life and that thing could possibly be me. I had always assumed that music was his first and only love and there was no extra room in his life for something as ordinary as a daughter.

He'd rented a second room for me, right next to his, so I could enjoy some privacy. *A mate of mine usually lives there, but I paid him to piss off for a while.*

We staggered downstairs to collect my bags from the dining room and then he showed me back to my room, rather sparse but impeccably tidy, with a single bed. We kissed each other goodnight and, just for a few seconds, he rocked me gently in his arms.

I was surprised to find he now had a day job, working as a cleaner at the men's clothing store Gowings. I thought it was a shame that, after having sacrificed his family and former girlfriend for music, he was now struggling to make a living from playing jazz. He was, however, his usual optimistic self: *I'm supposed to work eight hours, but I get it done in four. At eleven am, I just slip out the back door, and I've got the rest of the day to practise the drums!* He had his kit set up in a corner of his room, the cymbals covered with small blankets. I was impressed by his dedication, by his absolute stubbornness to never give up the one thing in the world he loved doing most. It made me want to be like him, so sure of who he was and what his life meant.

The following afternoon, over beers in the bar, he introduced me to a friend of his called Rich, a pasty-skinned man in his mid-thirties with narrow grey eyes who looked as if he drank too much. He and Rich were *in business together* and they were *going to make a killing.*

Oh, yeah? I asked. *Like how?*

My father smiled, as if he knew the answer to a great mystery. *Disco*, he announced, smiling broadly. *Y'see, I figure that no one wants to listen to jazz anymore – let's face it, it's 1979 – and you gotta move with the times.*

But no one actually plays disco live, I said. *In discos, they only play records.*

My father smiled smugly again, as if he were about to beat me at poker. *That's just the point. Y'see, Rich here is a brilliant DJ – y'wanna see him, he's fucking brilliant.*

Rich smiled self-deprecatingly and lit a cigarette.

Anyway, my father continued, *one night I see him in action – spinning the records and playing all that shit, and everyone's dancing and going wild – and that's when I get my big idea.*

He paused for effect and took a few gulps of beer. I sensed my cue and prompted him to go on.

So what we do is this, he said. *Rich, he plays all the records, just like he always did – and he's really good at talking on the microphone and all that crap – while I have a full kit of drums set up on the stage. But this is the difference, see? While I'm playing along to the disco music, every drum is wired up so that whenever I hit a certain skin a bright coloured light flashes through the air while everyone's dancing. So you don't just hear the rhythm of the tune – you also see it!*

He beamed at me, as if he were still amazed by the brilliance of his idea. I smiled and nodded, impressed by his enthusiasm, by his willingness to perform any kind of music as long as somebody was listening. He was fifty-eight years old, living in a room above a pub and working as a cleaner, and yet he was ready to *move with the times* and *really make it as a drummer again*. I also thought it was a good idea and asked if I could see the act some time.

We're still fine-tuning it, he said. *But it's going to be the next big thing.*

Late in the mornings, when he came home from work, we'd

sit in front of his heater and eat a breakfast of wholemeal toast with tahini and honey, and drink cups of herbal tea that I'd bought in a shop around the corner. He only had a hotplate in the room, for boiling water and toasting bread. *The prick who's just bought the pub, Roger – he's the old bloke who tried to bash down my door – well, he won't let anyone cook in their rooms.*

Why not?

My father shrugged. *Fire regulations or some bloody thing. He hates me because I've got this big room with harbour views for just fifteen bucks a week.* My father laughed then, and I could tell he enjoyed deliberately riling the new hotelier.

In the afternoons, he'd take me for strolls around The Rocks, telling me stories about its history. I was surprised he knew so much about the area, and by his keen interest in something other than music. He walked me up to Observatory Hill, where a breathtaking panorama widened before us – the Harbour Bridge, the various coves and points stretching to Balmain and beyond – and described sword fights and duels by nineteenth century English gentlemen on the very ground upon which we now stood. Then we lay down on the hill, with our feet pointing upwards, because my father thought it was therapeutic to *let the blood run to your head.*

We spent the rest of our time drinking in pubs around Millers Point and The Rocks, my father entertaining me with more stories and jokes. At around 7.30 pm, we'd wander arm-in-arm down to a buffet restaurant in Pitt Street, which served only vegetarian food. I was happy about the fact that he approved of my not eating meat, because he no longer ate meat either. He also liked the clothes I wore, my overalls and vintage dresses, my gumboots and felt hats. *You always were different*, he'd say, grinning. *You're definitely a Sayer.* For the first time in a long while I felt as if I belonged somewhere, or at least with a particular person.

Throughout the first week of my holiday, he refused to let me pay for any drinks or our nightly dinners, and this made me feel ambivalent, as he was living on the wages of a cleaner, and I figured that would not be very much. I thought about buying him a present in return, or perhaps lunch. *Don't worry about it*, he said. *Just having you here's enough.*

What if I cook you something? I asked. *How would you like that?*

Oh, yeah? he said, interested. *Like what?*

I only know how to make pumpkin soup, I confessed. *But it tastes good with crusty bread.*

That sounds great, he said. *Pumpkin soup it is.*

Another thought suddenly occurred to me. *But you're not allowed to cook in your room*, I said. *What if the owner finds out?*

That goose? said my father. *Don't worry about him. He won't even know.*

The following morning, I did the shopping for the meal. My father had no running water in his room, so I had to carry the hefty piece of pumpkin into the shared bathroom down the hall. It didn't fit in the hand basin, so I had to put it in the bath. As I was kneeling on the floor washing the pumpkin, I heard the door open, and turned to see a man standing there, holding a roll of toilet paper. It was the same man who'd helped the publican, Roger, bash down my father's door the night I'd arrived at the pub.

Sorry, I chirped, *I'll just be a sec!*

The man glanced sideways at the wet pumpkin, backed away, and closed the door.

My father soon arrived home from work and we had our usual tea and toast by the heater. Later, in the afternoon, he decided to take a nap, and that is when I began preparing the soup. I selected a large pot from his various utensils and heated two litres of water on the hotplate. When it came to the boil, I added the chopped pumpkin, turned the heat down, and allowed it to simmer. I cut up the onions and garlic and, after about twenty minutes, added them to the pot. I had just turned the heat up to bring it back to the boil, when three harsh raps sounded against the door. I froze, too scared to answer, assuming that if I just stood still long enough the person in the hallway would go away.

Suddenly, the door swung open, and Roger the publican marched into the room, followed by the man who'd glimpsed me earlier washing the pumpkin in the bathroom.

I angled my body directly in front of the hotplate and pot so Roger couldn't see them directly.

Are you two COOKING? he demanded, as if cooking were tantamount to robbing pensioners or torturing domestic animals.

N-o-o, I pleaded, as the steam from the boiling soup rose up my back and billowed above my head.

Don't bullshit to me! he cried. *I can see the bloody smoke!*

My father finally stirred, sat up and put on his glasses. *What's up?* he asked, climbing out of bed.

Roger's hands balled into fists and his eyes bugged. *That's it, Sayer! Pack up all your stuff and piss off! I want you outta here by tonight!*

With pleasure, countered my father. *Another day in this dump and I'd probably end up as bitter and stupid as you two!*

The men walked off in a huff and slammed the door behind them.

I'm sorry, I said. *I got you chucked out.*

Don't worry, love. It's not your fault. That bludger's been looking for any excuse to get me out of here. That's why he bashed the door down that night – he was probably hoping to find me dead!

I couldn't believe how composed he was; in fact he almost seemed happy.

And keep on cooking that soup! he added. *We're going to bloody-well have it for dinner tonight, no matter where we're living.*

I turned down the heat on the hotplate, then walked up to Millers Point and collected some boxes from the corner shop. By the time I'd returned, my father was already lifting suitcases and bags onto the back of a white utility parked beside the hotel. I carried his drums down, and then my own luggage, while he packed the last of his clothes. By five o'clock, everything he owned was on the back of the truck, except his hotplate, which he finally unplugged and took downstairs, while I carried the steaming pot. His friend Rich came out of the pub and started the engine. My father climbed into the front cabin beside him. I sat on the tray in the back, amongst all his belongings, still feeling responsible for getting him chucked out, the incriminating pot of pumpkin soup now wedged between my feet.

We doorknocked along Argyle Place, looking for another room, but no houses had any vacancies. We tried several hotels: the Hero, the Harbour View, the Mercantile; each was either full or no longer let rooms. We tried a grand Victorian home, the attic of which my father had once rented with my brother, but old Mrs Grant, the landlady, no longer took in tenants. All this time, Rich was waiting in the parked ute in Argyle Place, smoking and working his way through a six-pack of beer.

It was now completely dark and our last resort was to make our way down the west side of Lower Fort Street, which was lined with three-storey terraces. We started at number 77, knocking on door after door like two travelling salesmen, and at each house we were promptly turned away. By the time we'd reached the fourth and last block, I was feeling defeated. My father, however, was undeterred – in fact he seemed invigorated, as if we were on some grand adventure. We came to the last terrace in the street, number 1, and banged on the door. Within moments, a tall, white-haired man opened it. He had a pipe between his teeth.

Gerry! he exclaimed, as if my father were a long-lost brother. *Great to see you again!*

My father introduced the man to me – his name was Dennis – and explained he was desperate for a room.

Well, we've only got one, said Dennis. *It's on the third floor and it's pretty small.*

I'll take it! said my father. *I wanna move in now.*

Within an hour we had moved all his gear into the top floor room that overlooked the harbour and Sydney Opera House. I carried the pot of soup up the three flights of stairs and reheated it on the gas stove in the hallway. At eight thirty that night we sat on the floor of his room, ripped up a loaf of bread, and began eating.

Well, I gotta tell you, love, said my father. *It was worthwhile moving. This soup tastes fucking brilliant.*

My father reminded me of Sydney itself – cloudless and light. He was effortlessly optimistic, always turning a negative into a positive. When his son married his girlfriend, he declared that *Gene did me a favour.* Getting fired from a job was fine because it gave him *more time to practise.* He was glad he'd been evicted from the Glenmore Hotel because he could now *cook every day.* Each setback seemed to amuse him, as if it were some entertainment performed for his benefit only and without any real consequences. Sure, I realised some of his behaviour was just bravado and a way of saving face, but his humour and grace made him so easy to be around, and I felt a sense of ease in the presence of someone who seemed so confident about the world and the unwanted surprises it could bring.

After two weeks I returned to Melbourne with a stronger sense of purpose, with the idea of finishing high school as soon as possible. The coordinator, Leon, had already permitted another girl to do this, a tall, attractive sixteen-year-old called Cedar. Her parents were wealthy and American, and the father, a businessman, was being transferred back to Texas at the end of the year. Since Cedar was so *mature* and *bright*, the father had argued, might she not be permitted to skip two years and complete her leaving certificate before the family moved home?

Leon had relented and the mature, bright Cedar now sashayed around the school as if she were a combination of Marie Curie and Marilyn Monroe. I hated her because she was naturally beautiful, had rich parents, and never seemed to do any schoolwork apart from taking photographs. If she could have two years shaved off her education, I thought, surely I would have a chance, even though I was only sixteen and there were no particular extenuating circumstances to justify the special consideration.

The real reason was that I was eager to explore a life of my own, without the pressure of living with my mother and her increasingly erratic behaviour. One night, a parent/student general meeting was held at school. My mother had been drinking brandy all afternoon and turned up so drunk that she walked straight into a noticeboard. The meeting began and, when the chairman asked for ideas about how to raise money for the school, she put up her hand a little too high, teetered sideways, and fell off her chair. All the other kids, their parents and the teachers watched silently as I helped her up and brushed down her skirt. I then took her arm firmly and marched her out of the hall. As I guided her down the path towards a taxi, embarrassed, I knew I wanted to escape her as soon as possible. But what I told Leon was that *I need more challenges*, that *I want to go on to college as soon as possible*. And since I was always busy and productive at school, this seemed reasonable to him, and he allowed me to collapse my time there so that I would complete my Tertiary Leaving Certificate at the end of the year.

Now that Grace was single, she was becoming more expansive and eccentric. She dumped her old Austin and bought a bright red vintage Peugeot with cream leather upholstery, which she drove at an alarming speed. She began taking lessons in modern dance. When she went out she always drank Pernod on ice and occasionally we'd drink a bottle of it together on the veranda off her room. The dance classes began to correct her posture and she was soon embracing her natural height rather than diminishing it with a stoop.

This exuberance was infectious and spread throughout most of the classes she taught. During our writing class she came up with the idea of an all-night poetry session, which entailed everyone piling into the school bus and her driving us around various venues for twelve hours straight. We'd have to write a poem about each place we visited – spontaneously, à la Jack Kerouac. Fuelled by lots of strong coffee and the occasional alcoholic drink, we started off at Leo's Spaghetti Bar on Fitzroy Street – where the teaspoons had holes drilled into them so the junkie patrons wouldn't steal them. Then it was off to St Kilda Beach, Luna Park, a coffee shop on Acland Street, a bar in Little Bourke Street, all of us students and even Grace scribbling madly in our respective notebooks. Later in the evening, when venues began to close, Grace suddenly hit the accelerator and let out a whoop and when we asked her where we were going, she cried, *The airport!* After we'd all written several stanzas about Tullamarine, we ended up at Johnny's Green Room in Carlton, where we played several games of pool and wrote a verse about the seedy atmosphere before heading across the street to Genevieve's for breakfast.

It was around this time that kids at school presumed that Grace and I were having an affair, and occasionally one or two would pull me up and inquire about the status of our relationship. *Youse two are on together, aren't you?* asked one girl, who always seemed to have a bad cold.

No, I replied. *We're just good friends*.

The girl rolled her eyes and sniffed. *Oh, sure*, she said. *Everyone knows, you know. Youse two are always together.*

To supplement my baby-sitting income, I found a job as a house cleaner, but only lasted a month because one day I failed to dust a windowsill. I then scored a job as a children's swimming instructor at an indoor south Carlton pool. I was a strong swimmer and good with children and assumed I'd be suited for this kind of work. It was only for three hours on Saturday mornings, and paid three dollars an hour, but I hoped it might lead to a better position with higher pay. My boss, Travis, was in his late thirties, unnaturally muscled, heavily tanned, and with hair dyed egg-yolk blond. I noticed he employed four other teenage girls as instructors, and a woman in her mid-twenties, named Jan, who was a general manager.

After my second Saturday of teaching, Travis stopped me as I was leaving and asked if I'd like a lift home. When I hesitated, he announced, *I've got a Mini-Moke!* as if it were a Jaguar or convertible Porsche. I didn't much like Travis but I didn't want to get on the wrong side of him, so I shrugged and said, *OK*.

As we sped down Elgin Street, the wind in our hair, Travis prattled on about the teaching rosters and the percentage of chlorine in his pool. After he pulled up in front of my apartment block, he looked down at my legs and asked if I'd like to have dinner with him that night.

Sorry, I'm busy, I lied. The following Saturday, he gave me my cheque and explained: *It's not working out. You're not dynamic enough. And frankly, if I looked like you and one of the mothers saw me I'd be humiliated. You know we wear white T-shirts and white socks.* (I was wearing a white singlet with maroon socks). *Look, Mandy, you're a nice chick and I like you, but Jan says you're not dynamic enough.*

One day at school, a tall, blonde nineteen-year-old girl named Sally, who studied nothing but existentialism, noticed me going through the employment classifieds and tapped me on the shoulder. *Why don't you try nude modelling for art classes?* she said, wobbling on her orange patent-leather high heels. *I've just finished doing it. It's great money.*

Me? I asked, glancing at her long neck and slender frame. *I'm too fat.*

You're not fat, said Sally.

Well, I said, *I don't look like you.*

The students prefer women who are a bit more rounded – they're easier to draw.

Sally ripped a piece of paper from her notebook and wrote down the name and phone number of an art instructor at Swinburne College. *And how old are you?* she asked, almost as an afterthought.

Sixteen, I said, presuming I was too young.

Tell him you're eighteen, she said, handing me the number. *The job pays five dollars an hour.*

I was nervous as I undressed in the storage room of the studio. I still felt plump and unlovely – my thighs too wide, my belly too big, and I now noticed I had a hair growing out of the side of my right nipple. I changed into a robe and, when the knock came, I opened the door, threaded my way between the easels and students, walked up three stairs and onto a dais mounted at the front of the studio. There were two electric heaters on either side of the dais and a chair placed in the middle. *OK*, said the instructor, *we'll start off with some quick warm-up sketches. We'd like six poses in succession – thirty seconds each. When I say* change, *that's when you change the pose.*

I nodded, pulled off the robe and immediately assumed my first pose: standing on an angle with my hands on my hips. I'd practised in front of the mirror in my bedroom the night before, finding ways to hold my body that were comfortable, yet not too visually boring. I was just thinking about this when the instructor called *Change* again, and I spun in a circle and leaned on the back of the chair. The next few minutes passed in a blur of poses and flapping paper. After that came a twenty-minute pose, then two half-hour poses, and that is when I decided to lie on the dais and use the folds of my robe as a prop.

By the end of the two-hour session, I wasn't stiff, as I had expected, and I was no longer feeling shy and self-conscious. After I put my robe back on, the instructor invited me to join him as he walked from easel to easel and critiqued the students' work. I had expected to see some bloated creature with a big hair growing out of her nipple, and was surprised to see so many young women in charcoal, sitting on stools, leaning on chairs, lying against drapes, almost looking beautiful.

You're a very good model, said the instructor as he paid me my fee. *Interesting poses. We'd like to have you back.*

I skipped down the hill to the railway station, the money safe in my pocket, my heart racing with happiness: I was finally good at something.

I could feel my life opening up, growing away from my childhood, and into a world that was tranquil and almost mine. The instructor not only kept his word and invited me back to Swinburne several times, he also recommended me to other art departments – RMIT, East Melbourne Tech, the Gallery School at the Victorian College of the Arts, which paid a staggering six dollars an hour and employed me for six hours at a time. I began to enjoy the work more and more – it was much better than cleaning houses or teaching snotty-nosed kids the breast stroke, and it was fun coming up with more inventive poses for the artists, ones that would challenge both them and me. My biggest challenge, however, lay just ahead, and it had nothing to do with art.

It began on the afternoon of Mother's Day, 1979, when there was a loud knock on the door. I was in the living room, reading *The Ballad of Reading Gaol.* My mother and brother were asleep, so I put down my book, walked across the dining room and peered through the peephole in the door. At first, all I saw was a bunch of yellow chrysanthemums, then I took in a hefty beer paunch, and a man with thinning hair. I assumed it was one of my mother's various drinking buddies who lived in the neighbourhood. I flipped back the lock and opened the door.

The man proffered the flowers, smiling nervously. *Hello, Mandy*, he said, and it was only when he said my name that I recognised the voice. He was about fifteen kilos heavier, his hair was now greying, and he had an oval-shaped bald patch on his head. The only familiar thing about him was his accent. After three years of searching, Hakkim had finally tracked us down.

11

I walk onto the stage of the school hall, alone. I am wearing white pantomime makeup on my face, a red spot on each cheek. I can hear the children breathing in the auditorium as I search the stage, looking behind the curtain, underneath a chair. My name is Slippery Slippers and I made my dress myself: the top half is gingham and the bottom is blue-and-white polka-dots. I like my red shoes and pink socks because they look pretty together. I lift a square of carpet and look underneath, then up at the ceiling, to my right and left. I drop to my knees and crawl to the edge of the stage, gazing out into the hall. The front row is only inches from my face and I reach out to a little boy and draw him up from his seat. The children are giggling as I look down his shirt, go through his pockets, spin him around and begin searching through his hair. I do this to the next kid, then the next. They are laughing now as I back off, disappointed, and begin going through my own pockets.

Suddenly, a small rubber ball drops out from under my skirt, as if I've just laid an egg. I pause and stare at the ball, astonished, as it rolls to a stop in the centre of the stage. Intrigued, I walk slowly towards it, as if it might bite, and give the ball a nudge with the toe of my shoe.

It rolls a little more and I'm wide-eyed now. I drop to my knees again and sniff it. The scent is rather pleasing and I smile. Then I get another idea: I stand, pick the ball up, and abruptly sink my teeth into it, as if it were an apple. But one taste of the rubber has me reeling back, gagging.

I throw the ball down hard against the floor, wanting nothing more to do with it, and it bounces so high it arcs over my head and hits the curtain behind me. I pause and regard the ball again as it rolls towards me. I pick it up and bounce it gently in my hand, a smile slowly widening across my face, pleased with this new discovery. I throw it higher and higher, then from one hand to the other. I toss it into the air, spin around and catch it, then rock back and forth on the balls of my feet, grinning.

As I'm doing this, another ball suddenly drops out from under my skirt and rolls along the floor. I glance at the ball in my hand and the one a few feet away and realise they're exactly the same. Another idea strikes me: I pick the second ball up with my free hand and squeeze them both, as if they're two oranges. I throw one into the air and then the other, and then both at the same time. Each time I toss them they fly higher and higher. I beam at the children, so proud of my cleverness, when yet another ball drops onto the floor. I pick the third one up, but I'm stumped now, as I have only two hands. Passing each ball to my free left hand, I throw them up one at a time. As I do this the rhythm gradually grows faster, like an old machine warming up. I'm growing more excited as the momentum builds. My mouth is open, my knees slowly bend and, in one spectacular moment, I'm astonished to find myself suddenly juggling the three balls perfectly, each bouncing off my palms and making patterns in the air. The children jump to their feet, clap and cry out, as if I've performed a miracle.

*

As soon as I recognised Hakkim, I slammed the door and locked it. He began banging on it again as I ran into the main bedroom and woke my mother up.

It's Hakkim, I said. *He's at the door.*

My mother's eyes widened, her face suddenly white. *Are you sure?*

Of course I'm sure! My first concern was for my brother, now three, who was still asleep in the nursery. Even though we lived on the first floor, I was afraid Hakkim would climb up the drainpipe and onto the veranda, or find some other way to break in. I locked the windows of my brother's room.

Come on! I cried to my mother, who still seemed paralysed with shock. She rose from her bed and helped me lock the rest of the apartment's windows, while Hakkim kept hammering on the front door. It was only when she heard him call her name that the reality of the situation hit her. I glanced at her standing stock-still in the living room, her face so blanched I thought she would faint. There was no phone in the flat so we were unable to call the police. She sat down in her chair and lit a cigarette. I could see that her hands were shaking.

After about half an hour of banging and crying out, Hakkim gave up and walked down the stairs. I peered between the curtains and saw him climb into a parked brown Holden station wagon and throw the chrysanthemums onto the back seat. I presumed he would start the engine and drive away but he remained inside the car all afternoon and on into the evening. I thought he'd need a toilet break or would buy some food, but he kept up his vigil like a military guard. When we went to go to bed that night, we peered through the curtains again and found him still hunched over the steering wheel, staring up at our window.

As I lay in my bed, every rattling windowpane and rustling tree made me think it was Hakkim breaking into our apartment. Over and over, I could hear him shinning up the drainpipe and onto our balcony (I'd made the climb many times myself, after having mislaid my keys). And between hearing these dreaded noises, I wondered how on earth he'd found us, after all this time and distance. I dared not fall asleep, in case he came crashing through my window.

The following morning, all the windows and doors were firmly locked, but when I glanced through the curtains again, just after dawn, the car was still there and I could see he was smoking a cigarette.

I knew that Hakkim's first priority would be to kidnap my brother and use him as leverage to force my mother and me to return to Sydney. When Jason woke up that morning, I kept him away from the windows, not wanting Hakkim to see him.

I didn't bother getting ready for school, as I knew I wouldn't be leaving the flat any time soon. When my mother got up, she seemed hunched and exhausted, as if she hadn't slept much either. Hakkim remained in his car all morning, still staring up at our flat. I could tell he'd parked it in such a way that he'd be able to see the first-floor landing outside our door, preventing one of us escaping the flat and running to a neighbour for help.

At around lunchtime, I peeked outside again and was relieved to see the car had vanished. I wasn't sure how long it had been gone or whether he was, in fact, trying to outwit us. I talked this over with my mother, weighing up the possibilities. Finally, in order to test the situation, I decided to make a dash to the letterbox at the bottom of our stairs to collect the mail.

My mother locked the door behind me and I bolted down the

steps. I had just slipped my hand into the box when I saw his car suddenly swerve around the corner, heading straight towards me. I dropped the mail and shot back up the stairs, shouting, *Quick! Open up!* and ran back into the flat. He was now obviously parking in Canning Street, where we couldn't see him, but where he could still watch us.

I didn't dare leave the flat again. Fortunately, we had enough food to last us several days and I tried to keep my restless brother entertained by playing hide and seek and allowing him to splash about in the bath for hours. I was hoping one of my mother's friends would drop by – I would even have welcomed Herb the fruit man at this point – but no one came up the stairs and knocked on the door.

By twilight, Hakkim had stopped spying on us from a distance and had moved the car back to its original spot outside our flat. He kept his vigil up all night again. Occasionally, when I peeked out at him, I could glimpse cigarette smoke escaping from the driver's window, framed momentarily by the glare of a street-light. I wondered if he'd been searching for us relentlessly these past three years, or if he'd just got lucky one day and bumped into someone who happened to know us. The only thing I was convinced of was that time hadn't treated him well. At thirty-five, he already looked like an old man.

The next day was the same. I was hoping that one of the neighbours might grow suspicious about the continued presence of a strange car and man lurking outside their block, but no one seemed to notice. We ran out of milk. My brother started crying because there was no cereal left either, and he refused to eat anything else for breakfast. He wanted to go outside and ride his tricycle and had to be content with continually ramming it into his bedroom door. My mother was down to her last two cigarettes and I missed another day of school.

I decided to make my move at about four thirty that day, after I heard the car start up and saw Hakkim drive away. Of course, I realised his absence could be yet another trick but, after three days of imprisonment, I knew I had to do something. My mother still seemed paralysed with fear, and I didn't think she had the stamina to cope with this situation.

My plan was deceptively simple, and I wondered why I hadn't thought of it earlier. First of all, I pulled on a heavy coat. After summoning my mother to the kitchen, I opened a drawer, rattled around, and drew out the largest knife I could find, a sharp blade my mother used to carve up legs of lamb.

What are you doing? she asked, her voice trembling.

Lock the door behind me, I said, concealing the knife within my coat. *I'll be back in a minute.*

For Christ sakes be careful, she said, closing the door behind me.

Still gripping the hidden knife, I glanced along the landing and up the stairwell, expecting him to spring out of its shadows at any moment. I heard nothing as I moved quietly along the railing. I turned and began climbing the steps to the second floor. A door suddenly slammed and I froze and tensed, ready to plunge the blade into his heart, his stomach, his face, but all I saw was a dog on the upper floor, nosing a ball about. I took the rest of the stairs quickly, as quickly as I could, and when I reached the second landing, I began pounding on the door of flat number 3, praying that the Polish woman, or even Marco, was home.

After what seemed like an eternity, I heard footsteps, sensed somebody looking at me through the peephole and then, finally, the door swung open and there was Mrs Poticki, wearing a floral housecoat, staring back at me.

Please, I said. *Can I use your phone? It's an emergency.*

Twenty minutes later, Grace and her house mate were bundling us into her red Peugeot – now parked out the front – along with a couple of hastily packed bags. I was expecting Hakkim to appear at any moment and attack us, and I was amazed that when Grace hit the accelerator and turned the corner, there was no brown station wagon suddenly trailing us. Just to be sure, Grace chose a circuitous route back to her house in Clifton Hill, constantly checking the rear-view mirror.

My mother contacted a solicitor the following day. Penny Foreman represented the refuge and its many residents in legal disputes, specialising in family law. She advised my mother to contact the police and have a temporary restraining order served on Hakkim, after which time my mother would have to go to court to acquire full and legal custody of my brother.

Carlton police provided us with a restraining order, but there was one remaining problem: *You'll have to serve it yourselves*, they said. *You'll have to literally place it in his hands and explain to him what it is.*

But having to go near him, I said, *contradicts the whole point of the order. What if he tries to kill us?*

The cop shrugged. *We can't do anything until he breaks the law. I'm sorry, but being parked outside your house for three days isn't a crime.*

Grace and I decided we would serve the order together and that my mother and brother would stay back at the house. Grace would do all the talking while I would be there merely as a witness. It was twilight on a cold Friday night. We parked on

Nicholson Street, walked along the block and around the corner. There, in its usual spot outside our flat, for its sixth day straight, was the brown station wagon.

Hakkim must have glimpsed me in the rear-view mirror, because we were only halfway down the block when he leapt out of the car and came running towards us. Grace braced herself and pulled the order from her pocket. Before Hakkim could say anything she was pressing the envelope into his hand. *This is a restraining order. You are not permitted within five hundred metres of Betty Sayer.*

Where your mother? cried Hakkim.

You are not permitted within five hundred metres of Jason Sayer.

Where my son?

You are not permitted within five hundred metres of Mandy Sayer.

I look for three years!

If you come within five hundred metres of any of them you'll be arrested.

I look in Sydney! Hakkim pleaded. *I look in Brisbane!*

Do you understand? asked Grace. *Do you understand what I'm saying?*

Hakkim finally glimpsed the envelope in his hand, as if he hadn't noticed it before.

If you come near any of us again, I explained, *the cops are going to throw you in gaol.*

Grace and I backed away and began hurrying down the block.

Last year I hire detective! Hakkim called after us. *He steal my money. Two thousand dollar!*

But we were already rounding the corner by then and running towards Grace's car.

We spent several more nights at Grace's house. Grace shared

her bed with me while my mother and brother slept on a mattress in the lounge room. To keep herself busy, my mother cooked and cleaned, and got into trouble with one of Grace's house mates when she accidentally unplugged the light in the cupboard under the stairs that kept a small crop of marijuana plants growing. A couple of times a day, Grace and I would drive past my apartment block to see if Hakkim was still lurking about the area. Fortunately, after serving the order, we never saw him or his brown station wagon outside the flat again and, by the start of the following week, my mother, brother and I were back living in our own apartment, albeit uneasily. Hakkim was so unpredictable that his absence could mean the opposite of what it seemed; it could in fact mean that he was devising a more sophisticated plan to force us back into his life.

Winter came, and still there was no further sign of him. I wondered whether he'd given up and gone back to Sydney, or if he'd remained in Melbourne, and was now mounting a legal defence for the upcoming court case. Gradually, over the weeks, our fear of his presence began to wane. My mother stopped looking over her shoulder when she shopped, and we now allowed Jason back outside to play.

Meanwhile, it was my final year of school – mid-1979 – and I devoted myself to my twelve chosen subjects so I could leave in December, which became my new obsession.

It was around this time that Grace developed an obsession herself: she wanted to be a clown. Not a circus clown or some bozo who appeared at kids' parties and shopping malls, but one based on the art of improvisation. She began taking weekend workshops with industry professionals and sometimes drove her car about afterwards, forgetting she was still wearing a red plastic nose. At first, I didn't think she would stick with it – she had so many interests and couldn't possibly fit them all into the one life, but instead of declining, her passion for clowning increased and, by August that year, she'd assembled about a dozen students at school who were willing to become clowns too.

It started with a four-day workshop at the Drama Resource Centre in Bouverie Street, Carlton. Every morning Grace would lead us through stretching exercises, after which we'd practise general acrobatics: tumbling, handstands and cartwheels. On the second afternoon, Grace brought in a box of rubber balls and we spent hours trying to keep three of them in the air simultaneously. Grace could already juggle four at once and we were all in awe of her dexterity. The next day, she invited a professional juggler along to the studio and he taught us some more sophisticated tricks, the under-the-leg throw, for example, and the pirouette. Soon we were juggling different kinds of objects: hairbrushes, plastic cups, shoes. Grace then recruited her modern dance instructor, who led a movement workshop in a nearby park.

On the last day, she passed out theatrical makeup and encouraged us to find our personal clown masks. She explained to us that a mask was a licence to be a fool, to be as silly as we wished. While the other kids spent up to an hour trying to find their own particular clown faces, I applied mine immediately, as if I'd been painting it on every day of my life: white face, tiny red lips, a small dot on either cheek. When I gazed at myself in the mirror, the mask was so familiar to me I was startled, as if I'd just glimpsed my twin. Later, when we improvised skits, I found myself shedding my shyness: my voice was stronger, my laughter louder, and I felt as nimble and light as a child.

After the workshop, Grace began concocting an even grander scheme: to develop a sixty-minute show and take it on tour. The skits grew out of improvisations we performed for one another, which we rehearsed and polished in the back of the school hall. Some involved acrobatics, others juggling, but the main aim was to be funny. And the more we rehearsed, the more competitive we became – each of us striving for longer and louder laughs. I began to see the world through a prism of comic potential. A fork was no longer just an eating utensil, but something I could also comb my hair with. I could roll myself up in a long length of paper towelling and suddenly be wearing an entirely new dress. I could turn a chair into a dancing partner, a dinner guest, a lover.

In order to raise money for our clown tour, we baked cakes and sold them from a stall in front of the school. We did street theatre in Bourke Street Mall. And we held what Grace called a 'Clown-a-thon', during which we juggled and cartwheeled along the city streets while collecting money in our hats from bemused shoppers. This was a good experience for me because it made me aware of another way I could make money for myself. On Thursday nights, I would dress up in my clown mask and clothes and play the flute on a street corner, netting about ten dollars an hour – an absolute fortune for me. One night I even painted my three-year-old brother's face with the same makeup and, as I played, he danced and cavorted across the pavement, grinning at the crowd and, every so often, passing the hat around.

With my new sources of income I began to buy and drink alcohol more often, especially if I had to socialise with people. I found the booze was a lot like the clown mask: it immediately removed my inhibitions. Through the clown troupe I befriended a couple of other girls, and whenever we went to a party or to hear some music, I would take along a bottle of Stone's Green Ginger Wine. When I drank, my jokes were funnier, my dancing more fluid – I even felt slimmer and more attractive. Drinking also lessened my anxiety and depression, however temporarily.

Even though I was striving to outgrow my childhood, I was often aware that it still lurked behind me, like a shadow. The sudden appearance of Hakkim had left me shaken, and I was always wary because he now knew where we lived and could do something totally irrational, despite the restraining order. And I came to think of the past as something that was impossible to transcend, that I would carry it around with me always, like a terminal disease.

I began applying to every Melbourne college and university that would accept a tertiary certificate from an alternative school. I felt as if I'd entered some academic lottery that would decide my fate for me and thus relieve me from the pressure of having to make a decision on my own. Because there was no grading system at our school, I no longer really knew what subjects I excelled in and what path I should be following.

As the date for our ten-day clown tour neared, Grace scheduled even more clowning and improvisation workshops – during school, after school, and on the weekends. Once we had eleven skits well-rehearsed, we did a few free shows in local schools in order to refine our timing. I found it curiously thrilling to perform in front of a crowd, considering that I was usually so shy, and again attributed my sudden extroversion to the power of the clown mask. I briefly considered wearing it around all the time, like a favourite hat, so no one could see my true self.

Our tour would take us to Adelaide and back. Grace drove the school minibus, while our tall, lean sports teacher, Will, drove Grace's red Peugeot. We'd be performing in public schools along the way and, at night, pitching tents in caravan parks and mostly cooking our own food. We left Melbourne on a Sunday morning and drove along the Great Ocean Road. It was cold and raining when we pitched our tents by the Cumberland River, near Lorne, and I warmed myself with a bottle of cheap port, which I shared with another student, Anna, a short, bubbly Greek girl who always laughed raucously when I said something funny. When I woke the next morning I was wet and slightly hungover, but at least it had finally stopped raining. After we repacked the bus and car, we did our first show at Lorne Primary School. Even though I was still dry-mouthed and had a headache, I was proud that I didn't drop a single juggling ball or forget any of our routines.

The tour was divided between performing and partying, yet sometimes the line between the two blurred into one long, dizzying carnival. In Adelaide, Friday night saw us all tipsy, conducting piggyback races in Rundle Street Mall. At one point I was on Grace's back as she ploughed straight between two bemused policemen. As we drank more, we began singing and dancing along the streets, eventually fetching up at a cheap Lebanese restaurant, where I announced, *Innkeeper! More wine for my friends!* which the owner dutifully supplied. There were more songs and dancing around the tables as platter after platter arrived. I left with a glass of red in my hand as we headed back to the beach for a midnight swim.

The following day we drove up to Hahndorf, a quaint German village in the Adelaide Hills with thatched roofs and bay windows.

We bought local wines and beer and picnicked by a river, wading into its currents and floating downstream. When we ran out of booze, we piled into the bus and headed down the highway until we found a country pub. Inside, we each ordered so many different kinds of drinks that the barman threatened to throw us out. The last thing I remembered of the afternoon was sitting cross-legged on the bar, sipping a glass of port. I woke up inside a tent early the next morning, not knowing where I was or how I came to be there. Anna explained to me later that I'd passed out on the bar and they couldn't rouse me. They tried shaking me, pulling my hair, even holding my nose, but nothing worked. Of course, I found this unnerving, but not unnerving enough to make me stop drinking so much. It was the first time in my life I'd felt totally relieved from my inhibitions and this euphoria even carried over to the hangovers that followed, when I was clowning in front of an audience and making children laugh.

This strategy didn't always work, however, like the morning I was performing my solo juggling skit at a school near Apollo Bay, tired and slightly nauseous. I didn't make any obvious mistakes in the routine – like dropping a ball – but my energy was obviously lagging. When I completed the skit, I expected at least a round of polite applause. Instead, about seven or eight kids jumped onto the stage and tackled me to the ground. They pummelled me with their fists and feet, bounced the juggling balls against my chest, screwed up my hat, and ripped my dress and petticoat. Finally, the other clowns ran onstage and rescued me, and I fled backstage, deeply shaken. *You need to command your space more*, said Grace, *to mark out your performative territory*.

When we arrived back in Melbourne, I was sad that the tour was over and we would each have to return to our separate lives.

I was surprised by how much I missed camping by rivers, swimming on deserted beaches, the boozy camaraderie and laughter.

The clown troupe was not the only bright thing that was coming to an end: I was about to complete my high school studies and catapult myself into my own life. While I'd been away, a letter had arrived from Melbourne State Teachers' College, offering me a place in the departments of Film Studies and Drama. This meant that I would soon be receiving a regular students' allowance, perhaps enough for me to eventually live on my own.

My relationship with Grace was also coming to an end. Since she'd been studying dance and clowning, she'd begun to make different sorts of friends, people closer to her own age who were mime artists, modern dancers, sword swallowers, and theatre directors. She had an affair with a handsome actor whose family owned an island; then she had an affair with his current girlfriend, which the actor didn't seem to mind. She was now part of a bohemian crowd who *lived for their art* and who thought monogamy was a *bourgeois construction*. Of course, she didn't want her sixteen-year-old student tagging along as she made her way into this shimmering new world. I understood this intellectually, but it was still depressing to be left behind in a Housing Commission flat with my mother and brother, and no other close friends of my own.

I finally concluded my friendship with Grace one Saturday afternoon, just after the school year had ended. We were visiting a friend of hers, and in the living room we encountered a couple of women we'd never met before. Grace said, *Hi*, and introduced herself. The women introduced themselves in return.

And, oh, Grace added, cocking her thumb in my direction, *this is my dog*.

There was an awkward silence as the women regarded me. I was so devastated by the remark, I couldn't shrug it off as a joke and tell them my own name. All I could do was back out of the room, red-faced and slightly trembling. I never contacted Grace again.

My mother, in the meantime, had taken up with an alcoholic army cook and small-time crook named Tom. In his early sixties, his face was usually covered in grey stubble and the bags under his eyes were so big they looked like pouches that could have contained a newborn joey. He'd spend all day in our living room in his singlet and boxer shorts, drinking and smoking with my mother and trying to teach my four-year-old brother how to throw a left hook. He'd work six weeks at a time at the Puckapunyal Army Camp in northern Victoria, and when he was on leave he'd stay at our flat.

We're just friends, my mother insisted, as she still did about Herb, the fruit man. When Tom arrived back from Puckapunyal, he'd always be accompanied by boxes of ham, steaks, sausages and canned goods – stolen from the army mess – which my mother happily accepted. Sometimes he'd go out and *pull a job* with some of his mates and return bearing watches, jewellery, crystal figurines, a portable television. One day he even took a late-model 35-millimetre camera out of his bag. *If anyone asks ya*, he said, palming it into my hands, *tell 'em it fell off the back of a truck*. For this reason I liked Tom more than I did Herb, but not enough to stay in our small flat with a man I didn't know very well taking up so much space inside it. When I received a letter from my father, telling me that he now had the telephone on and that I could ring him any time I wished, that is exactly what I did, one Saturday morning, from the phone box on the corner. I asked him if I could visit again and he replied, *Of course. Anytime.*

I raised one hundred dollars by working in a laundry for three days and, in the new year, caught an overnight train to Sydney. My father was now living in a huge studio flat, in the same house he'd shifted to after our episode with the pumpkin soup. It was downstairs from his former room and boasted high ceilings and a fireplace. The kitchen had wide windows overlooking Sydney Cove and the Opera House. Every few minutes trains would rumble overhead, across the Harbour Bridge. By the rhythm of each one my father could tell the direction in which it was travelling and could imitate perfectly a north or city-bound train, hitting the accents against the laminex table with his open hands.

My father now had some proper furniture: an overstuffed old velvet couch, which I slept on, matching chairs, a wardrobe and chest of drawers. He had a single bed, the bottom end of which was propped up on two stools, so that he slept all night at a forty-five degree angle. This, he maintained, was good for his brain – all that blood pooling into his head every night. He even had enough room in the flat to set up his kit of drums in a corner, which he muted with old grey blankets.

It was January 1980 and Sydney was incandescent with midsummer light. In the mornings, the flat was filled with the scent of salt water and the sound of squawking seagulls. After skipping out early from his cleaning job at 11 am, my father would arrive home, eat breakfast with me, then pull out his round, hard-rubber pad and practise a single hand exercise, over and over, for four straight hours while watching the midday movie, a couple of sitcoms, and an episode of 'Sesame Street'. The exercise involved holding a drumstick at the base of his thumb and index finger and, with his palm rigidly straight, snapping it onto the rubber pad and back up to its original position in less than a nanosecond. It was supposed to improve his wrist action and strengthen his fulcrum. I'd sit beside him through all this, watching whatever he watched on TV and turning down the sound when the ads came on. *What happened to the disco idea?* I once asked, curious.

My father shrugged and shook his head. *Rich shot through with all the equipment. He still owes me two grand.*

On Wednesday nights I'd pack up his drums, carry them downstairs and load them into the back of a red panel van. Then a young mechanic named Mark, who lived on the ground floor, would drive us down the hill to an old wharfie pub called the Australian Steamship and Navigation Hotel. Mark had only one hand, and I always watched with fascination when the fleshy stump that was his right wrist guided the steering wheel.

I was now officially my father's 'drum boy', which meant I helped carry the drums into the pub, cleared the drunks from a corner of the bar, and set up the kit. In return, my father would buy me beer all night. Early one evening, as I was bending over, tightening a wing nut on the high hat cymbals, a wharfie declared loudly, *Gee, I wouldn't mind getting into your knickers.*

That'd be hard, mate, I replied. *I don't wear any.*

My father laughed so suddenly he spouted a mouthful of beer all over the bar.

There was nothing more pleasurable to me than making him laugh. It was like a double shot of rum or a great compliment. And occasionally, when I surprised him with a witty remark or comeback, he'd grin slyly and I'd notice him gazing at me, but as if from a distance, as if he'd just met me for the first time and was startled by how much we seemed to have in common.

Sometimes, while he was practising his one-hand exercise in his room, I'd paint on my clown face, walk down to Circular Quay and play my flute for the passing crowds. I'd perform simple classical pieces and a small repertoire of jazz standards, averaging up to ten dollars an hour. To fill in time while my father was doing his cleaning work, I took a free street theatre workshop for teenagers. The teacher was a professional clown in his mid-thirties, a suntanned Jewish man with curly black hair, a strong, aquiline nose and a delicious sense of irreverence, as if all the regular rules that most people obeyed did not apply to somebody like him. He lived half of each year in Rome and the other half in Sydney. He played several musical instruments, including the jew's harp. He could not only walk on his hands, he could do the tango on them. Sometimes, after class, he'd invite me to have a beer with him at the pub, where he'd sit telling jokes. One night we had drinks at a wine bar and strolled through the warm, sultry city arm-in-arm as if we'd been together for years.

Later, in a reserve by the harbour, as a ferry chugged by and the red light from a nearby buoy blinked on and off, he took me in his arms and kissed me slowly, moving his tongue around in my mouth in such a way that made feel as if he needed the taste of something that only I could give him. And as his hands moved beneath my blouse and up, cupping my breasts, I was surprised by how deeply I wanted him. As we continued to kiss, the hat I was wearing blew away, and as it skimmed the surface of the harbour, we pulled back and laughed. We didn't make love because there was nowhere to go. He was staying with his uncle and I of course was sleeping on my father's couch. Later that week he flew to Rome, and I found myself left with an unusual sense of longing: it was the first time I'd experienced any kind of romance and, in spite of my feminist beliefs, I was surprised to realise how much I wanted that man to hold me again, to have him deep inside me.

In the meantime, the relationship with my father was flowering. On Saturday nights he had a gig out at Punchbowl RSL, playing in the band of an old family friend, Jeff, who'd allowed my twelve-year-old brother to steer our car home after one of the Musicians' Picnics. On my first visit to the club, as I was carrying the drums into the foyer, I was stopped by the doorman, probably because I didn't look eighteen and because I was dressed unconventionally: in a silk and lace blouse, a pair of men's woollen cream shorts, a 1940s crepe jacket, and a pair of leather sandals.

Don't worry about her, mate, said my father, sweeping past him, *she's just my roadie.*

As my father played jazz standards that night, I could feel the best parts of my childhood returning, like a shimmering dream I'd long forgotten. I found myself reconnecting to that earlier sense of ease and joy, when he'd throw impromptu parties and I'd crawl out of bed and join in. Buoyed by this feeling, during the second set I performed a solo soft shoe on the dance floor while the guest artist sang 'Fly Me to the Moon'; later, I climbed onto the stage with my flute and played a solo of 'Summertime'.

My father was grinning widely as he backed me up, even though I was slightly out of tune.

Throughout January, he and I enjoyed each other's company so much, and created so much havoc in the process, that it startled almost everyone around us. After that first night at Punchbowl, the management of the club banned me from returning. *They said you're too young*, explained my father, *but I reckon the real reason is that you freaked them out!* He seemed particularly pleased with this outcome, as if my banishment from the club were some distinguished honour. In addition to this, my father's neighbours were growing more hostile towards us because we often sat up talking and playing jazz long into the night.

They're just a bunch of poor, lonely men, announced Gerry, after one-handed Mark had complained. *They can't stand the sound of us having fun.*

But it was impossible to spend any time with my father without there being noise. When he wasn't riffing on one of his stories, he was playing jazz and slapping rhythms against his thighs. Sometimes he'd pick up a spoon and play backbeats against a glass or the table. When he grew more excited he'd lean over and begin hitting accents against my head, as if I were a tom-tom, alternating counter beats on my shoulders, my arm, and it felt good to be a part of his excitement, to feel it beating through me. Soon I, too, would be slapping my thighs, finding a way into the music. These extended jam sessions would go on for hours and through them I absorbed my father's sense of timing, his rhythmic repertoire and favourite licks. Even when he was cooking dinner he could not resist putting on a tape, pausing frequently to tap out a rhythm on the kitchen table. One night he was stirring some stew when he suddenly swooned at a piano solo. He swung the wooden spoon from the pot, hit a rim shot against the wall and, as he did so, half the stew arced through the air, fanned across the ceiling and began dripping over our heads.

The house was run by a man named Gordon, who looked like a retired high school principal – balding, with thick-rimmed glasses, and always a little too much spittle on his lips. He lived rent-free in the basement flat with his yapping fox terrier, Cecily. Gordon, however, never missed an opportunity to mention that he owned a home of his own. The house was in the grungy inner-western suburb of Erskineville and Gordon and Cecily often spent their weekends there, in the comfort of a carpeted and well-appointed three-bedroom home. On Friday afternoons, my father and I would lean out the kitchen window and watch him bundling a bag plus the barking and writhing Cecily into the back of his yellow sedan. Gordon would then hitch up his trousers, glance up at us and announce, *We're off to Erskineville!* as if he were about to spend the weekend at an exclusive tropical resort. One Friday, I saw him bundling in more than a bag and Cecily: also clambering into the sedan was Mark, the one-handed mechanic, and Dennis, an English retiree who also lived downstairs. Now they were all *off to Erskineville!*

See? muttered my father, leaning over the windowsill, shaking his head. *Nothin' else better to do. Gordon's tried to get me to go over to his house on the weekends, but I won't have a bar of it.*

On Sunday afternoons, my father and I would sit out in the kitchen, open the wide windows, and listen to big band music from the 1940s. I'd tie the hems of the curtains back so we could enjoy a stronger harbour breeze and watch the sailing boats glide beneath the bridge.

On one such afternoon, Gordon climbed out of his car with yapping Cecily and gazed up at the window in horror. Moments later, there was a pounding on our door.

My father opened it. *What's up?*

From the kitchen I could hear Gordon hyperventilating over Cecily's short, sharp barks.

The kitchen curtains, he said, *they're tied up in a ball! They can't be tied up in a ball. They have to hang straight! You got that, Gerry? They have to hang straight.*

My father returned to the kitchen, shaking his head. *He looks up here and sees us having a good time together. And he's gotta do something to interfere.*

He began untying one of the curtains. *See?* he added. *Now, that's loneliness.*

By early February, when I was preparing to return to Melbourne to begin my college studies, Gordon informed my father that *women are not permitted to live in the house* and that I would *not be welcomed back.*

But she's not a woman, my father protested. *She's my daughter.*

Those are the rules, Gerry, he said firmly. *No females in the house.*

My father was always making fun of these isolated, elderly men, and liked to think he was much happier with his own life, but when he came to see me off at Central railway station he was unusually quiet and seemed depressed. Before I boarded the train, I asked him if anything was wrong.

I'm gunna miss you, he replied, his eyes fixed on the door of the next carriage, as if I were somehow too bright to look at directly.

I held on to my suitcase and was surprised to see him blinking back tears. Never in my life had I seen him cry – not even after his near-fatal car accident – and it made me wonder if all his bravado were just a good front and, in an hour's time, when he returned to his flat alone, he'd feel just as lonely as the men downstairs, as lonely as I would soon be.

Over the following months, I took any opportunity to fly to Sydney: long weekends, the Easter holiday. Now, my father would have to smuggle me into his flat, which he rather enjoyed, and whenever I showered in the communal bathroom, he'd have to keep a lookout so no one would see me when I emerged, wet-haired and wrapped in a towel.

I might have been banned from his house, and from Punchbowl RSL, but in early April I was accepted into yet another college, the City Art Institute, to which I'd applied on the off-chance that I could transfer my study allowance and finally move out of home. I didn't particularly like Melbourne State Teachers' College – the instructors were patronising and treated the students like children – and I wasn't getting along very well with my mother.

Your father never wanted you! she'd cry when she was drunk. *He wanted to have you aborted!* As I packed my bags, I thought to myself, *Well, I'm pretty sure he wants me now*.

Once, however, just days before I was due to move out, she hugged me and stroked my hair. *You're just as mad as your father*, she admitted, *you might as well be with him*. I knew the hardest part would be leaving my four-year-old brother, who was so close to me he'd still cry whenever I left the flat without him.

But I ended up having to delay my departure so I could testify at the custody trial between my mother and Hakkim, which was slated for the end of April. In the meantime, my mother had to be interviewed by a psychiatrist to see if she were *a fit parent*. On the morning of the trial, Hakkim walked into the courtroom with a harried migrant woman in tow. She had straggly bottle-blonde hair and wore blue eyeshadow, and she looked so tense it seemed as if she'd been standing in a strong, cold wind all morning. They were also ten minutes late, which infuriated the judge, and Hakkim received a firm rebuke before the proceedings had even begun.

Events then took a more ridiculous turn when Hakkim was asked to present his case. He stood up, shuffling papers on the table in front of him, and announced that he'd just sacked his lawyer and would now be representing himself. I knew this was not a good thing for anyone to do, let alone an unstable man with only a tenuous grasp of the language. And it made me realise just how crazy he really was, to fire the only person in the world who could have helped him through that morning.

In stilted English, he tried to tell the story of the relationship he'd had with my mother, how we'd run away, and how the private detective he'd hired had ripped him off for two thousand dollars, but the monologue rambled on like one long, unfinished sentence, never quite making a point or completing an idea. And I almost felt sorry for him with his tight shoulders and furrowed brow, struggling to find a word. He said he now lived with another woman – pointing to the sad blonde in the back row – who already had two children. They lived in a suburban Sydney house and would be able to provide a proper home.

Then he pointed directly at my mother and his right eye narrowed, as if his finger were a gun and he was taking aim. *She no good mother. She pisspot. She drink and drink and drink.* He performed a little mime of someone guzzling out of a bottle. *Always drink*. He turned on one heel and deliberately staggered, as if acting out in a charade what he was unable to articulate with words.

The judge brought up the point that my brother had been independently tested and was deemed healthy and well-cared for.

That the girl, he said, pointing at me. *The girl take care of boy, not mother.*

He struggled on through his arguments and I could see that the judge was growing more and more alarmed, as if he'd been locked in a room with a lunatic. After the lunch break, when we reconvened, Hakkim and his girlfriend were late yet again and the judge was furious by now. He told Hakkim that if this happened one more time, he would throw the entire case out and deny him any custody at all. Hakkim bowed his head and said, *Sorry*.

My mother's solicitor then asked me to take the stand. I knew my testimony would be important because the solicitor had explained the case was basically Hakkim's word against my mother's and I was the only independent witness. Wearing my best clothes – a mushroom-coloured vintage crepe dress and brown shoes – I climbed up into the witness stand and took my oath.

Now, Mandy, said the solicitor, *in your own words, just tell us what it was like living with Hakkim for three years.*

I had known beforehand that I would have to do this, but now the time had arrived, with Hakkim only a few metres away from me, staring at me with his yellow-flecked eyes like a dingo stalking prey, I could feel my legs begin to tremble. It started with a slight quivering around my kneecaps and moved down my calves, as if I were experiencing some minor epileptic fit.

Mandy, pleaded Hakkim, *I know you good girl. I know –*

Silence! yelled the judge. *If you interrupt one more time I'll have you removed from the court!*

Hakkim cowered a little then – again like an animal, like a dog who knows he's done something wrong but who isn't quite sure what that thing could be.

Proceed, Miss Sayer, said the judge, turning to me and nodding.

I clasped my hands together and inhaled deeply, and I reminded myself that I had been waiting for a moment like this since I was eleven years old, since the day Hakkim slammed me against the living room wall and slapped my face over and over until I was blue and swollen and feeling my own blood pooling at the back of my throat. And I thought about my little brother, how happy and uncomplicated he was, and how it would be a tragedy to have him grow up in a home with a father like Hakkim inside it. And that was all I needed: I looked the judge directly in the eye, opened my mouth, and the stories came pouring out like one unbroken river – the constant beatings, his heavy drinking, his nightly visits to my bedroom while my mother was giving birth. From the witness box I could see my mother paling over this latter story – probably because I'd never mentioned it before and she was now hearing it for the first time in a public courtroom. Still, I thought it was worth the added anxiety, and that hanging a bit more dirty laundry on Hakkim could only strengthen her case. Finally I finished with a rebuttal of Hakkim's accusations against my mother. *My mother's not an alcoholic. She only drinks socially. I've never seen her drunk*. And with that, I left the witness box, avoiding Hakkim's gaze, and sat down beside our solicitor.

My life now fitted into seven cardboard boxes and, a week later, I travelled with them to Sydney on the *Southern Aurora*. Saying goodbye to my mother had been harder than I'd expected. It was only in the act of leaving that I realised how much we had endured together and, even amidst the chaos, we had loved – and still loved – one another. Before I left, we shared a couple of cold beers and she said she wished me nothing less than happiness. After I kissed them goodbye, however, and walked out the door, the only one crying was my brother.

I was travelling on the same train that had carried my mother, brother and me to Melbourne after we'd fled Hakkim and the Bexley house. It now seemed so long ago – those nights when he'd knock me to the floor and drag my mother by the hair through the house. At least I was leaving my mother and brother secure in the knowledge that they wouldn't be seeing him for a very long time: only the day before, the judge had ruled against Hakkim. Not only was he denied custody of his son, he was forbidden to come within fifty metres of him until Jason turned sixteen. Apparently, my testimony had helped, but it was finally Hakkim himself who'd sabotaged his chances of ever seeing his son again. His erratic behaviour in the courtroom had convinced the judge that he was an unfit and possibly dangerous parent.

As the train cut through the darkness, heading north, I sensed the vestiges of that other life peeling away, like dry, unwanted skin. And with every new town, I could feel myself growing lighter and more effusive, as if I were levitating.

I hadn't told my father I was moving to Sydney: I didn't want to turn up as some kind of burden, expecting to be cared and paid for. I now earned my own money and could make decisions for myself. I knew I wouldn't be able to stay at his place very long and I was reluctant to impose myself upon him. At Central station, I put my boxes in storage and, since it was only eight o'clock on a brilliant Sunday morning, I caught a bus to Coogee Beach and swam in the ocean for a couple of hours, coasting on shimmering waves and frolicking in the breakers, just as I had as a toddler, when my family was together and everything ahead of me had seemed as if it would always be as happy and secure.

I didn't want to ring my father too early in the day, in case I woke him prematurely. By the time I did ring, however, no one answered the phone, and once again I found myself trailing around the pubs in The Rocks, looking for that familiar helmet of yellow hair.

I finally found him at around two o'clock, in the beer garden of the Orient Hotel. Shaded by the fringe of an umbrella tree, he was sitting on his own at a wooden trestle table, drinking a schooner of Guinness and gazing up at the sky as if there were something up there that was going to give him the answer to a problem he'd had for a very long time. I hovered in the shadows of the doorway for a few moments, unsure how he would react to my sudden appearance, to the fact that I'd moved to Sydney uninvited so I could be closer to him.

Part of me wanted to back away right then. If he didn't wish to have me there, it would be too awkward, too embarrassing for us both. I was already planning to return to Central station and book a ticket back to Melbourne – to stop yearning so much for someone to accept me. But right at that moment, he lowered his eyes, blinked, and glimpsed me standing in the doorway. And before I could say anything or make an explanation, he jumped to his feet and opened his arms, as if he'd been expecting me. I stepped into the sunlight of the beer garden, inhaling the scent of a nearby frangipani, and my father engulfed me, like someone in love.

Acknowledgements

The writing of *Velocity* was assisted by a two-year fellowship from the Literature Board of the Australia Council. My thanks for their support.

The first chapter of *Velocity* first appeared in *The Bulletin Summer Reading Series*, 2003. Thanks to editors Kathy Bail and Ashley Hay.

Lastly, I'd like to acknowledge my husband, Louis Nowra, without whom this book wouldn't exist. He threatened to steal the stories herein and use them in his own work if I didn't write them down. I thank him kindly for such a prompt.

Dreamtime Alice

I danced and danced because the neon light across the road had just blinked on, because it was the middle of spring, because I was twenty-one, because my father was playing beside me . . .

In this vivid, seductive, gorgeously written memoir, Mandy Sayer recounts the fascinating years she spent performing on the streets of New York and New Orleans with her father. Gerry Sayer was a jazz drummer, a beguiling Irish charmer with a million stories and an insatiable love for jam sessions and all-night parties. Mandy grew up captivated by his outrageous tales, even after he left the family for good and her mother descended into the distance of drink. When her siblings failed him by rejecting the bohemian performing life, Mandy saw her chance to become a character in his stories, part of the only life he really loved. So she learned to tap-dance, and they set off together to satisfy their grand ambitions on the toughest stage in the world – New York.

Driven by the dream of making it big, Mandy and Gerry arrived in the city with no place to stay and only costumes to their names. They became part of the thrilling, precarious world of street performers – jugglers, magicians, fire-eaters, dancers – who eked out their livings at the mercy of the elements, the cops, complaining neighbours and lurking thieves. In cinematic detail, Sayer tells of the first exhilarating season in New York City, earning $200 a night on Columbus Avenue; offsetting the physical pain of endless performance with the incomparable rush that accompanied it; the long, difficult winter in New Orleans, surviving on avocados and raw vegetables in unheated apartments; and their final unforgettable return to New York.

Entwined with this singular story of a busker's life is the deeper, more intimate story of Mandy's transformation from a girl searching for her father's love into a woman who could invent her own language and find her own voice. For ultimately *Dreamtime Alice* is a triumphant record of a young woman's discovery that she could create her own story at last.

Mood Indigo

Winner of the 1989 *Australian*/Vogel Literary Award, *Mood Indigo* explores the underbelly of Australian urban life through the point of view of Rose, aged four as the novel opens, almost a teenager when it ends. Her father is a failing, eccentric pianist and her mother is lost between lovers and cocktails. The family's movements grind on like an old blues song, but it's Rose's love for her family that sings clear above the din.

This edition also includes Mandy Sayer's second novel, *Blind Luck*, the sequel to *Mood Indigo*. A teenager now, Rose is street-smart and nobody's fool. As Rose steers a course through the disasters that beset her mother's life, she develops an almost Dickensian ability to navigate her way beyond the hard facts of poverty.

In these two novels, acclaimed writer Mandy Sayer creates an unforgettable individual, one who endures and shines above the powerlessness of childhood. There is, literally, music running through these novels, not only in Sayer's descriptions of pianos and piano players, but also in her writing style, which arouses the reader's mind and feelings in much the same way that great music can.

15 Kinds of Desire

For weeks, for months she had anticipated this, had waited with a gradual, agonising pleasure . . . the savoury taste of his mouth, the sound of his breath in her ear. Inside the small train compartment everything felt vertiginous and possible . . . Martin slipped off Esther's underpants and brassiere and cupped her breasts in his hands. He pressed her front-first against the glass, against the rush of night and stars.

A teenage boy in Kings Cross masquerades as an American sailor so he can pick up girls. A desperate man makes love to his wife in order to wake her from a coma. An eleven-year-old girl braves the dark streets to visit her transvestite grandfather, an adolescent falls for his father's first wife, and a woman makes her philandering husband magically disappear.

Vogel-award-winning author Mandy Sayer has created a collection of linked stories with a twist. From the brothels of Sydney's Kings Cross to the bayous of New Orleans, from the Australian outback to the French countryside, the eccentric cast of characters in *15 Kinds of Desire* appear and reappear in each other's encounters, setting the scene for stories as intricate and involving as a novel. Assured, intriguing and beautifully written, these desires will haunt the reader long after the final page has been turned.